A Migrant Music

by C.A. Barnhart

Editorial Offices: Glenview, Illinois • Parsippany, New Jersey • New York, New York
Sales Offices: Needham, Massachusetts • Duluth, Georgia • Glenview, Illinois
Coppell, Texas • Ontario, California • Mesa, Arizona

Every effort has been made to secure permission and provide appropriate credit for photographic material. The publisher deeply regrets any omission and pledges to correct errors called to its attention in subsequent editions.

Unless otherwise acknowledged, all photographs are the property of Scott Foresman, a division of Pearson Education.

Photo locators denoted as follows: Top (T), Center (C), Bottom (B), Left (L), Right (R), Background (Bkgd)

Opener: (CR) ©Bettmann/Corbis, (BL) ©Bettmann/Corbis; 1 ©Bettmann/Corbis; 3 ©Bettmann/Corbis; 4 ©Bettmann/Corbis; 5 ©Corbis; 6 ©Bettmann/Corbis; 7 ©Bettmann/Corbis; 8 ©Leonard de Selva/Corbis; 9 ©Corbis; 10 ©Bettmann/Corbis; 11 ©Bettmann/Corbis; 12 ©Bettmann/Corbis; 13 ©Corbis; 15 © Frank Driggs Collection/Getty Images; 16 ©Renato Toppo/Corbis; 17 (T) ©George Rose/Getty Images, (CL) ©Frank Driggs Collection/Getty Images; 18 ©Bettmann/Corbis; 19 ©Bettmann/Corbis; 20 ©Bettmann/Corbis; 21 ©Lynn Goldsmith/Corbis; 23 ©C/B Productions/Corbis

ISBN: 0-328-13681-6

5 6 7 8 9 10 V0G1 14 13 12 11 10 09 08 07

TABLE OF CONTENTS

Chapter 1
And Then Came Jazz

No one really knows where the word *jazz* came from. However, we have a fairly good idea of where and when jazz, the music, began.

Around 1913, the word *jazz* referred to a kind of dance associated with ragtime. Ragtime music depends on **syncopation**, a rhythmic technique that places emphasis on beats that are usually weak or unaccented. Ragtime started among African American musicians in the late 1890s. Musicologists—scholars who study the development of musical forms—have traced ragtime back to New Orleans. One of its famous composers was Scott Joplin from Missouri. His rags achieved great popularity and were performed in both white and African American dance halls.

Scott Joplin

By the 1930s, *jazz* was the word used to describe the original, **energetic** music that African American musicians wrote and performed. Jazz built upon ragtime. As the popularity of jazz grew, it became recognized as a particularly American musical form. Jazz musicians were admired for their technical and creative musical abilities.

Jazz musicians followed a melody, added notes to it, and changed its rhythm. They were basically creating a new composition every time they played a song. This technique is called **improvisation**.

Jazz became popular in the United States at a time when African Americans and whites lived very separate lives. There was strict separation of the races, yet both races embraced jazz.

Jazz musicians enjoyed great popularity, and some built long and respected careers. More often than not, however, African American performers were not even allowed to **patronize** the very clubs they headlined.

The popularity of jazz did not break down the barriers that kept African Americans out of the mainstream of American life. It did, however, put jazz musicians firmly in the mainstream of American music.

Louis Armstrong is considered one of the greatest of all jazz musicians.

Jazz became popular at a time of strict separation between African Americans and whites.

Chapter 2
Jazz: A Window into the United States

Jazz was the creation of African Americans. In the 1920s, when jazz became a major musical form, the great African American jazz musicians lived segregated lives in the United States. It was not until 1954 that **segregation** in public schools was declared unconstitutional by the U.S. Supreme Court. Segregation was not fully outlawed until the Civil Rights Act passed in 1965. In some ways, the story of jazz has much to do with segregation.

The story of the development of jazz is also one of remarkable and widespread success. In fact, while jazz was new and maturing as a musical form, it was already a powerful cultural force, influencing other forms of music, art, literature, and even language.

Jazz acted somewhat like an American ambassador, especially to European countries. Many Europeans thought of American culture as less refined or less important than their cultures. In the view of Europeans, the United States had not been a country long enough to have established any literary, artistic, or musical traditions.

Like some generalized opinions, these observations about American culture were not necessarily based on facts. The United States had a long tradition of appreciation for the arts, although its artistic expression had been mainly influenced by European traditions. Jazz was something completely different because it was a reflection of American life and had sprung directly from it.

Since the United States was populated by immigrants, American culture was a collection of many, mainly European, cultures. It did not have a particular character of its own—that is, until jazz exploded in night clubs and on concert stages throughout the Americas and Europe. Then jazz became established as a respected and important **genre** of music.

What accounted for the spread of jazz, and who were the people who brought jazz to our nation's musical life? Much of the reason for the spread of jazz lies in the great movement of African American people from one part of the United States to another. These migrations of African Americans, especially from rural areas to urban centers, came about because of economic need. Jazz also spread, however, because African American musicians wanted to be in places where jazz was becoming popular.

Chapter 3
Slavery and Music

To understand the development of jazz, we need to understand the life of African Americans in the United States. Prior to the Civil War, most African American people came to the United States as enslaved people. Not only had they lost their personal freedom, but they were forced to live in a culture with different customs and practices than those they had known. They did not know the language, much less the religion, of their owners.

In expressing their religious beliefs, African Americans blended African and European musical traditions into what we now recognize as African American religious music. This distinct music, made up of spirituals and "sorrow songs," is considered by many musicologists to be a significant part of musical history.

There was another kind of special music made by enslaved people. It included rhythmic sing-song, call-and-response work songs developed by enslaved people working in the fields. Some of the songs were about injustice and hardship. These songs became the basis for the blues, on which jazz is based. The blues is also the source for rhythm and blues, country music, and rock 'n' roll—all of which remain popular today. These work songs did not need any instrument except the voice.

Enslaved people also used the African drumbeat in their songs. Even though it was often illegal to own a drum, they provided a throbbing beat with spoons, dried gourds, and pots. Enslaved workers often provided music for their owners' social occasions.

"Shouts" and "hollers" across the fields were the beginnings of the blues, ragtime, and jazz.

Chapter 4
Two Races, Two Cultures

With the end of slavery after the Civil War, African American life became freer but much less secure. In the South particularly, but actually all over the United States, there were two cultures: white mainstream culture based on European culture, and black African and slave-based culture.

A Civil Rights Act was passed by Congress in 1866, declaring that African Americans were citizens of the United States. The Fourteenth Amendment followed soon after, recognizing their citizenship. Still, African Americans were not treated fairly.

The maintenance of segregation of the races in the South was known as **Jim Crow**. This was a time of great economic and social difficulty for those who had been enslaved. African Americans attended segregated schools and churches.

They ate at separate lunch counters. They found it difficult and sometimes impossible to vote, and it was difficult for them to find good schooling or jobs.

Chicago in the 1920s

Due to the South's strict segregation policies, African Americans reached out to other immigrant groups for both friendship and music. For example, Caribbean Creoles who settled in New Orleans, Louisiana, contributed their unique drumming traditions, as did people from Latin America.

African American people also realized they needed to migrate from the South. Economic opportunities were more plentiful in the fast-growing cities of the North, such as Chicago. This movement brought African American music to other parts of the country.

In both New York and Chicago, where there were audiences with sufficient leisure and money to support jazz, the exciting new music became part of the popular culture. The newly arrived musicians from the South blended with the established musicians in the North, adding more depth and richness to the jazz sound.

Chapter 5
Increasing Acceptance

World War I, which raged from 1914 to 1918, helped bring international attention to African American music and musicians. Along with white soldiers, black soldiers joined the armed forces to help our allies fight and win the war. However, African American soldiers were as segregated in the military as they were in civilian life. In spite of this, African Americans distinguished themselves on the battlefield, proving that they were every bit as capable as any other soldiers.

African Americans also distinguished themselves musically during World War I. An army band led by James Reese Europe was made up entirely of African American musicians. It played an original military ragtime march. Commanders saw that the African American band created a mood of friendship wherever it played. African American musicians were gaining important recognition.

After the war, returning African American soldiers found the United States basically unchanged in its attitudes. Segregation still held sway. By the 1920s, shortly after the war, a period of great financial wealth brought great changes to the United States. This time was known as both the Roaring Twenties and the Jazz Age. It marked the solid entry of jazz into American popular culture.

The Europe band brought the sound of Dixie in World War I.

Chapter 6
Growing Appreciation for Jazz

One of the outstanding jazz musicians of this period was Louis Armstrong. He played the cornet and introduced the improvised solo to jazz.

Improvisation is a difficult art and central to jazz. The person who is improvising must have a great musical imagination. An improviser is aware of the structure of the music or the melody line. He or she **embellishes** the music with other sounds that blend well with the original sounds.

Some music critics thought jazz was undisciplined. They did not like its wandering melodies and unpredictable rhythms. However, ordinary people found it wonderfully exciting and free.

The great jazz improvisers became famous, and jazz spread far beyond the United States. The French, in particular, admired jazz and embraced African American jazz musicians. Even classical composers were influenced by jazz. George Gershwin used jazz in his works, *An American in Paris* and *Rhapsody in Blue.*

George Gershwin was a composer who incorporated many jazz elements into his classical compositions.

Louis Armstrong was a successful composer for his jazz band. While in New Orleans, Louis Armstrong was in a successful band called the "Hot Five."

Jacob Lawrence lived and worked in Harlem, home to many African American artists.

During the Jazz Age of the 1920s and beyond, the African American community exploded with many forms of artistic expression. Jacob Lawrence made an extraordinary contribution in visual arts. When asked about influences on his painting, he remarked that he was surrounded by color in Harlem, where he lived. Harlem was home to many African American people and was an important artistic center. The Apollo Theater and the Cotton Club in Harlem attracted huge audiences of both African Americans and whites.

Duke Ellington

Chapter 7
Music and War

Hard economic times followed the Jazz Age of the Roaring Twenties. The Great Depression of the 1930s was a time of financial and emotional loss and distress.

Even so, jazz and jazz-based music in the form of swing music were doing very well. This time, the spread of the new music was not the result of migration, but of radio and recordings. Jazz became international.

Duke Ellington, who became a successful jazz musician in the1920s, went on to become equally successful with his swing band. He was a great pianist and composer. He and his band created an orchestral jazz sound.

During World War II, one million African Americans were in the armed forces. They were again subject to segregation in the army, even though they were risking their lives to save democracy in Europe.

Both black and white entertainers were sent all over the world to bring entertainment to the soldiers. One jazz musician, Artie Shaw, said that all the soldiers wanted to hear was the sound of jazz, which was, for them, the sound of home.

After the war, more African Americans moved to urban areas. This concentration of African Americans in cities energized the musical scene. By the 1950s, another large migration from the Caribbean was bringing new musical traditions to U.S. cities. These Latin musicians brought a different sound and beat. They began to play with American jazz musicians and created yet another version of jazz. Some called it Latin, or Afro-Cuban, jazz.

Dizzie Gillespie

The Beatles

Chapter 8
Jazz Grows Up

The free flow of musical ideas between musicians from different cultures created an exciting musical scene in places such as New York City. Jazz of all kinds was played in clubs all over the city.

Jazz had grown and spread throughout the country as the musicians who played it migrated. Jazz also grew and changed as new musicians from other cultures added their contributions. By the 1960s, other musical influences seemed to overwhelm jazz, especially rock 'n' roll.

The tremendous success of the Beatles, a rock 'n' roll band from England, combined with the influence of television on the genre, hit jazz musicians hard. Many felt as if they had been struck by a thunderbolt. Some turned to rock or rhythm and blues in order to maintain a career. Older jazz musicians wondered if jazz was dead.

Of course, such music does not die. It is claimed and reclaimed by musicians who play it and who develop new sounds and audiences. American jazz, the music that migrated along with the people who developed it, has continued to migrate and adapt. There are internationally recognized jazz musicians all over Europe, the United Kingdom, Latin America, Africa, and Canada. These musicians, like the early jazz musicians, have blended American jazz with their particular musical roots.

In the United States, jazz is regarded as important and serious music. For example, trumpeter Wynton Marsalis began his career in the classical concert hall and is now head of Jazz at Lincoln Center in New York City.

Jazz, whose roots sprouted in the soil of slavery, migrated with musicians from the rural South to become a permanent part of American culture. Jazz is still migrant music, traveling to other cultures just as it was originally spread by its performers in the United States.

Wynton Marsalis

Now Try This

After reading *A Migrant Music,* you probably have more questions about jazz and its history. Here are some ways to find out more about the role of jazz in American culture. Break into small groups—perhaps based on interest. Choose one of the following activities and explore more about jazz of yesterday and today. Plan to share your information with the class.

Here's How to Do It!

1. The book does not talk specifically about the role of women in jazz, but there were many famous female jazz performers. There were also many all-female bands that toured during the Depression Era (the 1930s). Here are some names you can investigate: Marjorie Hyams (trumpeter); Elsie Smith (saxophonist); pianists Dolly Adams, Mary Lou Williams, and Emma Barrett; and singers Billie Holiday, Sarah Vaughan, Bessie Smith, and Ethel Waters. See if you can find their recordings or articles about them.
2. The book mentions the role African Americans played in the military during wartime. These men and women contributed to the armed forces and to our victories. Many were medal-winners for their bravery. How much can you find out about their outstanding deeds? After you gather the information, you might wish to create an "honor roll" to remember them.
3. Many young people play in small jazz bands in school. Perhaps you know some students who do, or perhaps you play jazz. You could arrange a mini-jazz festival featuring your fellow students, or you could develop a jazz program for your class. Present recordings of several jazz pieces, and write a program booklet that explains the different jazz selections. Include something about the artists who play the music and something about the jazz artists who made the songs famous.

Glossary

embellishes *v.* makes more interesting by adding details; adorns; decorates.

energetic *adj.* active; vigorous; full of energy.

genre *n.* category; style of art, music, or literature.

improvisation *n.* something that is made up on the spur of the moment.

Jim Crow *n.* systematic discrimination against African Americans.

patronize *v.* to be a regular customer of.

segregation *n.* the separation of one racial group from another.

syncopation *n.* in music, the practice of beginning a tone on an unaccented beat and holding it into an accented one.

constructing
IDEAS

constructing IDEAS

understanding architecture

Lance LaVine

KENDALL/HUNT PUBLISHING COMPANY
4050 Westmark Drive Dubuque, Iowa 52002

ISBN 0-7575-1412-X

Printed in the United States of America
10 9 8 7 6 5 4 3 2 1

ACKNOWLEDGMENTS

My thanks to Mary Musson, Linda LaVine, and Martha Abbott who read and made helpful suggestions about the text, The University of Minnesota Department of Architecture who have supported this effort beyond institutional requirements, to my wonderful students who helped to forge the contents of this book, and to Ed Siemek, Renae Heacock, and Emily Cabbage of Kendall Hunt for their invaluable help in preparing this manuscript. A large debt of gratitude to those who graciously contributed photographs for this book including Simon Beeson, Andrzej Piotrowski, Dale Mulfinger, Edward Allen, Martha Abbott, Stephen Weeks, David Samela, John Archer, and Erik Olson.

Additional thanks to Catrina Corcuera, Director of Casa Barragan for her help in obtaining photographs of the house and to Federica Zanko of the Barragan Foundation for their use.

Graphic design: Canek Sánchez Guevara
Computer graphics: Benjamín Ibarra Sevilla
Editors: Anne Carroll
Ellen Boroughf

To my wonderful wife for all that she is
Thanks Linda

CONTENTS

Chapter 6: Chartres Cathedral and Architectural Technology

Technology as symbolic construction; the general problem of the use of technology in architecture; defining climate, gravity, and sunlight as technological problems; metaphorical technology; Chartres Cathedral; the flying buttress and technical elegance in Chartres Cathedral; Scholasticism and the section of a column in Chartres Cathedral; architectural technology as the intersection of metaphorical and empirical thought; summary

Chapter 7: Technology in post 1850 Architecture

Industrialization and mass production, machine as metaphor, and perennial technologies; changes in circumstances after 1850; the development of modern architectural technology; the Crystal Palace and an architecture of mass production; Centre Pompidou and the machine as metaphor; Casa Barragan and natural light as a perennial architectural issue; summary

Chapter 8: Katsura Imperial Villa and the Idealized Landscape

Rearranging nature to become what she ought to be; two landscapes; visions of nature; nature as counterpoint to human construction; Katsura Imperial Villa; Buddhism and the Japanese tea ceremony; the building and gardens; formal analysis; summary

Chapter 9: The Idealized Landscape after 1850

Nature as poetic image or as ecological process; Pastoralism as a poetic image of the ideal landscape; Machu Picchu and the landscape as acquired experience; Woodland Cemetery and the landscape of death; Central Park and the landscape as the center of the industrial city; the Kings Road house and the domestic ideal landscape; nature as process, ecology, and Ouroboros; summary

Chapter 10: The Difference That Architecture Makes

The role of canonic buildings in architecture; canonic buildings and every day environments; comparative interpretations of Villa Savoye and the Kings Road House as idealized landscapes, a Dogon Village and Central Beheer as domains, Katsura, Centre Pompidou, and Exeter as technology, and Casa Barragán and the Robie House as the order of natural light; people as the subject of architecture; the problem with architecture as image; architecture as a positive pursuit; summary

List of Illustrations

Index

INTRODUCTION

For all of its pervasiveness, history, and significance, architecture remains a relatively unconsolidated discipline. Our era has not developed core definitions of the purpose, content, and means of architecture that might allow us to understand this body of work as a whole. It is not that contemporary propositions about architecture are scarce. The problem with these definitions is that they are often partial and tend to develop from current stances in philosophy and literary criticism. Few develop from the material of architecture itself. The result is a scattered and often borrowed sense of the roots of architectural design thought, leaving us without the sense of an architectural center.

One way to begin to identify such a core is to ask what difference architecture makes in our lives and communities. This question shifts the focus of our understanding of buildings from aesthetic to symbolic architectural issues in an attempt to explore the broad significance of the why, what, and how of designed environments. The following study outlines one set of possible answers to this question by analyzing twenty great architectural environments and the ideas that they propose. My hope is that these analyses will open up the rich world of architectural thought for your consideration.

ARCHITECTURE:
IDEAS, DEFINITIONS, PURPOSES
Architecture as an idea-making discipline

Architecture creates a tapestry of rich ideas that explore the human problem of habitation. It houses us in our everyday lives, creates our cities, and endures to tell us how people lived and what they valued in the past. Architecture helps create ways we are families and neighbors just as it creates places of political and religious power. Buildings and landscapes that have been designed by someone at some time do indeed, as Michael Benedikt suggests, provide a "stable matrix for our lives."

But if architecture in the broadest sense creates the context for our lives and links us to other lives, the question arises as to how it does so. Why are some buildings and landscapes considered significant while so many others are not? What is the difference between a great building and those that we occupy every day? Is there a way to understand designed environments of other cultures and times in contemporary terms? Why should we be concerned about the quality of our constructed environment?

Various eras and individuals would respond differently to these questions. A place to begin understanding these viewpoints is to ask what we mean when we use the word architecture.

The most common contemporary use of this term defines architecture as a licensed profession. The words *architect* and *architecture* are derived from the Greek *architekton*, from *arche* meaning leader and *tekton* meaning builder; an *architekton* was thus a master builder. Today's definition is more modest. Architecture is recog-

01 A megalithic burial marker in southern England

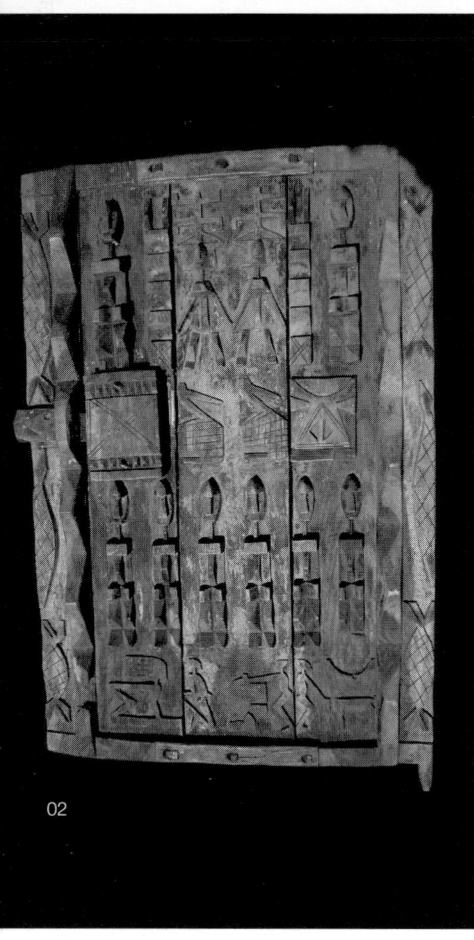

nized as a profession that requires special education and expertise. Architects take registration examinations to qualify for a license to practice. This tradition of professional architectural education began in France with the École des Beaux-Arts and the École Polytechnique in the 18th century and continues today in our schools of architecture.

But architecture is more than a profession. It is what you and I live and work in every day. Architecture is the sum of all the environments that have been transformed by humans to meet the special needs and desires of people. Such a definition includes the families, organizations, and businesses that have required shelter as well as the streets, parks, gardens, and natural areas that people have created to organize buildings into villages and cities. These places have been constructed as permanent domains since organized agriculture began 12,000 years ago. Unmodified nature can be frightening without paths to locate people or places to accommodate human needs. It was by creating paths that humans first created order in nature, followed closely by fire, burial mounds, and dwellings. These are the human constructions that let us know who and where we are.

But architecture is more than the sum of all the places that have been created. It is the sum of all the ideas that have been interpreted from these constructions. These ideas include the ways we think about nature, the ways we think about how we live

02 A Dogon granary door
03 The dining room of Villa Mairea

04

together, the ways we think about how we construct places of habitation, and the ways our constructions express our values. This is a broad kind of idea-making that crosses many of the conventional boundaries of thought. It is at once concrete and symbolic, cerebral and emotional, empirical and rational. Architectural ideas cross all these boundaries of thought because they reflect the complexity of being human. We understand the world we inhabit with all our powers of understanding our human circumstance. Architectural ideas arise because a place we are in strikes us as being particularly significant.

The primary sources of architectural theory are environments that have survived over time from every culture and period of human development. Texts have been written and preserved that deal explicitly with the characteristics that made buildings significant to us throughout architectural history. But these texts remain secondary to the actual material of architectural design: the constructed environment that architecture has left in its wake. Like musical compositions, literature, paintings, and sculpture, these environments provide the base for architectural interpretation.

The common characteristic of the environments that we will explore is that they are capable of sustaining analysis. People have constructed a vast store of places of habitation over human history, but few are worthy of our attention. Environments that prove worth studying are those that reward our extended attention. These environments are typified by the rich stream of interpretation they are able to sustain.

These ideas do not emanate solely from those environments that have attained the status of architectural canons. While the Parthenon remains a continuing source of architectural thought, so do a 17th-century Japanese farm house and a suburban shopping center. Architectural thought is not divided into the high-minded and the common but rather into the interesting and uninteresting. Those environments that capture our attention normally do so for good reason: they point to something in our constructed environment that has significance to us. Our search will be for the basis of that significance wherever it may occur in our designed environment.

05

04 Sea Ranch condominiums from the coastline of the Pacific Ocean
05 A detail of the exterior cladding of Sea Ranch condominiums

Architectural ideas

Our first problem in this search is to define what constitutes an architectural idea. We might begin with the contention that an architectural idea is composed of symbols representing what we value about a constructed environment. Consider, for example, Akiko Busch's definition of a front door in her lovely little book, *Geography of Home.* Busch begins her chapter on front doors by describing all the houses she has occupied. In her experience, front doors have been more ceremonial than useful. Like many people, Busch enters her house through a side or garage door that offers more direct access to the working parts of a house such as garages and kitchens.

Busch asks of her seldom-used front door, "Isn't there an enormous difference between something that is never used and something that is useless?" Her reply is that the front door is an architectural symbol of social congeniality that is less important in functional terms than as a representation of how individuals belong to a larger social world.

Describing a front door as "congeniality" is a different kind of mental process than measuring its dimensions. Even the words *front door* connote more than a location in a house by suggesting that this is the primary place of entry into a domain, even if less frequently used. This connotation requires an intellectual leap from a tangible to an intellectual experience: from architecture as material construction to architecture as immaterial interpretation of value. The front door has become an architectural idea.

Think of the process required to come to these conclusions. First, we must be able to distinguish a front door from all other doors. Most of us can discriminate between a back and a front door even if the former is more frequently used. Front doors are normally a bit grander and more richly decorated than back doors; and more importantly, they face the larger social order of the street. People are able to recognize this distinction in their own homes, in the homes of their city and country, and often in homes from other cultures and historical periods.

Each of these distinctions represents a complex mental process. First, this idea is initiated by a literal front door. Most architectural ideas emerge from a tangible construction. Secondly, we must be able to collect all front doors into a category of openings sharing common characteristics. Without this gathering, all architectural thought would remain anecdotal. As a specific door is generalized to become the abstract formal idea of front door, so personal value might be extended as the base of corporate meaning. Busch's thoughts about her own front door might be connected to those of people in general through this process.

The steps in this analysis differ little from those of other creative modes of human thought. Major differences in modes of thought such as music, literature, philosophy, mathematics, and painting come from the human experiences their abstract symbols

06 Central Beheer office building in the Netherlands

07

attempt to explain. Musical ideas, for example, are expressed as clusters of notes. These notes take special forms to accurately and concisely tell musicians when and how to play sounds on instruments. Musicology would be at a loss without these symbols to help explore the significant musical ideas that have been forged by composers. Novelists and philosophers use words, scientists use numbers, and painters use graphic media to capture other perspectives of our world. Each discipline of human thought uses a symbolic language that is uniquely suited to test human understanding of a particular category of issues that concerns us. This symbol system and the issues being explored form a complementary pair of material form and interpreted value.

What then are the symbols that allow us to explore architectural ideas? These symbols are as particular to the problem of constructing habitation as notes are to musical composition, words are to literary and philosophical explorations of human nature, numbers are to the mathematical ideas that expose the structure of the universe, and graphic media are to capturing the essence of human identity.

Architectural ideas are put forth by floors, walls, frames, openings, roofs, and gardens.

These very familiar symbols are at once tangible and abstract. The tangible nature of Busch's front door allowed her to make this environmental element real to us. We can picture a front door from her description because we have all seen and touched a front door. We are able to generalize from that front door to others because all front doors have similar formal characteristics. Busch is able to convey the emotional significance of her door to us because we all have experienced front doors that move us and those to which we are indifferent. Beneath these common experiences lies the abstract formal root of a front door as an opening in a wall for passage from one domain into another.

07 The Parthenon atop the Acropolis
08 The Robie House in Chicago

This is true of all other architectural ideas. They are built from a ubiquitous and relatively universal vocabulary of architectural elements. Floors always provide a surface on which we stand and relate to the ground. Walls always separate. Frames always organize space as they reference the regularity of gravity. Roofs always cover us from the sky. Openings always reconnect us to the world from which walls and roofs have separated us. Gardens always rearrange natural resources to present a landscape that is what we think nature ought to be.

As these elements take on individual shape, they express very particular thoughts about standing, separating, regulating, covering, connecting, and rearranging the landscape. It is in this particularity of form that architectural ideas arise. There are an infinite number of architectural environments that might be created by these symbols, just as there are an infinite number of musical compositions that might be created with notes of a musical scale. What creates an architectural idea is the particular material shape and relationship to other material shapes that architectural symbols assume. As these elements are added to one another to form this whole, complexity of thought and potential for interpretation increase dramatically.

How, then, might we discriminate between those architectural environments that might reward our attention and those that will not? Philosopher Susanne Langer defined good ideas as those that give rise to other good ideas. To her, the role of ideas in our thought was not to be right in the limited sense of this word but, rather, to be fecund. Fecundity is a word not often used now. It means the power to produce or give birth abundantly. Langer's good ideas gave birth to other good ideas. Good buildings do the same. What makes a building significant in the history of the discipline of architecture is its ability to sustain analyses that give birth to ideas that yield other good buildings.

How does this happen? Though formal imitation undoubtedly plays a role in architectural design, it does not represent the core of this process. What is required for

08

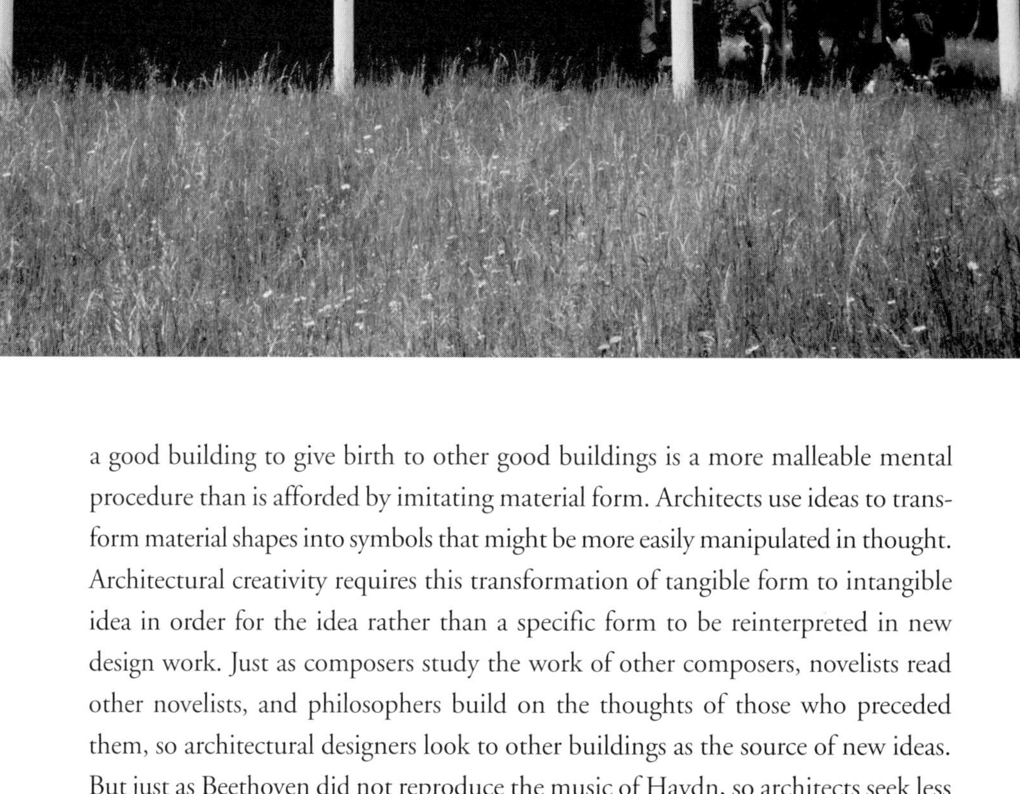

09

a good building to give birth to other good buildings is a more malleable mental procedure than is afforded by imitating material form. Architects use ideas to transform material shapes into symbols that might be more easily manipulated in thought. Architectural creativity requires this transformation of tangible form to intangible idea in order for the idea rather than a specific form to be reinterpreted in new design work. Just as composers study the work of other composers, novelists read other novelists, and philosophers build on the thoughts of those who preceded them, so architectural designers look to other buildings as the source of new ideas. But just as Beethoven did not reproduce the music of Haydn, so architects seek less to imitate than to understand. Literal parts of buildings are an unwieldy thinking device in design. Giving birth to new good ideas represents a different and more abstract process.

What makes this set of ideas so special is that we inhabit them. Few other ideas made by people are as direct and intimate as those made by architecture. Any time we are any place other than unmodified nature, we are within an architectural idea. Like all other ideas, these range from the profound to the superficial, from the emotionally moving to the boringly bland, and from the specific and temporary to the universal and transcendent. We might divide significant ideas of habitation into four categories: domain, order, technology, and the idealized landscape.

Domain is the way in which architecture establishes boundaries to contain us with our values. These boundaries are nested inside each other. They extend from the boundary of our skin that includes only us, to the universe that includes everything. Architecture is particularly interested in domains at the lower end of this scale. Body, furniture, room, house, street, institutions, and cities are the boundaries that occupy most of architectural thought. Each of these contains a smaller demarcation of territory and each, in turn, is contained by the next larger demarcation. The essential condition of this material demarcation is a pairing of formal and cultural ideas.

Order is the way in which meaning emerges from material pattern in architecture. People seek out these patterns because they must. Without pattern, we would be cast adrift in a world of episodic events. None would relate to the other in any generalizable way. The inability to recognize a pattern of events is synonymous with being lost. People are located in time and place through the recognition of pattern. The meaning to be located is the outcome of understanding the pattern of one's context. Because order in architecture is the sum of patterns that might be identified in buildings and landscapes, it is not a closed list but one that grows with each new insight into what order might mean.

Technology in architecture is composed of the symbolic forms of architecture that redirect natural force. This use of technology is not the same as that of engineering. Technological form in architecture does have a special mechanical responsibility. It must empirically redirect the natural forces of gravity, climate, and sunlight in order for buildings to exist at all. But in so doing, these forms accomplish much more. Gravity becomes a symbol of permanence and regularity through the form of the frame. Climatic boundaries define a social inside from an outside. Sunlight gives birth to all form allowing us to order our surroundings through sight. These symbolic distinctions arise because people inhabit the technology of architecture. The particular material forms of architecture that are charged with redirecting the forces of gravity, climate, and sunlight are thus asked to do more in buildings. They are asked to relate these forces to us by suggesting what these natural forces might mean in human as well as mechanical terms.

09 The side façade of Villa Savoye in Poissy, France
10 Sculpture in the German Pavilion in Barcelona

10

The idealized landscape is the human transformation of nature to become what we think nature ought to be. Homo sapiens are a tampering species. We are animals apparently uniquely gifted with the need to know why things are the way they are. We are also the species that speculates on how things ought to be. This speculation includes the natural landscape. Rearranging the natural landscape to suit human rather than natural purpose reflects the uniqueness of the human animal among all other natural creations. We alone think that our natural context can be remade to be just a bit better.

11 Exterior façade of Exeter Library at Phillips Academy
12 Construction of the Crystal Palace

12

Definitions of architecture

Architectural theorists have addressed these issues in a variety of ways over the course of architectural history. Each of the following definitions of architecture taken from *The Theory of Architecture: Concepts, Themes, and Practices* by Paul-Alan Johnson places different emphasis on the issues of domain, order, technology, and the idealized landscape.

> *Architecture consists of "commodity, firmness, and delight."*
> — Vitruvius, 1st century BC
> (English translation by Sir Henry Wotton, 1624)

Vitruvius was a 1st-century BC Roman architectural historian who produced a compendium of classical thought about the purpose and means of architecture in his *Ten Books on Architecture.* Rediscovered in the Renaissance, these books have since served as a benchmark of architectural thought. The Vitruvian triad of firmness, commodity, and delight might be loosely translated in modern terms to speak of architecture's response to natural force, the need to accommodate human activities, and beauty. These, in turn, reference architectural obligations to technological, social, and aesthetic functions.

> *Architecture is "the art of designing sculpture for a particular place, and placing it there on the best of principles of building."*
> — John Ruskin, 1884

Ruskin wrote about architecture when the Industrial Revolution was threatening traditional architectural values derived from classical models. New materials, technologies, and social problems began transforming the industrial world in the mid-18th century; and by the mid-19th century, these forces had become so formidable that they were changing the ways people lived and constructed their domains. The railroad locomotive was the symbol of this change and the railway terminal the architectural expression of its presence in the modern city. Ruskin hoped to differentiate between the architectural meaning of such domains as being purely utilitarian and therefore not architecture in a true sense of the word and those that were truly architectural. For Ruskin and many who followed him, architecture is fundamentally a fine art, charged with manifesting aspirations higher than biological survival. Thus, Ruskin compares architecture to sculpture as a fine art, with a fundamental purpose of speaking to us about meaning in our lives after our utilitarian needs have been met.

"When we come across a burial in the woods, six feet long and three feet wide, then we become serious and something inside us says: here lies someone buried. That is architecture."

— Adolf Loos, 1910

13 A bundled column and vault of the Cathedral at Chartres

14

Adolf Loos was a Viennese architect and architectural theoretician in the early 1900s when that city was the intellectual capital of Europe. Loos wrote when Otto Wagner, Sigmund Freud, Ludwig Wittgenstein, Gustav Klimpt, and Arnold Schoenberg were all residents of this city that was the locus of thinking for a new era. As a member of this brilliant group, Loos sought to redefine the purpose of architecture. Rather than restate the Vitruvian triad of commodity, firmness, and delight, Loos seeks a basis for understanding architecture that is lodged in the person who inhabits it. Birth and death are seminal human events, and the burial mound is a way of memorializing the latter. It reminds us of the significance of life, the inevitability of death, and our need for symbolic treatments of significant events in human lives. The burial mound recalls at once the richness of life, our capacity to care for one another, and the human capacity to remember that which no longer exists. Loos thus re-centers the purpose of architecture in the human psyche.

> *Architecture is the "creat(ion) of forms out of the nature of our tasks with the methods of our time."*
>
> — Ludwig Mies van der Rohe, 1923

Mies van der Rohe was concerned with rectifying the forces of industrialism that Ruskin sought to deny with traditional architectural values. Instead of ignoring the power of these changes, he sought to incorporate them within a larger design framework. In this theory, history becomes a cascade of events that always produces a new context for building design from which new problems and new technologies arise. The role of architecture is to reinterpret traditional architectural issues within these new conditions. History produces an evolving set of conditions which require architectural forms to emerge that rectify what changes with what remains the same.

14 Front façade of Centre Pompidou, Paris
15 Casa Barragán, Mexico City

> *"(F)or architecture is an undeniable event that arises in that instant of creation when the mind, preoccupied with assuring the firmness of construction with the desire for comfort, finds itself raised by a higher intention than that of simply being useful, and tends to show the poetic powers that animate us and give us joy."*
>
> — Le Corbusier, 1930

To many, Le Corbusier was the central spokesman of architecture's modern movement. The classic period of this movement extends from the late 19th century to the beginning of World War II. Its problems were those of the modern world: industrial production, the problems of the industrial city and workers' housing, and the kinds of abstractions that grew from late 19th- and early 20th-century art and science. It is therefore especially interesting that Le Corbusier chose to restate the purpose of architecture as the modern version of the Vitruvian triad. Certainly "firmness of construction," "desire for comfort," and "higher intention than that of simply being useful" are a nearly literal restatement of Vitruvius' position. The last part of Le Corbusier's definition, "poetic powers that animate us and give us joy," lays more emphasis on delight than might be interpreted from a balanced interpretation of the Vitruvian triad.

> *"There is architecture, and it is the embodiment of the unmeasurable."*
>
> — Louis Kahn, 1964

15

Louis Kahn was concerned about the meaning of architecture. Kahn thought of architecture as a perennial set of issues, much like the human problems of gathering and learning. His contention was that architecture resolves these problems in each architectural era. His sources of inspiration were classic architectural models. Beneath the material forms of these models and of his architecture lay the idea that architecture has an "unmeasurable," transcendent meaning — an essence. These meanings were initiated by a more fundamental sense of the purposes of architecture than are conveyed by words like technology, usefulness, and beauty. The "unmeasurable" in architecture suggests not how but why people have constructed places of significance. These reasons cut across time and culture, transcending both because they come from a human core that remains unchanged. When that core is manifested in a building, the outcome is felt, not thought. It reaches inside us to initiate what might be dormant

feelings that have grown from the human ambition to understand why and how we exist. Uses of a building and styles of architecture may come and go, but this underlying meaning shows through in great buildings.

> *"Architecture like the other arts produces 'cultural capital'... by which people display their upper-class status through their tastes and possessions."*
>
> — Dana Cuff, 1991

It would not be difficult to reduce architecture to a commodity much like all the others that middle-class people buy. Much of architecture is exactly that. Vast suburban developments, big-box stores, and office buildings create a large majority of our contemporary constructed environment. Though these structures may foster other values, their major concern is with identifying the social status of inhabitants. These structures are far more socially interesting than they are architecturally interesting. Yet they say much about who we are and what we value in our constructed domain.

Purposes of architecture

Each of these definitions touches on a different dimension of what we may consider as the primary purpose of architecture. The Vitruvian triad attempts to be comprehensive by claiming that people construct buildings to redirect natural force, be useful, and be beautiful. This categorization of architectural purpose has served architecture well as evidenced by its restatement by Le Corbusier nearly 2,000 years later. Ruskin imagines the best of architecture to be a fine art like painting or sculpture. Loos and Kahn search for something different in architecture, both concerned with a less tangible and more psychological definition of architectural purpose. Both the burial mound that Loos discussed and the "unmeasurable" of Kahn have their roots in a sense that as we have always been human; architecture has always reflected the core values of our being. It is the search for those unchanging aspects of being human that propels great architecture. Mies van der Rohe might be seen as striving toward the same transcendent purpose but with a special emphasis on the modern means and needs of a particular era. Cuff abandons all of the above as a thin veneer applied over a human desire to visibly proclaim one's place in an economic and social structure.

For many architects, beauty is the larger construct that holds together these disparate ideas. Firmness, commodity, delight, artfulness, existence, the immeasurable, the

16 A teahouse of the Katsura Imperial Villa, Kyoto
17 Machu Picchu, Peru

17

18 Woodland Cemetery walkway, Stockholm
19 Central Park, New York

issues of our times, and even social status are connected by aesthetics. It is what a building looks like that really counts. Image is all. The aesthetic quality of a designed environment is what elevates it from the ordinary to a significant piece of architecture.

But what if this aesthetic quality were shifted from being an input of architectural purpose to being the product of architectural insight into a range of other issues? Perhaps what is commonly referred to as the poetics of a building is actually shorthand for the ability of a design to reveal something insightful about us and the way we inhabit the world. Designs become powerful when these revelations bring into focus a condition of habitation that was obscure. In architecture, these revelations are forged in material forms. Beautiful architecture connotes insightful architecture. This beauty is not skin deep but flows from a revelatory understanding about the issues of architecture.

Architecture allows us to belong with one another in nature.

The underlying purpose of these revelations is to create a world where we can belong. Habitation begins with the idea of nesting. Like all other animals, we need a place to raise a family. But biological nesting is inadequate to fulfill our species' need to belong. We seek to understand the structure of what exists around us in order to belong intellectually, emotionally and spiritually as well as biologically. People need to belong within the natural and social world or they remain lost among the forces and forms that comprise these worlds.

Domain, order, technology, and the idealized landscape are simply subcategories of the ideas of habitation shaped by architecture in our collective search for how we belong within nature and our social world. While domain and order may be primarily about our social and cultural need to belong with others, and technology and the idealized landscape about our need to belong in nature, these terms are more complex than they might first appear. The best way to understand the meanings they might suggest is to study great buildings.

19

THE DOGON
AND THE ISSUE OF DOMAIN
Containing us with our values

Issue

What is an architectural domain?

Human beings share with other animals the need to mark territory that they are able to control. Within these limits, organisms dictate acceptable rules of behavior. Outside of these limits, different rules of behavior may prevail. We call the area within these limits a domain. Architecture's first social task is to create these limits for individuals, families, and larger organizations of people.

Domain begins with a sense of our own bodies and a distance around them that we consider to be our own territory. Invasion of this boundary produces discomfort. Try sitting face to face with another person you don't know very well. Now move your face progressively closer to theirs until you both feel the discomfort of being too close. Too close means that you have violated the other person's domain. Everyone has a ring of space around them that is theirs. It is an extension of their body, it belongs to them, and they control what happens within it. The size of this column of space varies by culture, but it exists for all people.

This personal domain might be extended to the distance that two people maintain between them as an acceptable social distance. Lot lines and fences define the domain of a family. My street defines the domain of my immediate neighborhood. Stores, institutions, and landmarks within walking distance identify the larger domain of my neighborhood. This boundary might be enlarged in suburban settings where the automobile rather than walking can establish neighborhood boundaries. The city and state that we reside within define larger social and physical domains, as do nationalities. Finally, there is the domain of the earth within the cosmos. We somehow see the universe as the farthest extent of the territory that we possess, at least in terms of thought.

01 The Dogon primal couple

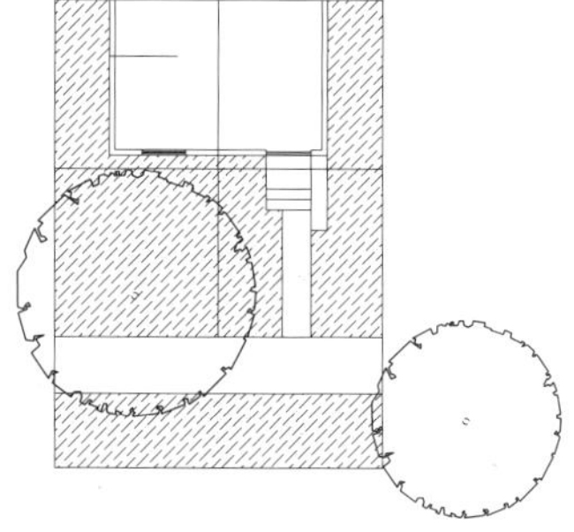

02

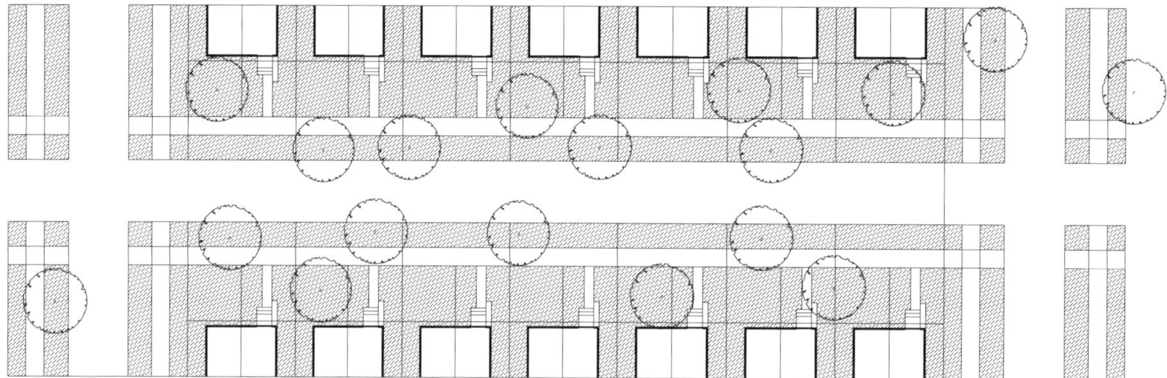

All of these are physical circumstances. Each has an inside and an outside. Each locates us in relation to our surroundings. The act of creating physical boundaries that have insides and outsides is the act of creating domains. These domains structure our daily locational conversations with the natural world and with each other. Chair, fireplace, room, house, front yard, block, neighborhood, and settlement are conventional architectural definitions of domain. At one end of this scale is the horizon where the air, land, and sky meet to form the farthest extent of our immediate domain. At the other end of this scale is my skin that defines the boundary of my personal being as opposed to that of everything else.

Domain is such an important word in architecture because it allows us to know where we are and how we belong in that particular location. This is a location and sense of belonging that is initiated by physical architectural forms but represents the social and cultural rules that those forms manifest. Even if I am able to, I cannot simply pass through your front door without your permission because I would be passing from what constitutes the public domain into what constitutes your private domain. Sidewalks, stairs, porches, and front doors become architectural symbols in the assembly of entry that connote this shift in domain. Our physical residence within the cosmos is by and large constructed of such boundaries. As an assembly of places and paths, they create a three-dimensional setting for life. Parts of this setting will change over time but it will, in major outline, retain its central identity over extended periods of history. This ability to conserve a conceptual map of our places of being is the purpose of constructing architectural domains.

02 Diagrams and photographs of the organization of a Midwestern residential street
03 Dogon river with fields adjacent to it
04 Naturally created forms of rivers, earth and vegetation
05 Humanly created forms within a natural context

How have people established architectural domains?

03

In hunter/gatherer societies, the way that people marked the land left only temporary traces of architectural domains. Housing and villages were assembled and disassembled as people needed to move to find sources of food. The paths that were annually trod in this search were overgrown between migrations. As berries were picked, they grew back. As animals were killed, new young were born to replace them. People left few marks that indicated their presence in a location. Their existence was typified by transience. Dwellings were portable and artifacts had to be of a size and number that could be easily carried. Subsistence was, for the most part, a day-to-day affair. Demarcations of social territory were carried on in the minds of the hunter/gathers.

Our modern sense of domain was born in the agricultural revolution that took place roughly 12,000 years ago in the Middle East. It was based on the discovery of the hybridization of native grasses to produce a larger kernel of nutrients. When two kinds of natural oat grasses were artificially crossbred, the product was a grain with a much larger edible head than either of its parents. Though nutritionally beneficial, this large-kernel grain had a problem: it could not reproduce itself. Agricultural plants were annuals rather than perennials. People were required to annually replant seeds produced by crops of the previous year if they wanted to reap the increased nutritional content of future crops. Farming was born from this relationship. Farmers were required to till, plant, weed, and reap crops annually. Their reward was a surplus of wealth. They could annually produce more food than they could eat.

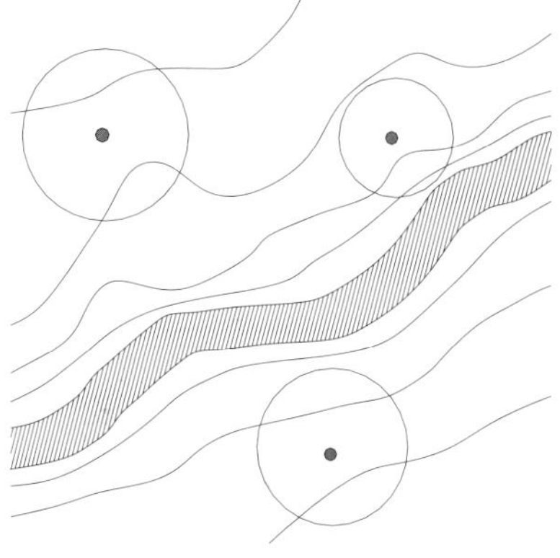
04

Repetitive acts required to tend crops suggested the demarcation and ownership of land required for fields. It probably did not take people long to discover that some land was more fertile than other land, that land once tilled was easier to prepare the next year than was virgin turf, or that water was more accessible in some places than in others. Once these realizations occurred to people, it was an easy step to marking a patch of soil as one's own. To be useful, that marker had to be permanent. It could not be easily moved because to do so would destroy its benefit. The stone corner field marker probably grew into a stone wall that made the demarcation unambiguous as land was divided among people to become their farms.

As people invested this labor in land, they became tied to it. Their source of biological survival was now located in a single place. Their houses needed to become permanent; and as groups of permanent houses became villages, the modern concept of home and city were born. Social organizations of families and tribes were reflected in the physical organization of these houses. The surplus of wealth created by agriculture allowed some of the people of these villages to perform tasks other than those biologically necessary for the group. A form of government was required to maintain civil order. Religious customs and rituals could now be housed in permanent structures. New buildings were required in the village to accommodate these new activities. Much of our current definition of domain as room, house, neighborhood, and village originated with these events.

05

Demarcation, ownership, wealth, and specialization became the hallmarks of the pattern of habitation that accompanied the agricultural revolution. Permanence both allowed and required that a physical fabric grow up to house agricultural people. The architectural vocabulary that emerged is one that we recognize today. Land was subdivided by paths that served to connect residences made of walls, floors, roofs, windows, doors, and frames. Fields represented the idealized landscape in these communities as they reorganized the natural landscape to provide a surplus of food. Homes were related to one another and were organized by a larger order of community spaces that were deemed necessary to serve and regulate the whole. The whole gave an identity to all those who resided within the limits of the settlement, giving rise to a permanent culture. These same architectural definitions of domain remain true for our settlements today.

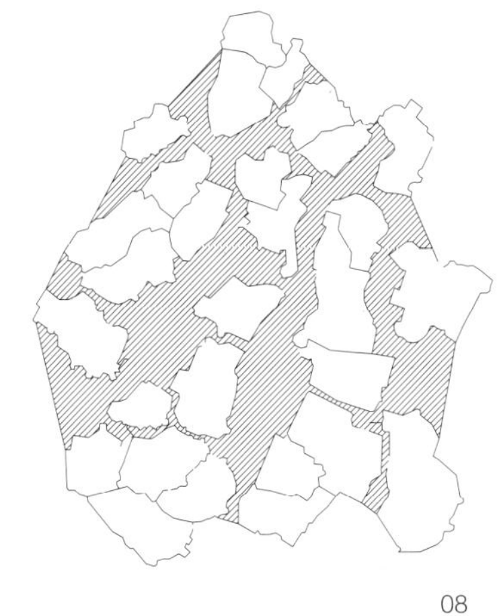

08

07

06 Three young Dogon children
07 A Dogon village
08 Public areas of a Dogon village
09 Walled compounds of a Dogon village

How have our definitions of domain changed over time?

Agriculture acted as the base economy of settlements until the Industrial Revolution. The invention of the steam engine and the power loom in the mid- to late 1700s marked the beginning of the Industrial Revolution in England and Scotland. This revolution was important to the definition of domain because people were no longer tied to the farm field as their source of wealth. Machines replaced agriculture and manufacturing replaced farming as the economic driving force of societies. As steam allowed the concentration of power and production, so manufacturing called for the centralization of people to operate machines. The modern city was born in this concentration. All the trappings of the village were carried along in this new organization of domain but increased scale signaled not just a change in degree but a change in kind in this settlement. There were now so many people gathered from so many different villages that variations in social structures and beliefs collided instead of emerg-

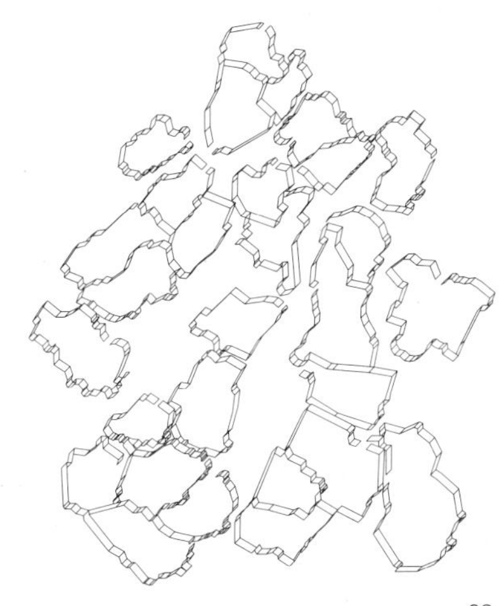

09

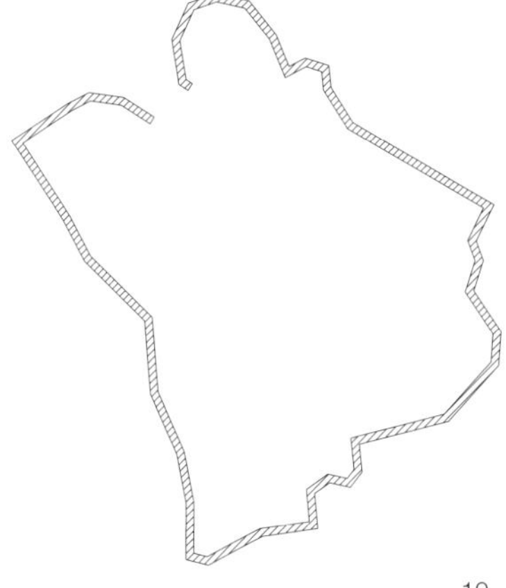

10

ing from the singular history of isolated groups of people. The result was a friction that could produce social discord, or as Lewis Mumford has pointed out, serve as a great stimulus to human imagination.

The specialization and rate of invention that emerged from the organization of the city was similar to that which had emerged from the agricultural revolution, but at a greatly increased pace and scope. The city became the place of change. Where the village had been fundamentally a conservative force in architecture for over 10,000 years, the city was dynamic. Architecture was asked in this city to accommodate rapidly emerging new needs in terms of domain. These requirements changed again in the mid-1800s when the base of industrialization became coal and steel. The major difference was one of size. By 1800, London became the first modern city to exceed 1,000,000 inhabitants; and by 1850, Paris followed suit.

Our shift from an agriculture-based to a manufacturing-based order of domain is registered in the shift of residence in the United States from farm to city in the 20th century. At the beginning of that century, 75% of the U.S. population lived in a rural setting. By 2000, 80% of the U.S. population was urban, and only 4% were farmers. This rate of change registers a progressive increase in the rate at which conditions, needs, and definitions of the architectural domain have changed. It required 11,800 years for the agricultural revolution to run its course in the development of permanent villages. The reorganization of that definition of domain as cities required only another 200 years. We are now only 50 years into our third major revolution, the information revolution, with consequences for the architectural definition of domain that are yet to be fully understood.

What is architecturally interesting is to note which characteristics of these conditions of architectural domains have changed and which have remained largely unaltered over the course of this history. Our bodies, furniture, rooms, and homes have remained conceptually the same over this period. A room with a table, bench, and a fire pit of 12,000 years ago is easily recognized by contemporary people because it is so

11

10 Walls of a Dogon compound
11 A common area between two Dogon compounds
12 Enclosed sleeping rooms and entry porch of a Dogon compound
13 Granaries within a Dogon compound
14 The central social space of a Dogon compound

familiar. The paths of the village that were to become streets of the city remain the same in intent if not in form. A place of communal decisions and a temple of spiritual beliefs were not uncommon in early settlements. These constructions were slow to change in form and in meaning. The room joined to other rooms remained the definition of the family. The front door remained the definition of the relationship between communal and family domains. The path gathered homes together to form a village. Institutions like temples and meeting houses gathered disparate families together within the common bounds of culture. And the means of biologically and economically supporting that culture were demarked by material boundaries that signified ownership of this productive capacity. Domain in architecture became a stable pattern of social and physical organization.

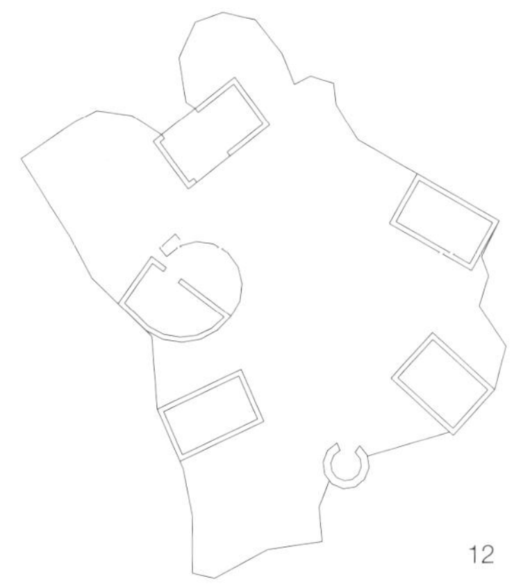

12

The institutions that arose with the industrial revolution, however, produced kinds of structures that were unknown before 1750. Schools and libraries for middle-class citizens of cities, manufacturing structures, and places to sell the goods that mass production brought forth were all new building types. Railroads and automobiles altered the organization and distances that could be traveled in cities. The size of cities grew until there were hundreds of settlements in the world that contained more than 1,000,000 people. All of these factors contributed to the urbanization of the world we recognize today.

How might we think of domain today?

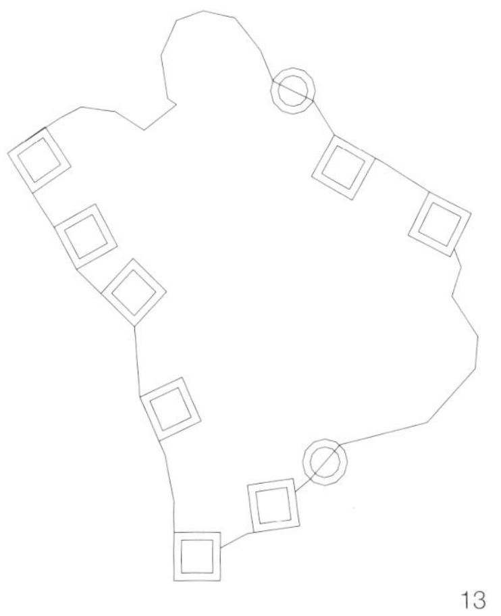

13

Architectural domains play a crucial role in our everyday lives though we often do not notice them. Two stories illustrate the role of these domains in our lives. The first stems from the complexity of social and physical demarcation of territory that accompanies a front yard. My house sits on a small, 40-foot by 120-foot lot in south Minneapolis, Minnesota. It once had a large front porch that was turned into a sun porch and has since become a part of my living room. The result is that the windows in the primary living space of my house are only 20 feet from the public sidewalk that allows pedestrians to transverse our neighborhood. That's a bit too close to the street for me. For 25 years, I have advocated a lovely arborvitae hedge, about 8 feet high, to capture the front yard from neighbors for my living space. My wife replies "Over my dead body." Why?

My front yard is a much more complex issue of territorial boundary and social custom than it may appear to be. To understand it requires an examination of our responses to a number of issues. Let's begin in the street. The city owns the street. Cars may pass at will. My front walkway terminates at the curb. If someone repeatedly parks in front of my walkway, what might I say? The boulevard belongs to the city. Who mows it? The public sidewalk belongs to the city. Who shovels it when it snows? How do neighbors feel about other neighbors who fail to shovel their public sidewalk after a snowstorm? We all grow (or try to grow) grass in our Midwestern front yards. Growing grass is an unnatural act here; it clearly was meant for another climate. Yet we all march to the same horticulturalist on my block and grow only to mow grass.

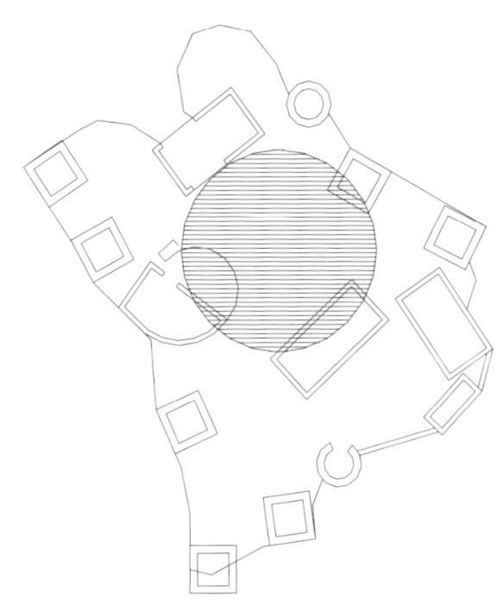

14

15

When pedestrians turn up my private walkway, they cross an invisible boundary. They are now, clearly, entering my domain. When I sit out on my small front porch on a sunny day reading the newspaper and glance up, I'm obliged to say hello to anyone on the public sidewalk whether I know them or not. These are all familiar social rules that go with the physical boundaries of my front yard.

Our Midwestern blocks are socially organized so that our front yards belong to us, but they also belong to all of us who have houses along a street. In many ways, the front yard, while owned by individuals, represents common territory. It separates each house from the public sidewalk and street while binding us together as a community. My wife will not allow me to plant an arborvitae hedge around my front yard because to do so would be to disregard my larger social obligation to my neighbors. The rules of behavior of this territory have been established by this larger group. My private domain is a part of their larger social domain. Not planting an arborvitae hedge is one of the ways that I am able to belong within that domain.

Robert Bly, a well-known poet from this area, makes the importance of these values clear in his own story. As a young college student, Bly went east to an Ivy League school to become a writer. He did well, and his poetry was beginning to be frequently published in the eastern academic press. Then his father fell seriously ill, and Robert returned to his Minnesota farm home to be with his family. While there, he realized that something was missing in his poetry. He realized that he didn't really know what he was trying to say in his work. A sense of despair came over the young poet until he walked into the front yard of his farmhouse and leaned against an old oak tree. Bly realized that he understood that tree. He had grown up with it. He could say something genuine about his oak tree because he knew it so intimately. The values that we each attach to our domain permeate our thought as Bly's oak tree was fundamental to his understanding of the world.

16

15 A Dogon elder in the togo-na
16 Exterior of the togo na
17 Dogon ceremonial sculpture

The Dogon

18 Dogon granary
19 Detail of Dogon granary
20 Floor
21 Wall
22 Frame
23 Roof/ceiling
24 Opening

The Dogon people migrated to Mali in northwestern Africa sometime around 1300 AD. Currently about 200,000 Dogon people inhabit this area in four tribes: the Arou, the Ono, the Dyon, and the Domno. The land in Mali that they occupy is the Bandiagara escarpment and neighboring Gondo plain. This semi-arid land has a river running through it that supplies water for crops. Farm fields are laid out along the river with village houses nearby in nucleated settlements. The Dogon are an unusually artistic people whose art commemorates the wonderful story of their origin.

Description of a Dogon village

18

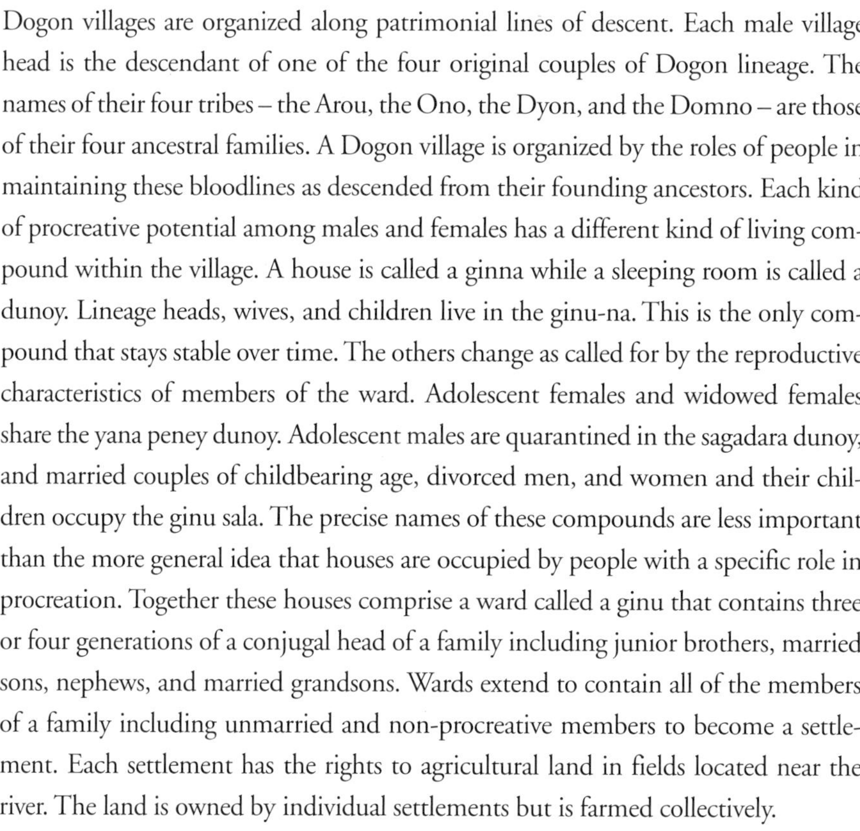

Dogon villages are organized along patrimonial lines of descent. Each male village head is the descendant of one of the four original couples of Dogon lineage. The names of their four tribes – the Arou, the Ono, the Dyon, and the Domno – are those of their four ancestral families. A Dogon village is organized by the roles of people in maintaining these bloodlines as descended from their founding ancestors. Each kind of procreative potential among males and females has a different kind of living compound within the village. A house is called a ginna while a sleeping room is called a dunoy. Lineage heads, wives, and children live in the ginu-na. This is the only compound that stays stable over time. The others change as called for by the reproductive characteristics of members of the ward. Adolescent females and widowed females share the yana peney dunoy. Adolescent males are quarantined in the sagadara dunoy, and married couples of childbearing age, divorced men, and women and their children occupy the ginu sala. The precise names of these compounds are less important than the more general idea that houses are occupied by people with a specific role in procreation. Together these houses comprise a ward called a ginu that contains three or four generations of a conjugal head of a family including junior brothers, married sons, nephews, and married grandsons. Wards extend to contain all of the members of a family including unmarried and non-procreative members to become a settlement. Each settlement has the rights to agricultural land in fields located near the river. The land is owned by individual settlements but is farmed collectively.

19

Dogon settlements are a collection of compounds. One to four houses are grouped around an open area of common use in each compound. The entire area of the compound is walled. Tall, rectangular millet granaries may either be part of this wall or located within it. Smaller granaries are used for storing secondary crops. Enclosed rooms in the compound are sleeping areas for wives. Stone seating platforms are placed within the central social area that is also used as a cooking space. This common central area is shared with livestock pens and chicken coops. A front porch serves as an entry to connect the compound to the larger social structure of the village.

Each village has a special structure called a togo na. This building is alternately called the house of words, the men's house, or the great shelter by the Dogon. The function of this building is to be a communal meeting place for the elder males of the village. Here they administer justice, fix the agricultural calendar, deal with emergencies, and make other administrative decisions for the village. This structure is generally 4 meters by 6 meters in plan but is only 1.3 to 1.5 meters high. This low ceiling is intentional. It forces all members of the governing council to remain seated, promoting discussion rather than physical confrontation over difficult issues.

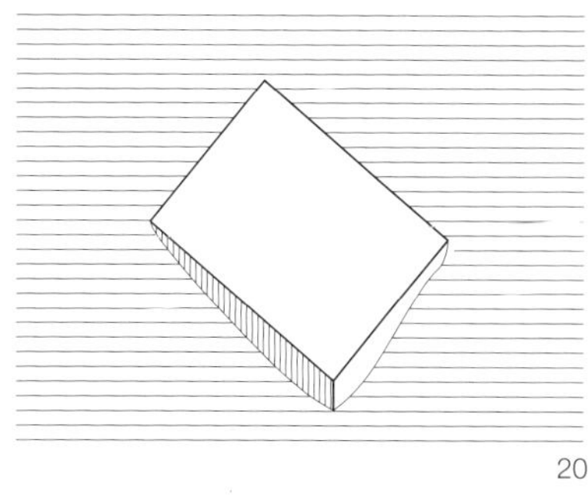
20

Dogon thought, values, and myth of origin

All of this would remain mere physical description without a set of values to animate it. The values that give birth to the Dogon domain emanate from the Dogon myth of origin. In this myth, the supreme being, Amma, precedes all existence within a cosmic egg. This is a marvelous symbol of fecundity for a people who cherish birth and bloodlines above all else. Amma, in this myth, is not an outside actor but an integral portion of that which can be literally observed to create life from the inert material of a yolk. This paired symbol of Amma plus the cosmic egg becomes the metaphorical structure of the Dogon universe.

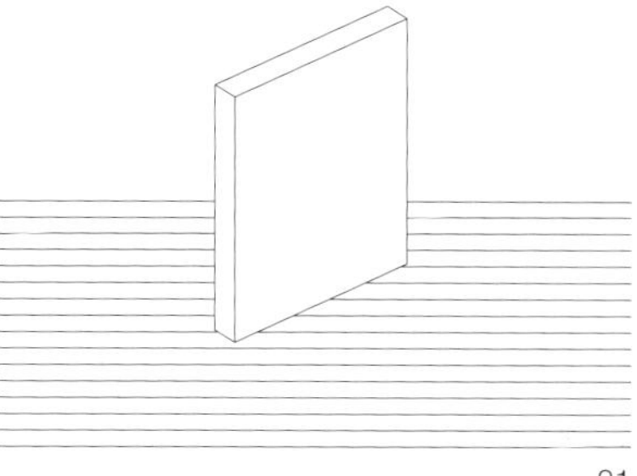
21

Dogon culture is a culture of signs. For them, signs precede symbols, symbols precede thought, and thought precedes reality. This notion begins within the cosmic egg when Amma has sex with himself /herself to produce the 266 signs of the universe. These signs are archives of the events, ideas, and rituals that allow people to regenerate themselves into the orderly workings of the universe. They constitute a kind of cosmic key akin to our conception of modern science.

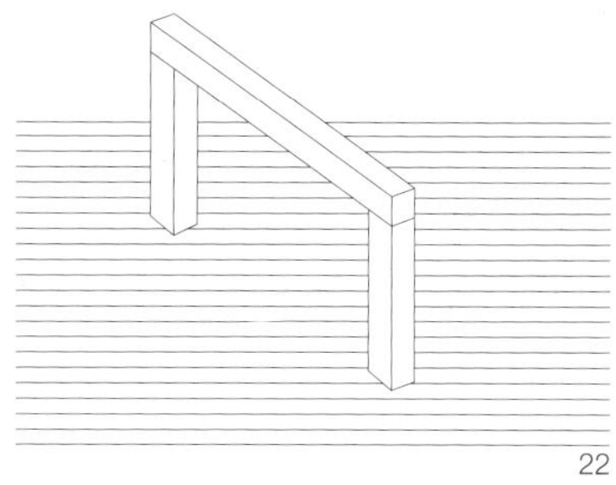
22

The birth of the world is prefigured by seven signs. First, there is the egg. Then there is Amma within the egg. Creation begins when the interior of the egg is partitioned into quadrants. These compartments come to symbolize many things including the placenta, the four cardinal directions, and the four initial pairs of ancestors of the Dogon. After the egg's interior is partitioned, the first seed, or word, leaves the egg. The fifth development of signs that prefigure the world is a horizontal line just below the egg, which signifies that after creation Amma becomes the prisoner of his/her own creative acts. This is followed by the arch that structures the world pictured at the lower end of the line that signified the seed of the word. Finally, the horizontal bar of Amma's imprisonment drops to become arms that signal the dawn of humankind.

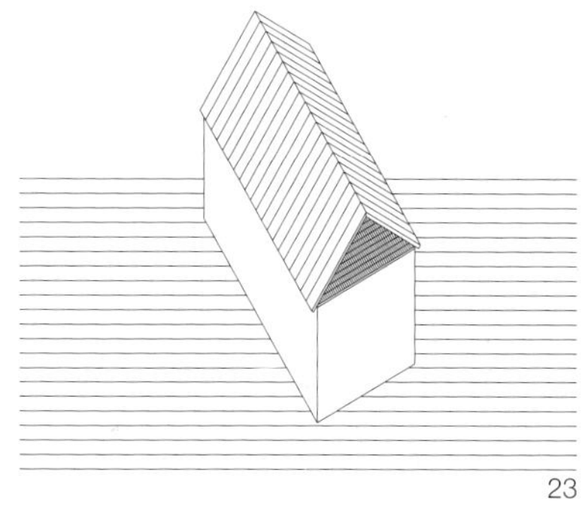
23

This sequence represents Amma's second try creating humankind. The first was aborted because Amma gave birth to humans as a singular entity rather than as two people of different genders. This singular entity was Ogo, who immediately after being born, stole a quarter of the placenta (one of the quadrants of the first internal partitioning of the cosmic egg) and brought it to earth as fire. Ogo, both because of his lack of a mate and his duplicity, was unable to procreate. Everything that he touched withered. Amma corrected this mistake by turning Ogo into a jackal and restarted creation on a more fecund base. There is something very human about a supreme

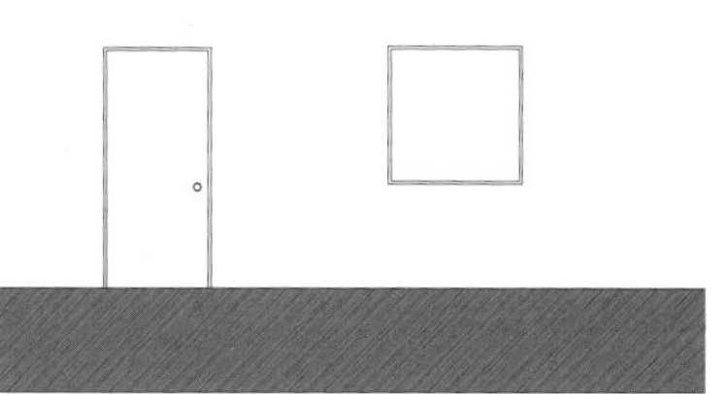
24

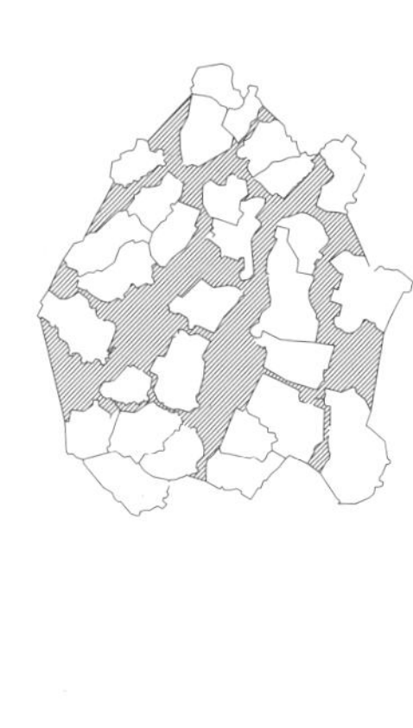
25

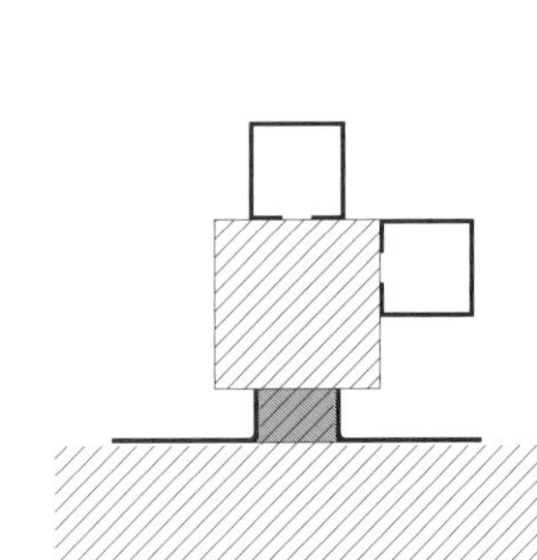
26

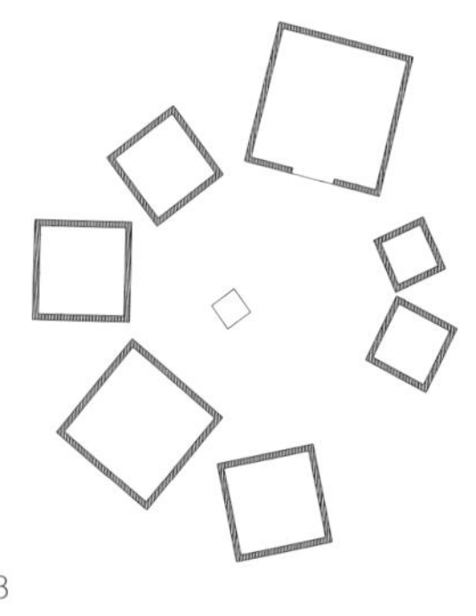
27

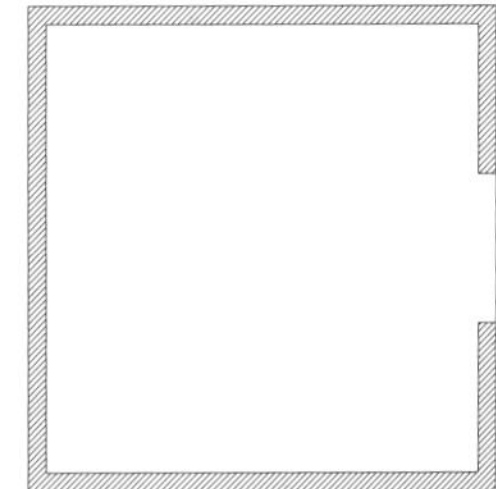
28

29

being who makes a mistake when he first tries to create the world and has to abort his experiment to correct the problem. On his second try, Amma begins with duality. The primal individual becomes the primal couple. The primal couple then gives birth to the four male/female pairs who are the ancestors of the tribes of the Dogon.

The construct of duality runs through Dogon thought in the signs used to structure their domain. Amma in the cosmic egg represents both what something is and what inscribes it. Amma and the 266 signs are both the energy of origin and the symbols that give order to the world. This kind of duality will be manifest in Dogon buildings in hundreds of ways.

It is this Dogon emphasis on symbol preceding form that creates such a rich pallet for the Dogon design of domains. For the Dogon, history is not lineal and progressive but static and conservative. The goal of the Dogon symbols is to preserve the sum of a people's knowledge so it will always be an intimate part of their lives. The Dogon granary provides a rich example of this kind of preservation of symbols that reenact the Dogon myth of origin. Construction of the granary is initiated with a foundation of nine stones in three rows. The nine stones might be interpreted as the eight original ancestors of the four Dogon tribes surrounding Lebe, the Dogon god of water. This base mates the idea of the fertility of the land represented by the storage of crops with the fertility of people as represented by the four primal pairs all given life by water in this semi-arid land. The seven floor supports which sit on top of these stones represent the seven vibrations of the cosmic egg that gave birth to the world. In this manner, the floor of storage that provides for biological survival is mated with the origin of the 266 signs that will provide the symbolic structure to the world of the Dogon.

Four inch thick mud walls are built on this rectangular base. They will rise to form a two-story granary that is circular on the top. The two stories represent the duality of heaven and earth. The rectangular base represents the impurity of the earth while the circular top represents the purity of heaven. A thatch roof above this wall is supported by nine radial rafters. These nine rafters restate the nine stones of the foundation and create symmetry between heaven and earth. The outline of the granary as a whole represents the cosmic egg with Amma in it. The doors of the granary are formed in a pair. The zigzag lines at the side of the doors represent the seven vibrations of the earth and are a graphic sign for the helix that portrays the Dogon structure of the universe. The primordial couple and their four paired offspring as the origin of the four Dogon tribes are symmetrically portrayed on the two doors. The paired doors symbolize the duality that is the foundation of the fecundity of the universe.

This description is a synopsis of ways that the symbolic content of the Dogon granary might be interpreted. What is important about it to us is that the structures of the Dogon so graphically portray their values. As graphic signs, these symbols are multi-vocal: they might stand for multiple meanings. History is a set of repeating primordial acts, and the results of all past acts are always present in Dogon culture because the forms of their domain preserve them.

Domains of the Dogon

A way to begin understanding this construction of the Dogon domains is to formally analyze the architectural elements that create them.

Domains are initiated by leveling the earth to become a floor. A floor signals an architectural domain in that it proposes that a broad range of human activities might take place on it. In a Dogon compound, special areas are spelled out on this floor by mats to sleep on, stones to sit on, and a fire pit to cook in. Sleeping mats are surrounded by four walls and a roof to create a private place to sleep, one that is separated from the other social activities of the compound. Granaries are similarly enclosed with walls and a roof to protect the millet that will biologically sustain the family. An 8-foot high wall separates these areas from all the other compounds in the village. Sleeping rooms and granaries are sometimes incorporated into this wall. A front porch, as the compound's front door, connects the interior of the compound to the larger community.

As compounds multiply, the shape of a village begins to emerge. The walls of each compound separate the values of those within from those of the group as a whole. These are the procreative values of childbearing capacity and lineage as offspring of one of the four primal couples of the Dogon myth of origin. The area outside of these compounds allows people to access them. They are a rough progenitor of streets in a city. Each compound is linked to the whole by its front door porch that connects the social area of the family within a compound with the social territory of the village as a whole. All is held together by the communal decisions made in the togo-na by the governing elders of the tribe.

Domain in a Dogon village is, thus, divided into three general categories. There is first the domain of an individual made by a mat to sleep on or a stone to sit on; then there is the domain of the family surrounded by a compound wall that encloses the social structure of that group along with the granaries and livestock that sustain its biological existence; and finally, there is the domain of the village that includes the compounds of the extended family of the male head of the tribe, the paths that connect these compounds, and the togo-na where communal decisions are made. All is animated by the Dogon myth of Amma and the cosmic egg.

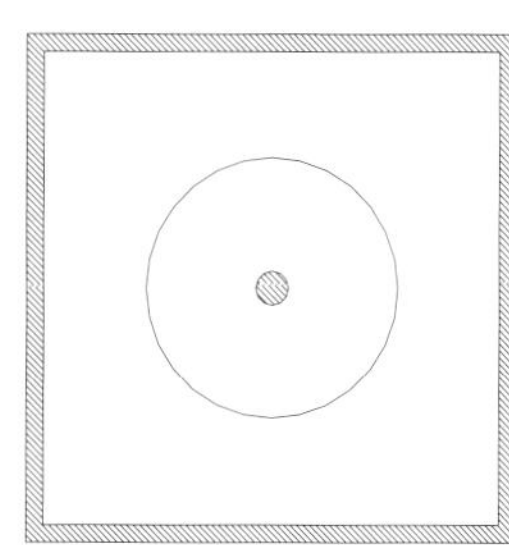

30

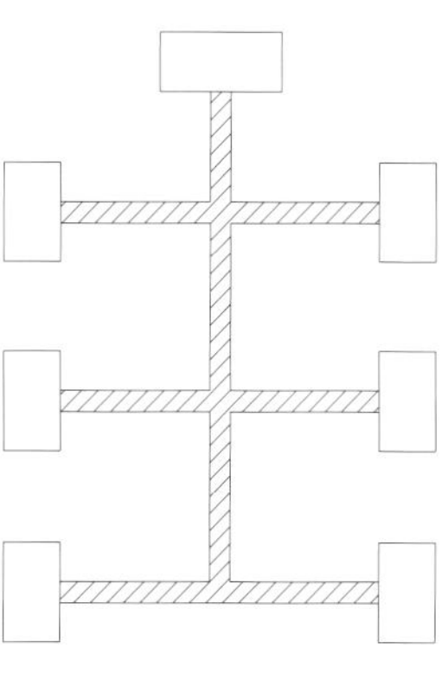

31

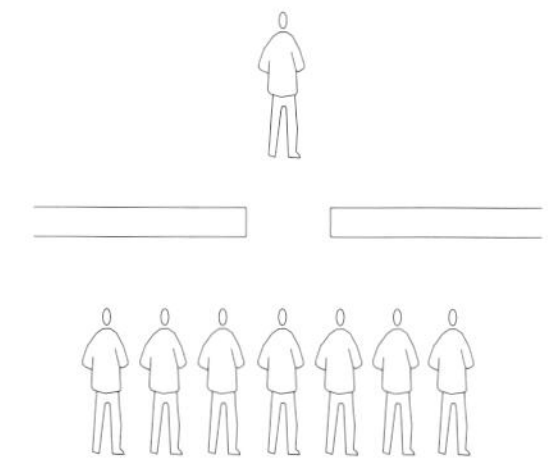

32

25 Settlement
26 Domain as boundary
27 Entry as the juncture between two domains
28 Dwelling as a collection of rooms
29 Room as an enclosed domain
30 Center and edge
31 Path and place
32 Individual and group
33 Inside and outside

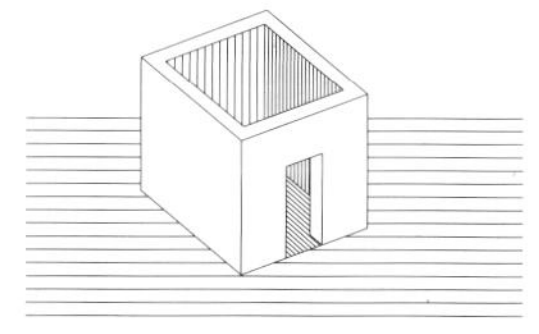

33

Closing thoughts

34 A Dogon granary door
35 Dogon ceremonial mask

The world of architecture begins in a natural landscape; a landscape sculpted solely through the interaction of natural material with natural force. Natural forms of the earth are the result of the energies and the material of the earth achieving equilibrium. Beaches are sculpted by waves and the inertia of sand pebbles, mountains by plates and internal pressures of the earth, rivers by rain, gravity, and the hardness of different kinds of rock, forests by trees, soil, and climate. The process for each is the same though the ingredients and outcomes are very different. These forms are a snapshot in time of the continuously changing outcomes of natural processes.

Human creations transform this natural world to accommodate the needs and desires of human beings. The first human act of marking a domain was the simplest of alterations to this natural landscape. Making a path by treading the same route frequently enough to break grasses and compress earth differs only slightly from waves making beaches in process or product. A human actor simply replaces natural force as an agent of temporary change. Tilling soil, as our species began to do 12,000 years ago, is a different matter. This process is foreign to the natural world as is its outcome. The tools made marks on the earth that nature had not seen before. The biological mating of two oat grasses to produce a hybrid wheat plant constituted direct human tampering in nature's organic order. The idea of the permanent field, selected for fertility and water and reworked annually, marked the earth as it had not been marked before.

Permanent dwellings developed hand-in-hand with permanent fields. The latter required the former. No longer were members of our species nomads but now had become members of a permanent community anchored to a single place they would call home. Their constructions of multiple homes made a village.

These dwellings consisted of elements that were to become the elementary ingredients of all buildings. Floors leveled the ground so that inhabitants could stand and move about; vertical walls horizontally separated an external landscape and climate from an internal landscape and climate; roofs and ceilings covered inhabitants from

35

the sky; openings reconnected inhabitants of interiors from all in the exterior that assemblies of these elements had separated them from; frames held elements aloft; fire powered an internal climate different from harsh weather outside; and gardens modified the organic shape of the land to fit human needs and desires.

A second order of architectural ideas emerged from the assembly of these elements. These ideas included boundary, room, house, and entry. These words let us generalize across particular assemblies of architectural elements. Territorial markers signify domain; six surfaces to enclose a space signify room; assemblies of rooms to fit the needs of a family signify house; and the act of crossing from one domain into another signifies entry. These assemblies reflect human social and physical needs. They are central to our ability to locate ourselves within but distinct from the organic order of the natural landscape that provides our context. They are just as central to the ways we have learned to live with one another.

But these assemblies would be in danger of becoming mere enclosures, shelter hollowed from natural force, without the addition of a last major ingredient. Each of these assemblies is material and social; but perhaps of even greater importance, each holds and reflects a set of values. Domains contain us with our values. A domain is separated from a transitory place to stay by just these values. No one expects a motel room to contain or reflect the things that matter most to us. This honor is reserved for the places we make for ourselves. This making of a place that contains our values might be as simple as placing a special photograph on a dresser or as complex as designing and building a house. In either case, it is our personal sense of significance that selects a particular architectural form as our residence. Among the Dogon, this shape and arrangement is animated by their rich myth of origin. In our industrial society, personal or societal belief may be a bit more difficult to discern in our buildings, but it is never absent.

The broader abstractions that we might associate with ideas that grow from constructed domains are, thus, never as simple as an analysis of their material shape. These material forms speak of other significant things. The way a society selects building materials and how it crafts the organization of these materials provides a base for social and cultural interpretation. But this message would fall far short of the richness of the ideas created by architectural domains in the absence of the social and cultural constructs that these assemblies might be interpreted to convey.

Inside/outside is not simply a physical demarcation but a social and cultural divide as well. My home contains my family and my particular sense of the importance of life as well as materially separating nature's domain from my own. Center and edge may refer to a geometric point versus a linear surround of my territory, or just as easily a dining table that gathers my family for meals and conversation, or an altar to my deity. Identification of the place of the individual versus that of the greater group signifies the difference between families and a community but also individual idiosyncrasies versus the common values of the group. Path and place indicate movement versus stasis but also common versus individual senses of value.

36 A young Dogon woman

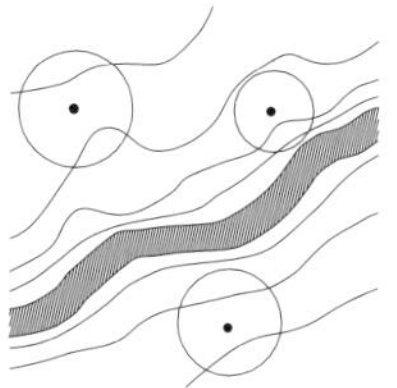

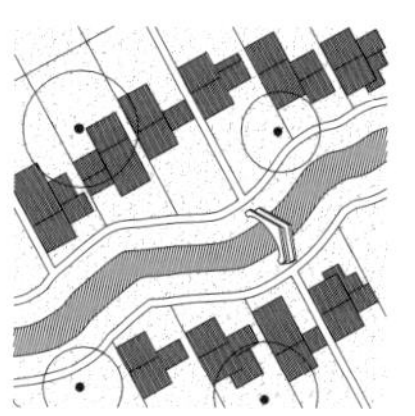

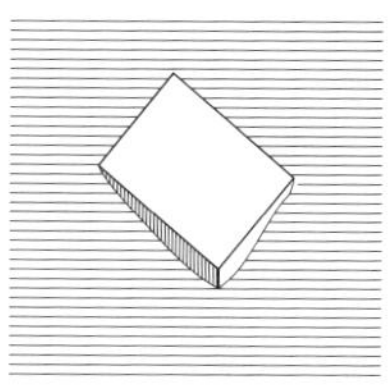

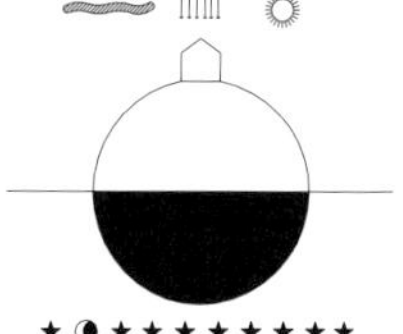

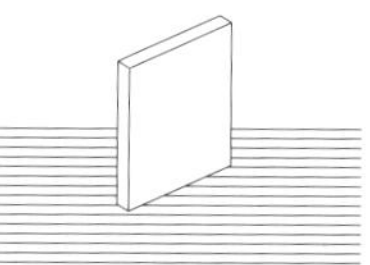

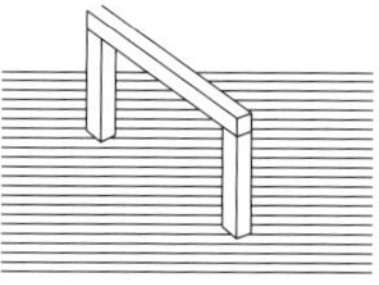

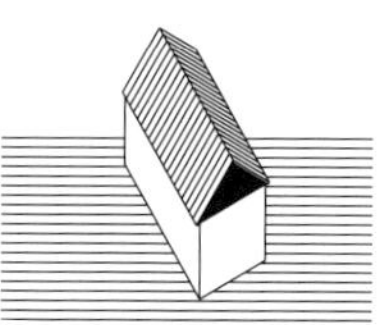

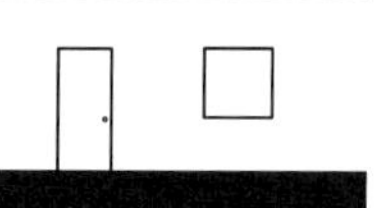

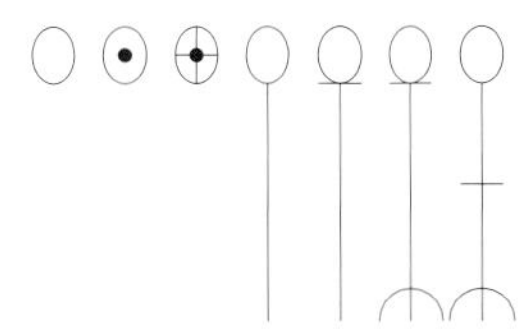

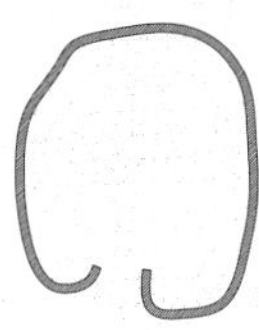

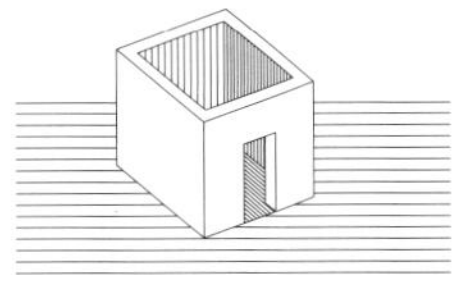

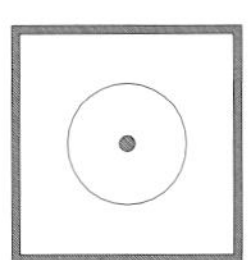

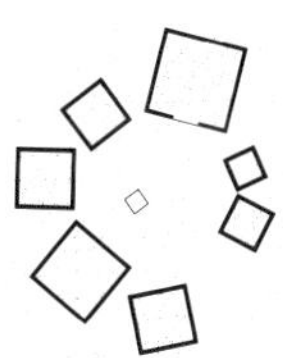

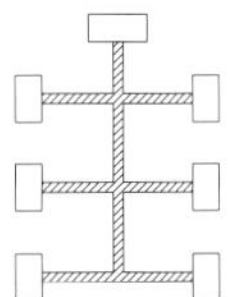

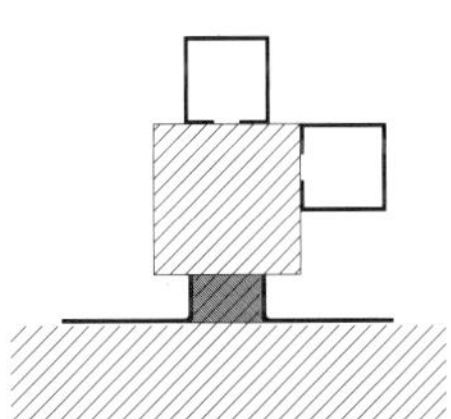

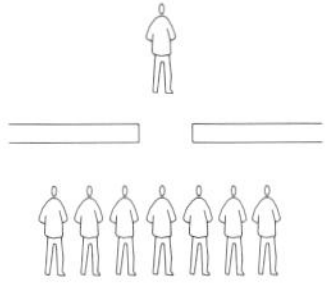

DOMAINS
IN POST-1850 ARCHITECTURE

Body, cultural history, personal identity, and consumerism as values of contemporary domains

Background

Given the central position of issues of domain in architecture, it is surprising that this issue has found so little voice in design thought after 1850. The early modern movement followed popular intellectual fashion and reduced people to measurable commodities. Hygiene replaced the rich array of possible definitions of the significance of domain, allowing clean and well-lit living conditions to replace richer definitions of a place to live. This reduction is partially understandable given the urban living conditions in the cities of the industrial revolution. Edinburgh, Scotland was justifiably called the sewer of Europe. Other cities were not far behind. But this reduction had continuing and damaging consequences for the 20th-century's definition of architectural domain. This objectification of life in a dwelling tended to allow buildings and cities to be designed as mechanical objects that processed rather than housed urban populations.

Architecture was slow to respond to this new definition of the significance of domain. It took half a century for the real impact of these intellectual roots to be felt in a large enough portion of our environment to become worthy of attention. When they were noticed, the response occurred at the fringes of architectural thought rather than at its center. A series of author/architects began to take issue with the modern movement's definition of domain in the 1960s. Aldo van Eyck and the Dutch led this attack when van Eyck published his now famous article on occasion and place. The modern movement and its historians had defined architecture to be concerned with time and space, issues that were held in esteem by modern science and philosophy. Architecture took up the scientific creed of time and space to become part of this revolutionary stance by association if not by actual thought. Van Eyck responded that

01 Villa Mairea in the Finnish woods

architecture was not physics, and architects dealt not with time but with occasion, not with space but with place. In so doing, he re-centered architecture in a subjective rather than objective vision of its products. Human beings with all their immeasurable qualities were reinstated as the center of constructed domains in this pronouncement. Van Eyck's design work in an orphanage and home for unwed mothers gave architectural substance to his writings.

The second attack on the scientific objectification of design came from an unlikely source. Christopher Alexander was trained as a mathematician at the Massachusetts Institute of Technology. His interests in architecture were systematic and addressed the role of computers in design thought. After Alexander had done extensive work in this area culminating in *Notes on the Synthesis of Form*, he rejected his own scientific stance in favor of a definition based in vernacular buildings. In these buildings Alexander thought that he had discovered transcendent patterns of the design of domains that emanated from core human values. He wrote the intellectual defense of this stance in *The Timeless Way of Building*. The actual patterns that he and colleagues found in their examination of vernacular buildings were conveyed in *A Pattern Language*. Together these two volumes supplied the ammunition required by a group of architects who had become disenchanted with the abstractions of domain enunciated by modernism.

In the 1970s, Norwegian architectural historian Christian Norberg Schultz joined this debate with a series of books that took issue with the way buildings had been dealt with by architectural historians who were trained as art historians. Schultz broke with this tradition by examining constructed environments on the basis of work done by 20th-century anthropologists and philosophers. He was particularly interested in the work of Jean Piaget and Claude Lévi-Strauss who suggested that societies were un-

02

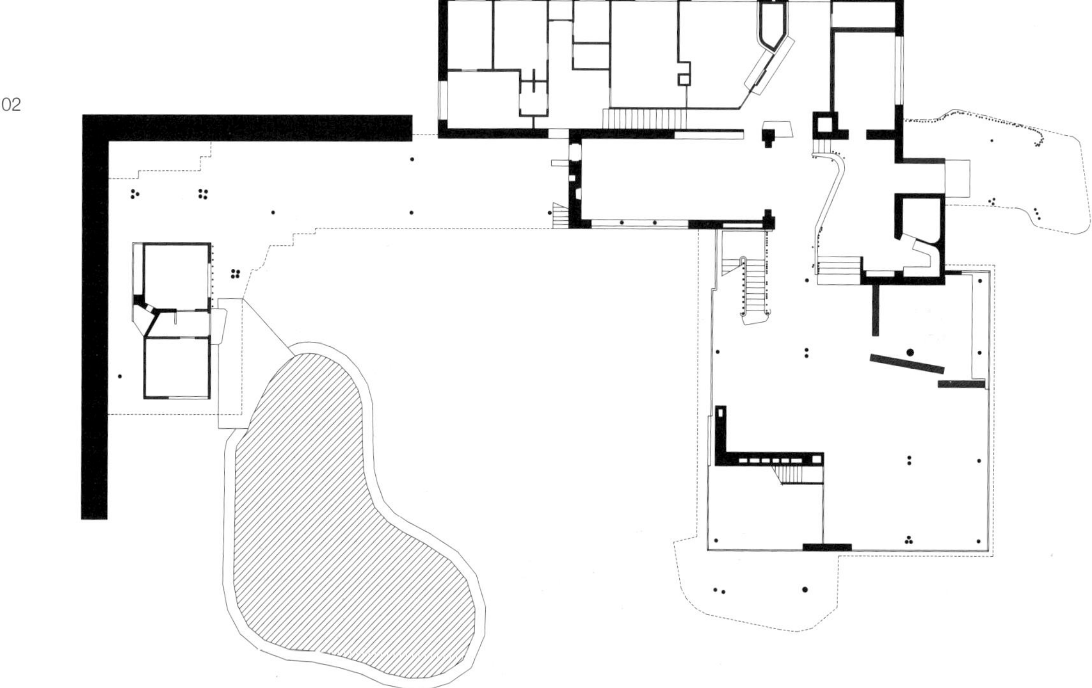

02 Plan of Villa Mairea
03 Entry canopy of Villa Mairea

derpinned by deep structures that determined their behaviors. Piaget dealt with pattern making as a fundamental trait of human thought. Lévi-Strauss was interested in the role of social acts like gift-giving as symbols of deep social structures. Together these two suggested to Schultz that the basis for the design of environments might be our desire to establish patterns that organized human social and cultural values which reflected deep structures of human behavior. *Intentions in Architecture* presented this manifesto to a larger architectural community.

Finally, there are the irreverent voices of Charles Moore, Donlyn Lyndon, William Turnbull, and Charles Whitaker. These four formed the firm MLTW in the early 1960s in Berkeley, California. The 1960s were an era of rapid social change in the United States, and nowhere else in the country took this revolution more seriously than did the people of Berkeley. At one point, the citizens of this city proposed seceding from the United States, a social act that had not been seriously contemplated since the Civil War. This wonderful group, headed by Charles Moore, decided to cast off the intellectual shackles of modernism to pursue an architecture that more intimately reflected the desires of people who lived in their buildings. Central to this movement was the notion that all people carried with them a rich sense of their own history. This sense was recorded in objects collected over lifetimes and memories of places they had enjoyed being in. A good domain was one that gave a home to these artifacts and remembrances. *Body, Memory and Architecture* and *The Place of Houses* analyzed their extant design work in these terms.

It may appear that these descriptions outline major directional changes in 20th-century architecture; and in some ways, they do. Place and occasion rather than time and space, the underlying values of domain found in vernacular environments, patterns and values underlying architectural intensions, and personal and corporate memory are all very distant from abstract and objective ideas of domain as time and space. But though some wonderful buildings came out of this movement, they remained largely peripheral to architectural thought. Architecture in the 20th century continued to take up issues of order and technology as its central driving force. The buildings that did break with this more general direction remain unusually interesting primarily because they are not common.

03

Villa Mairea

The modern movement, like all other movements, was never quite as coherent as it was often portrayed to be. A number of important architects of this era did not fit comfortably within the definitions of what constituted modernity as supplied by Walter Gropius, Le Corbusier, and Ludwig Mies van der Rohe. Le Corbusier cast the problems of modernism in cerebral terms, Mies van der Rohe as a manifestation of universal space, and Gropius as the problem of building in an era of industrial production. Chief among those architects whose work was difficult to classify under this rubric was Finnish architect Alvar Aalto. Aalto began practicing architecture in Finland just after that country became independent in 1917 after 800 years under Sweden and 100 under Russia. What is surprising is that the Finns managed to maintain a national identity over this extended period of colonial rule. That they did so was clear in the movement called National Romanticism that gave birth to composers like Jean Sibelius. Aalto's place within this history is probably responsible in no small measure for his divergence from mainstream European architectural thought.

04 Interior entry space of Villa Mairea
05 Sod covered logia of Villa Mairea
06 Dining room of Villa Mairea
07 Villa Mairea stair

The house

Villa Mairea is a complex set of interwoven domains that recall the cultural history of a people. It is a house that Aalto designed for a wealthy industrial family in Noormarkku, Finland in 1938. The house is composed of four major parts. A two-story stone rectangle contains service functions like the kitchen and servants' quarters below, and children's and guest bedrooms above. The central section of the house contains the front entry, a vestibule, a dining room, and an outdoor logia that terminates in a sauna.

04

On the other side of this midsection lies a two-story column and beam box that houses the living room, library, and winter garden on the ground floor with the parents' bedrooms, an art studio, and outdoor decks above. This column and beam box and the dining room/ logia/sauna enclose a courtyard behind the house that contains an irregularly shaped pool framed by a series of stone walls and earth beams. Villa Mairea is surrounded by the dense foliage of a Finnish pine forest.

06

05

Domains

Villa Mairea creates a series of overlapping domains that mirror Finnish attitudes about their cultural origins. The tripartite formal division of this house in plan is less about functional differentiation than the significance of activities in terms of Finnish social values. The center section of the house contains functions that link this house to a corporate sense of social value. Front door, entry, dining room, sod-covered logia, and the sauna all speak eloquently to the centrality of these values in Finnish culture. The front door of Villa Mairea serves the same purpose as the porch of the Dogon compound. The entry to Villa Mairea, however, is very different in form from that of the Dogon porch. The Villa Mairea entry is initiated by a canopy supported by columns of peeled logs and partially enclosed by a screen of smaller peeled branches. The sleek canopy of this entry might be seen to be an outgrowth of the formal vocabulary of the modern movement. The stripped logs and branches that hold it up and screen it from the rest of the site are a problem for mainstream modernists. These are not manufactured materials but objects only one step removed from their natural forms. The sense of these logs and branches is not as much an imitation of the trees that surround the house as a symbolic act of reverence for the products of the natural world. This construction is a carefully planned and detailed artifice that reminds inhabitants of a simpler time when nature was more directly a part of people's lives. This atavistic

07

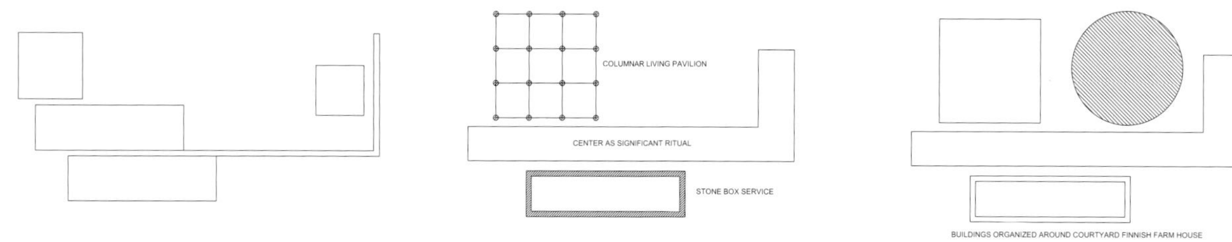

08

use of logs to support a sleek canopy is an artful reminder of the past and a symbolic indication that as a species we continue to inhabit nature even if the industrial revolution has distanced us from a direct appreciation of the natural world.

The entry continues into the small foyer of the house. The floor of this little room is at the same level and material as the floor of the porch outside. A difference in elevation occurs only when the entry rises four steps into the living area. This vestibule is suspended between the ground level stone of the outdoors and the elevated floor of the living room that signals entry into the house proper.

The third element in this central spine of cultural memory is the dining room. Here the family gathers to discuss the matters of the day as they have always done. Members of the family have their appointed places around the table specifying their role in this social unit. Gathering to eat and converse is a distinctly human trait. The table creates a domain in which participants in a meal are both held together as a group facing one another and separated by a distance that is congenial. This gathering around a center is a primal act of human domain formation with deep historic roots.

The sod-covered logia beyond the dining room is not made necessary by any specific family activity. The concrete frame of this logia is covered first with purlins, then with birch bark, and finally with sod. This construction harkens back to the first Finnish houses that were sod-covered pit houses. This roof is not the expected covering material of a modern concrete frame. Its presence atop a modern frame reminds us that domain is not its construction system but an aggregation in the present of elements that have made our domains in the past. These memories are carried along in our houses not because they make technological sense but because they preserve elements of former domains that have maintained their symbolic value in our lives. Like a fireplace in a contemporary suburban home, the sod covering of this logia does not represent nostalgia but rather the value of our domains that has been accumulated along a history to which we remain connected.

The sod-covered logia creates an appropriate transition to the sauna as the center of Finnish culture. Few other societies spend Saturday night in dry heat ranging from 180°-200° F. Other people do not consider a jump in a cold lake or a roll in the snow after heating the core temperature of their body in the oven of the sauna to be a source of great pleasure. Finns, however, take a particular comfort from this activity. It is both

08 The organization of Villa Màirea as a stone box service area and a columnar living room flanking a center of cultural memory and enclosing an idealized landscape
09 The overlapping territories of the living room, winter garden and library; the wife's bedroom, studio, and winter garden; the parent's bedrooms, hall and front terrace; the children's and parent's bedrooms and halls
10 Detail of roar façade of Villa Mairea
11 The living area of Villa Mairea

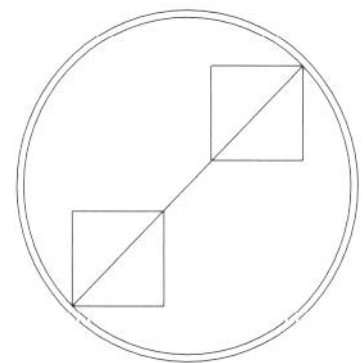
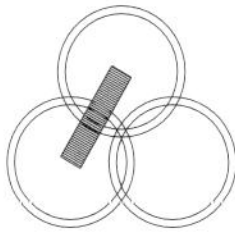
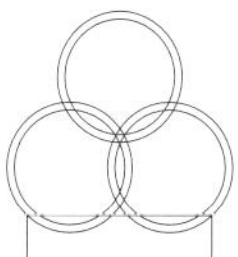

09

a cultural and a social rite, a place of mental and physical cleansing. The oldest Finnish houses were thought to be saunas. The sauna ceremony helps to identify a people as a tribe, much as the Dogon myth of origin helped to give them a group identity. The primitive sod-covered logia and exquisite sauna of Villa Mairea bring this old custom forward into contemporary Finnish life.

This central portion of the domain of Villa Mairea is flanked on one side by a stone box containing kitchen, pantry, servants' quarters, and office below and children's and guest bedrooms above. These activities have always been necessary to the operation of a home. Containing them in vernacular stone walls may be as much a commentary on past significance of these functions as it is to those of today.

This stone box is formally balanced by a modern frame structure on the opposite side of the house's entry/dining/logia/sauna center. This large frame contains the living area, library, and winter garden on its lower floor and the parent's bedrooms, halls, painting studio, and outdoor decks of the second floor. Unlike the stone utility portion of the house in which functions are assigned to rooms, domains overlap in this part of the house to create more complex relationships. The library and winter garden are inserted within the more general boundary of the living area. Parts of this living space are demarked by specific architectural elements like the stair and fireplace, while walls and floors separate others from the main body of this room. The library, initially intended to be enclosed by movable panels, hovers within the living space connected to the ceiling by a sinuous glass divider. The winter garden occupies a corner cut out of the room. Library, winter garden, fireplace, and

10

11

seating areas collect family members with different sensibilities and needs in a common area. The stair overlaps the parents' entry hall above, and that entry hall overlaps that of the children's bedrooms. Each of these domains is distinct yet is connected to its counterpart not by a doorway but by an area of floor that registers a much looser sense of demarcation.

Upstairs, the two parents' bedrooms are held together by a common bath. The interior hall at the head of the stairs couples them in a common seating area with a fireplace. A common deck provides the same service at the other end of these bedrooms. The wife's bedroom is adjacent to her painting studio on the second floor which, in turn, is linked directly with the winter garden, another special interest of the wife but one shared by other members of the family, through a small stair directly from the painting studio to this first floor space. The common hall of the children's bedrooms is designed to be a play area that gathers their three rooms into a social unit. Bedrooms for parents, children, and guests form an L-shaped enclosure around a common second floor deck that looks out over the courtyard at the rear of the house. This deck is joined to the lower space by a small stair.

The house as a whole curls around an inner courtyard. The living room, dining room, logia, and sauna cup a grassy area with a stone-lined pool at its center. This garden centers the house as the dining room table centers the family around meals. It recalls the yard of a Finnish farmhouse as home, sauna, barn, and numerous outbuildings gathered around a common outdoor working space. But the farmhouse courtyard of the past was utilitarian as opposed to the symbolic character of the contemporary central green area of Villa Mairea. Here the manicured grass and cut stone pool are clearly manmade as opposed to the pine forest beyond. This courtyard represents a kind of protected, excised nature as opposed to the organic form of the forest. Its significance to the idea of domain is as a domestication of nature. Like the farm field that provides food, this is a natural landscape that has been transformed to suit human purpose. Unlike the field for growing food, however, this purpose is symbolic rather than biological. This representation creates a landscape that is about what we think that nature means rather than about its literal evolution as the product of natural force. This excising by framing makes nature a part of the human world of symbols rather than a part of the world as natural selection. It is a nature that is able to belong to people rather than solely to the great forces that have formed the earth without us.

The parents' bedrooms wrap around a bathroom. The bedrooms plus bathroom are wrapped by a common living area on one side and an outdoor deck on the other. The parents' domain is attached to the children's bedrooms by the stair hall and to the living area by a painting studio and winter garden. The children's and guest bedrooms wrap around an outdoor deck that connects them both visually and literally to the courtyard of the house. The living room envelopes the library and the winter garden. The living room and service block hold the entry/dining room/logia/sauna between them as the social and symbolic center of the house. The living room with bedrooms above cups a domesticated piece of nature at the center of the house. Domain after domain is melded together in complex overlays of territory, social organization, and cultural values.

12 The library of Villa Mairea

13

13 Sea Ranch condominiums
14 Sea Ranch from the ocean
15 Sea Ranch entry road
16 Sea Ranch interior
17 Sea Ranch framing system
18 Sea Ranch corner domain

Sea Ranch condominiums

14

The design of the Sea Ranch condominiums comes from the 1960s, an era of experimentation in the United States. Rules were made to be broken. Even real estate developers could be caught in the excitement of trying out new things in this era. This was the case in the development of a large tract of land along the rugged Pacific coast of northern California called Sea Ranch. Here a real estate developer hired landscape architect Lawrence Halprin to design an ecologically sensitive development plan for this very special strip of coastal land. Halprin did so and also recommended some local architects to design the first vacation houses of this community as models for future development. MLTW, a very young architectural firm based in Berkeley, California was selected to design a 10-unit condominium structure right at the shore.

15

The condominiums

MLTW looked to both Western and Eastern architectural history as source material for their work. They described architectural form frequently as *aedicula*, a term derived from a Roman structure with four posts and a roof to house the statue of a god, and as saddlebags, a term that came from storage bags slung over a horse's back in the old West. They were less interested in the moral language that the modern movement had developed than they were in how people intimately fit in their homes. They abandoned the modern movement's penchant for steel, concrete, and glass for the wood, tin, and tar paper that characterized cheap, vernacular cabins that people built for themselves.

The plan for Sea Ranch began from a desire to use as little land as possible for housing so that what remained could maintain the wonderful rugged sense of this coastline. To accomplish this, the 10 housing units were compactly grouped around a central courtyard. Each unit was based on a 24-foot cube of space. The shell of this space was composed of wood walls supported by a heavy timber frame. Major elements of the frame were 10-inch by 10-inch fir posts with 4-inch by 4-inch secondary members. This frame was cross-braced inside by exposed diagonal fir joined by metal connectors to major orthogonal structural members. The result was a little like a modern version of a pole barn with structure exposed inside against a background of wood sheathing.

16

17

Domains

Inside this cube, rooms were developed as furniture. Designs often began from developing a special place for a bed. There is something more intimate and more protected about the place of beds in houses than for other pieces of furniture. It is the place we associate with the vulnerability of sleep, the intimacy of touching the skin of another person, safety from the social world of action, or the pleasure of dreams. Beds in Sea Ranch were placed atop towers within the shell. The tower is the place where people go to rise above the fray of the everyday world, the place where they feel protected in a medieval world, the place in the attic where children used to play dress-up. Sea Ranch beds are little nests at the top of internal towers. Parachute drapes could be released from the ceiling to shroud these spaces. They were often placed under large skylights that afforded a clear view of a star-filled northern California night sky or allowed rain to come close. Below the sleeping lofts were bathrooms and below these were kitchens. This three-story assembly of places stood like an independent form within the general 24-foot by 24-foot by 24-foot volume of the condominium. This internal tower's specificity of use was paired with the generality of place created by the shell of this cube.

18

Just as the tower represents a special kind of architectural form, so does the corner. Corners are different from the midsections of walls in that they hold people differently within them. A human body can slide along a wall. It is protected from the back but vulnerable at its flanks. By contrast, a corner protects a human body from both back and sides. A human body cannot slide along this surface but is tightly held by two intersecting planes. In this way, the corner is a special place of protection

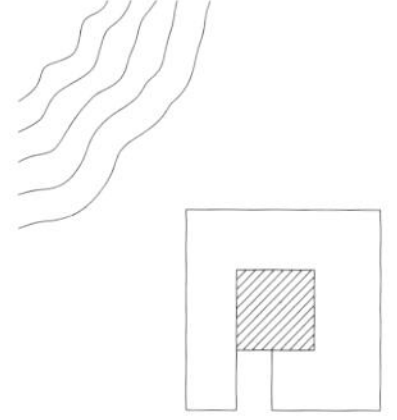

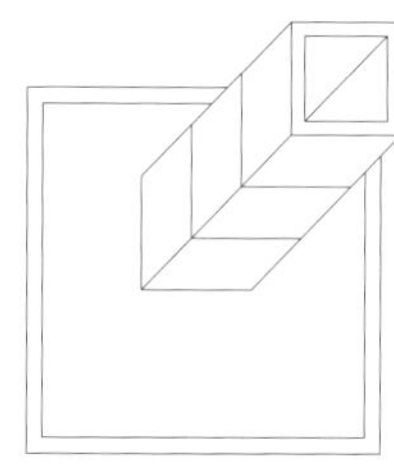

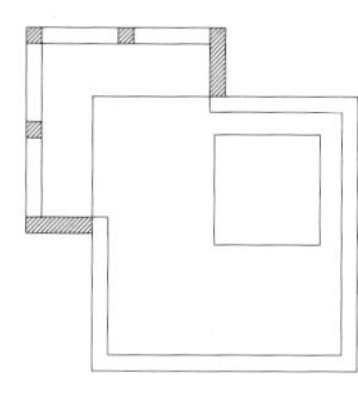

19

in an enclosure. It is this association that makes opening the corner up to the outside a dramatic architectural design decision. Frank Lloyd Wright understood this when he spoke of destroying the box. Wright destroyed the box-like containers of traditional rooms by opening up the corners with windows. In Sea Ranch, much the same effect is achieved by pushing a saddlebag of space out beyond the corner of the wooden 24-foot cube that defines the interior territory of the condominium. Windows bound this saddlebag with views up and down the rugged California coast. This is a very special place to sit or lie down. Unlike the bed atop the tower, this location is one of vulnerability. This window seat is suspended between the protected territory inside the 24-foot cube and the unprotected territory of the coastline outside. This suspension occurs just where the limits of a domain are most clearly spelled out as a corner. The window seat becomes a kind of entry porch to the natural landscape. Instead of affording passage like a normal entry, however, it affords a place between the inside and outside that powerfully references the characteristics of both. Inside is the domain of the social and cultural family. Outside is the domain of natural forces. To be in this window seat at the corner, outside the box but inside the weather envelope of the house, is to be suspended between these two worlds.

Beneath the seemingly simple architectural forms of this building lies a sophisticated idea about the modern meaning of domain. In contrast to the base of domain in Villa Mairea, this meaning is founded on a more primitive and fundamental sense of how we as people locate ourselves in a natural and social world. In Villa Mairea, domain could extend from the cultural history of a specific group of people. The entry, dining room, logia, and sauna reconnected inhabitants of this house to their cultural past. People of the United States often lack such an explicit definition of culture. We are an amalgam of cultures, one overlaid on the other until cultural distinctions between groups blur. Without explicit cultural references, where is this group to turn to find the values of their domain? The answer to this question, given by Sea Ranch, is that we should return to a core set of values that come from deeper memories than those of culture.

20

These values can be found in the way that domains have placed us in the natural world. If the fire pit was the first definition of a social domain, then all subsequent definitions of domain have the opportunity to as fundamentally and as powerfully place us in the natural world. The rudimentary skin of the Sea Ranch condominiums, the gathering of units around a protected social center, the towers within condominiums, and the corner window seats are all such definitions. Each depends on a primitive sense of how the human body is placed within its surrounds to engender a set of associations about what this visceral placement might mean. These primitive locations in nature are represented to us in these condominiums in modern forms, but their power lies in how each of these forms refreshes our memory of ways we have modified a natural landscape to fill our symbolic and biological needs.

Central Beheer

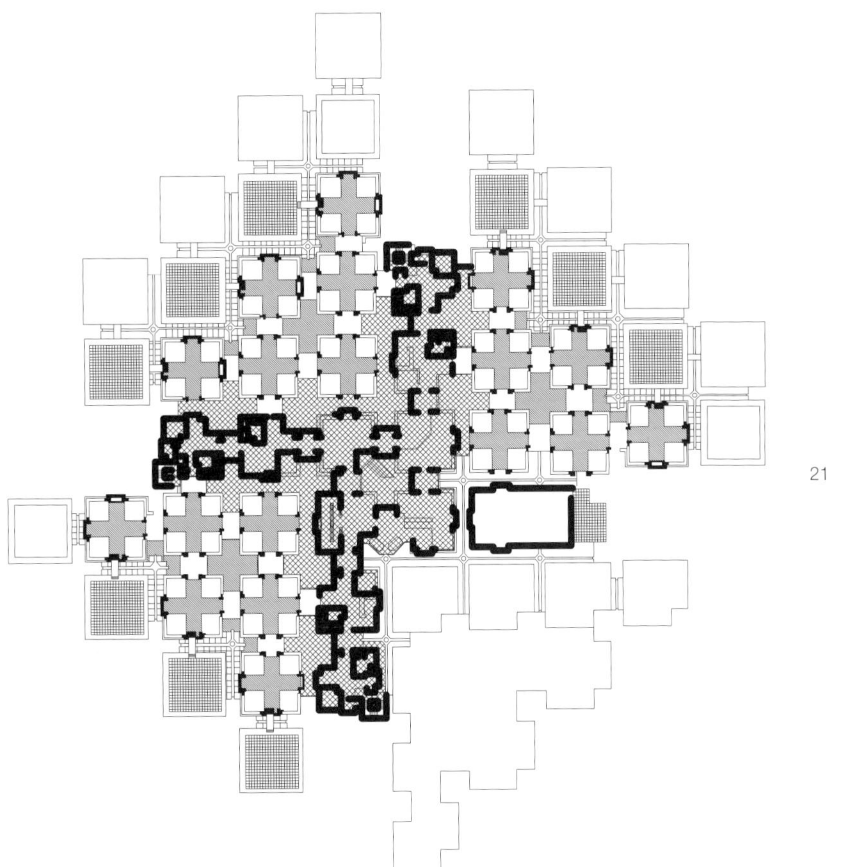

21

19 Sea Ranch exterior courtyard, interior tower, and extended corner
20 Sea Ranch bed atop interior tower
21 Central Beheer plan
22 Central Beheer social area
23 Central Beheer exterior corner

22

23

The Dutch have traditionally stood a little outside the mainstream of the modern movement in architecture. Their concerns about the social quality of domains did not allow them to wholeheartedly accept the abstraction of people as hygienic organisms that became popular in much of the rest of Europe. This interest in the quality of social domains sprang from the idea that, as vernacular houses and villages grew from a rich set of human needs, the role of modern architecture was to replicate this richness in spite of the fact that people no longer built their own homes or cities. This suggests a difficult task that architecture in general has been loath to take on. How can a place, designed and built by people who will not occupy it, reflect the values of domain of those who will?

Central Beheer, built in 1975, is a sprawling accretion of square forms with windows at the corners. It is a little like the honeycomb of a beehive in that these cells simply accrete to form the exterior shape of the building. The organization of the squares is canted at 45° to the orthogonal order of the city of Apeldoorn that provides its context. A transit stop and parking garage below allow workers access to the building. The building's interior organization is one of major corridors of space giving way to smaller corridors that service individual office spaces.

Domains

Central Beheer in Apeldoorn, The Netherlands represents one possible answer to the question of how a specialized part of an industrial society might make plans that accommodate the values of another group of people. This structure was designed by Dutch architect Herman Hertzberger to house the employees of a Dutch insurance company. Instead of conceiving of it as a conventional building with offices strung along corridors or as an open office landscape plan, Central Beheer is modeled on a village composed of residential units. This plan begins with the individual employee. This employee is allocated a space that is a bit like a plot of ground in a city on which to build a house. The lot lines of this land establish areas of responsibility and control, but each plot of land also fits into the larger structure of the block as blocks fit together to form neighborhoods. In Central Beheer, this plot of land is defined as the corner of a square of a larger territory that contains three other corner lots. The crossing paths that separate the square into four corner lots are like streets. The four lots with their two streets form a block. Blocks are assembled in a form that allows streets to be continuous just as they are in a city. Continuous streets are the organization of paths in a settlement that allow all members of that settlement to have access to all other individual plots of land. The plots of land themselves represent places as domains that can be filled with personal values. In this way, the structure of the whole of the building is like the structure of a village. The whole is ordered by a fixed set of organizational forms, streets, and lot lines; but within each lot line, individual definitions of domain are allowed to emerge.

25

26

24 Central Beheer interior corner
25 Central Beheer restaurant
26 Central Beheer interior street
27 Organization of Central Beheer as development of columns that delineate path and entry and corners that delineate degrees of enclosure

27

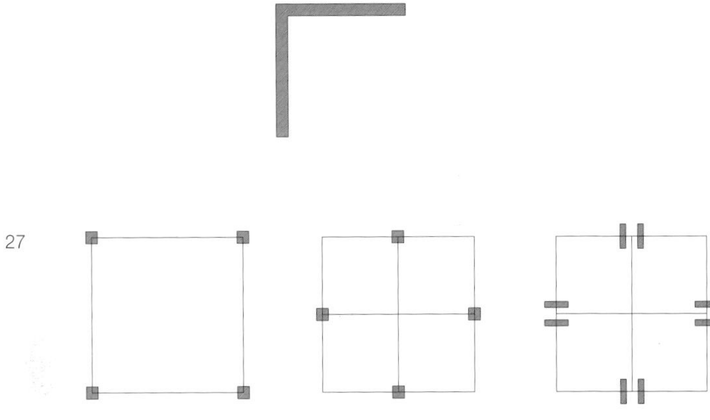

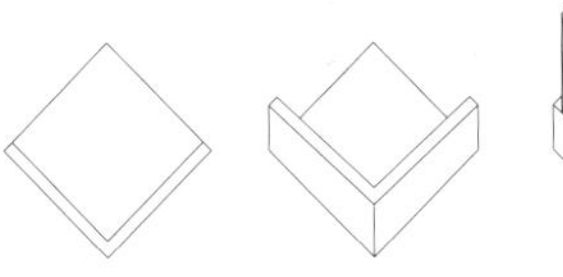

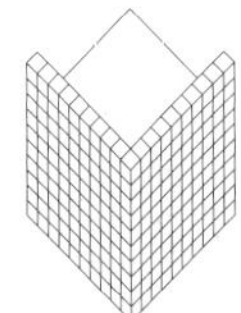

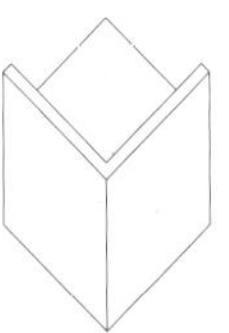

The dual architectural key to this organization is continuous streets ordering corners that might be treated in a range of ways. Streets in this structure are formed by bringing structural supports from the corner of each square neighborhood to a position at the center of its side separated by just enough space to facilitate passage. This placement of columns is a very clever rearrangement of an architectural element with one function—to hold the floors of the building up—to accomplish the goals of another architectural function—to outline the edges of a path.

The formal partner of path in this domain is the treatment of the corner. Each plot of individual territory as a corner of a square of Central Beheer shares two sides with neighbors on this block. These two sides always remain open as an acknowledgement of belonging to a larger social group. The other corner of individual domains faces the territory of other blocks. They may be developed in five different architectural ways. This corner might remain open all the way to the floor with just a handrail to outline inside from outside. It might be bounded by a kneewall that encloses the corner only to the height of a person's hips. It might have a window above this kneewall that allows visual contact but controls an auditory territory. It might be glass block from floor to ceiling allowing diffuse light but not images to pass through it. Or it might be an opaque material from floor to ceiling absolutely separating the outside from the inside. Each of these conditions suggests a different social relationship between the territory of an individual in this building and the larger social group. None of these

28

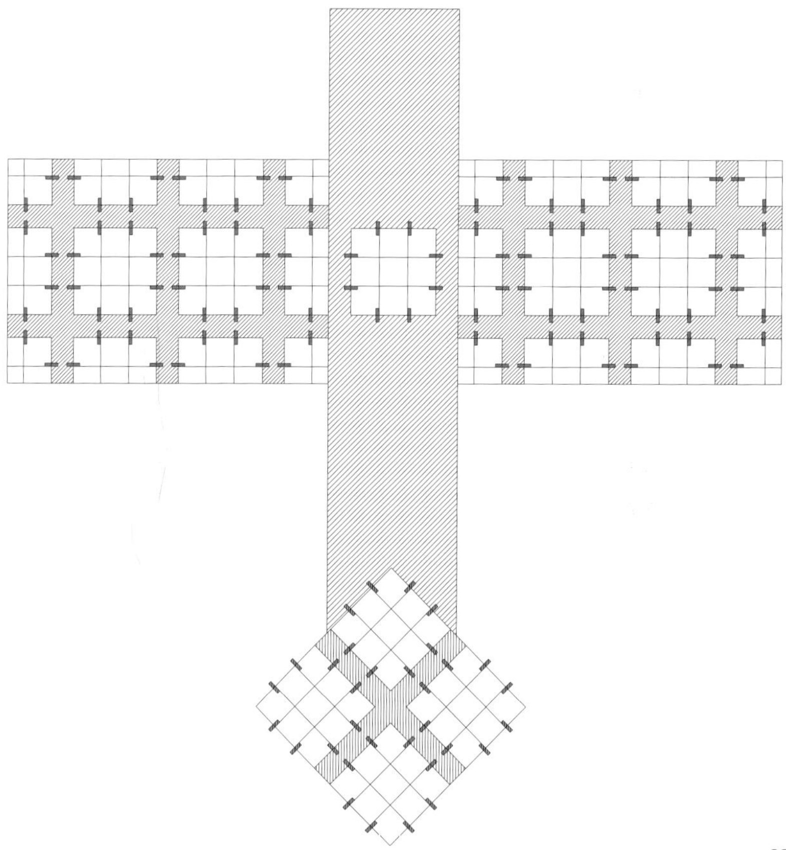

29

30

relationships will be as intimate and direct as those with neighbors on the four-person block because none will remain open to physical passage. But barring passage, each corner connects inhabitants to the space beyond in a different way. The hand rail suggests the most minimal of boundaries between domains. The kneewall is a little more substantial but still open. The window represents physical enclosure that maintains visual access. The glass block creates the domain of radiance. The opaque wall is the corner of absolute separation. This might be seen as a material vocabulary that is fundamentally responsible for all definitions of domain as separation compressed into the corner design of an office space.

There is at once a very methodical and scientific and a very humane sense of the design of different corners in this building. On one hand, all is regulated by a fixed grid that makes only an occasional formal nod to the richness of the organizational form of a village. The development of the corner is, likewise, composed of a rigidly fixed vocabulary. On the other hand, this limited pallet of architectural elements is capable of being arranged in an infinite number of ways. Each change in corridor definition and each change in corner development goes together with all others to create a condition that is akin to the location of pieces on a chessboard. Each time one of these pieces is moved the entire board is reconfigured. Each change in path and corner makes something new of the community as a whole. The struggle in Central Beheer is one between structure that keeps group relationships clear and a domain that allows for individual expression. In Central Beheer, a domain that we have come to expect so little of is propelled into a formal/social richness that opens up new horizons about what an office building might be.

28 Central Beheer office
29 Central Beheer as the order of the city
30 Central Beheer conversation corner

Southdale Shopping Center

After World War II, suburbs in the United States began to grow rapidly. Herbert Gans studied one of these early suburbs and concluded in his book, *The Levittowners*, that people moved from city to suburb in search of a richer social domain than that afforded by urban tenement living. Economic policies favored housing construction in the suburbs and propelled a reapportionment of residential populations that would continue for the next 50 years. As a result, about two-thirds of the residents of metropolitan areas in the United States now live in suburbs while one-third remains in core cities. Our culture is largely the product of this suburbanization. It was made possible by a growth of wealth among middle-class residents and the emergence of the private automobile as our primary mode of transportation.

The romance of the automobile in the United States and of ownership of an individual house surrounded by a large lawn drove the architectural form of suburbia. Among our people, there is a long-standing tradition of individualism that makes the flexibility of auto travel attractive. There is an equal appreciation of the natural landscape as a symbol of goodness. The suburban rambler on its own large plot of ground was made possible by the former value to fill people's desire for the latter value.

31

32

Suburbs have become a powerful force in American acculturation. A person can move to the United States from a small town or from another country, buy a suburban house and car, water and mow their lawn, and fit in with other suburbanites whatever their culture of origin. The center of this community is the suburban shopping center. This commercial center began as a simple strip of stores with a common walkway connecting them to automobile parking. It graduated to an enclosed courtyard structure with an enormous amount of parking for automobiles all the way around it. Southdale shopping center was the second such structure built in the United States. Victor Gruen Associates was a California firm that specialized in commercial architecture. Southdale was built in Edina, Minnesota, a relatively wealthy suburb of Minneapolis. In the early 1960s, it was clear that middle-class flight from central cities was going to call for a new community structure in American cities. Urban renewal, which bulldozed whole blocks of old buildings in core cities to attract new development, did little to stem this trend. People left core cities for better schools, neighbors with similar values, more land, lower prices and lower taxes, and a host of other reasons. But like all people, these émigrés needed services they had left behind in core cities. The services that they chose to make their center of value were not those of government but rather those of the mass production, mass consumption society that made possible the material wealth exhibited by the suburbs. The most powerful symbol of this emphasis on material wealth was the shopping center. Here all the goods produced by a society could be purchased by people whose new-found wealth made such purchases possible. The bazaar or market place of the old city was transformed in Southdale to meet the needs of mass production of goods and automobile transportation.

31 Southdale shopping center and parking lot
32 Southdale store

The shopping center

Southdale helped create a model for all the enclosed shopping centers that succeeded it. A large, central courtyard is naturally lit from above. This courtyard is surrounded by hallways that serve store fronts on two levels. These store fronts are largely glazed so that each store can display goods to passersby. At each end of the courtyard are large, well-known department stores. These are called majors as opposed to the smaller, less well-known stores that fill the space between them. The role of these major department stores is to attract consumers to the center. Once there, the smaller stores benefit from their presence. A small sidewalk café is located in the center of the courtyard as is a large commissioned sculpture. Shoppers in this harsh northern climate can come at any time of the year to Southdale, take off their coats, and shop in climate-controlled comfort. An abundance of free parking makes sure that access to these stores is both convenient and cheap. This organization was so successful that it has been duplicated thousands of times in the United States and has been copied in many countries around the world.

Domains

The suburban shopping center is a domain that propels more social and cultural than architectural interest. It is largely an organization of parking lots surrounding stores with a courtyard in the middle. The generic structure allows new stores to plug into this framework when old stores fail. Though it has public bathrooms and sometimes services like a post office, the vast majority of this building type is given over to the display and purchase of goods.

People of all ages come to this center for a variety of reasons. Teenagers hang out there, middle-class families shop or have a meal, and older people often take their daily walk around the corridors of the center in the morning before shops open. The uses of the shopping center have become so ubiquitous and frequent in suburbia that it has come to be identified as the center of the community. Far more people recognize the location of Southdale in Edina than would recognize the location of this community's city hall. Other community functions are located in other, distant structures. Public schools and libraries have their own buildings and parking lots. Sporting events attract either spectators or participants to another set of separate structures with parking lots. This community form is both made possible by and held together by automobile travel. The shopping center maintains the central position in this allocation of community values because it identifies the purchase of goods as a central cultural value.

In many ways, the suburban shopping center surrounded by suburban homes on large parcels of ground is emblematic of the development and triumph of the middle class in the United States. The 19th-century world was predominantly composed of peasants and aristocracy. It was in the new country of the United States that mass production was linked with mass consumption so effectively that after World War II,

75% of the American population was considered to be middle class. For the first time in history, a large amount of wealth was distributed to a large urban population. This group of people used this wealth to forge the kind of community that represented their values. These values, while sometimes criticized by the intellectual elite, do represent what a majority of middle-class people in the United States would call the "good life." The structures and the organization of suburbs represent these values just as the Dogon granary represents the myth of origin to be the central value of that society.

The power of the shopping center to serve as this symbol might be brought into focus by comparing it with a town center created before the industrial revolution. The Zocalo of Oaxaca, Mexico was drawn on the ground by the Spaniards when they came to the intersection of valleys that was to become Oaxaca in 1529. It is a square, open block at the center of the city. The role of this square was to provide a location for the church, government, and commerce for the village that would soon develop around it. Over time, this space has come to fulfill its promise. The street around the Zocalo

33 Southdale interior courtyard

was closed to automobiles long ago making this a purely pedestrian area. It is bounded on the south side by a row of arcaded government buildings and on the other sides by arcades that house numerous sidewalk restaurants. The northwest corner of the Zocalo gives way to the Alameda de Leon that provides an entry court for the Basilica. The center of the Zocalo is filled with large shade trees, fountains, gardens, benches, and a wind orchestra pavilion. From morning until late at night, the Zocalo is filled with all manner of people. Tourists come to stroll, listen to concerts, and have coffee and meals. Young people "strut their stuff" in search of possible mates. Families bring their children to play with balloons. Merchants sell goods at tables. Shoe shiners shine shoes. Beggars beg. All is a cacophony of human activity that somehow gives the impression of a centered culture rather than of chaos. Everyone belongs in the Zocalo.

The Zocalo has much in common with the suburban shopping center. It is recognized as the center of the community. People buy goods and take meals there. Young and old stroll – albeit for different purposes. But here, the similarities end. The Zocalo centers a dominantly pedestrian rather than automobile city. It sits cheek by jowl with the other portions of the city, not isolated by a vast ring of automobile parking. The institutions around the Zocalo include church and government as well as commerce. The level of social activity in the Zocalo is far more varied and substantial than that of the shopping center. It seems that everyone in the city comes to the Zocalo at one time of the day or another as part of their normal urban life. Shopping is not the central value of this place. Having a cup of coffee with friends is. In many ways, the Zocalo of Oaxaca represents what we think that social centers of cities ought to be rather than what they are. This contention is given substance by the number of tourists who visit Oaxaca to participate in all that goes on in the Zocalo.

But the Zocalo could also be seen from the opposite perspective. It could be seen as the remnant of a culture that has not built a middle class but retains an economic aristocracy and large peasant class. It could be seen as nostalgia recalling a pre-automobile city. It could be seen as a spectacle maintained primarily for the benefit of tourists. All of these observations would be correct to a degree. The Zocalo in Oaxaca, however, retains the ability to question whether or not the suburban shopping center is a rich enough domain to serve as a container for our community values.

Closing thoughts

Ideas of domain have fueled less architectural speculation in the 20th century than other organizing ideas of architecture that we will examine. Issues of technology and order have been far more central to 20th-century design thought. Nonetheless, a number of issues of domain might be found in post-1850 architecture. Alvar Aalto's Villa Mairea in Finland asks if we can really belong in a place without a material memory of our cultural past. The sauna, courtyard, dining room, and entry that form the midsection of this house recapture cultural memory in the center of this modern residential design. Charles Moore paid special attention to the role of the human body and personal memory in generating ideas of domain. The corner seating area and bed atop an internal tower speak of the power of locating the body to evoke ideas of how we belong next to the ocean or under the sky. Herman Hertzberger's Central Beheer examines the role of the corner in architecture to both demark the territory of the individual and of the possibility of linking the individual to the larger community. This work takes seriously the contention that a building is a small city. And finally, Southdale shopping center asks if our new form of community symbols are rich enough to represent our core values.

These are all difficult and provocative questions. They have not and will not reach certain resolution in the architecture of the future. What they do ask of this architecture, however, is that we reexamine the role of architecture as a container that holds us with our values. No one truly wants to be housed in places that clinically deny the values we feel are significant in our lives. Science fiction horror films are rife with such placeless environments. Perhaps in an era of mass production and mass consumption, it has become even more important for architecture to identify and represent issues that cannot be simply commodified. Perhaps our buildings, gardens, and cities should resist other forces that seek to reduce our lives to abstractions promoted by advertising.

Though 20th-century architecture has paid scant attention to the issue of domain as a central focus, that does not mean it has lost its place among architectural ideas. What you and I live in every day is largely a function of the ways in which we have chosen to construct domains. The story about planting an evergreen hedge in my front yard, Robert Bly's oak tree, the ways we arrange furniture and memorabilia in our own homes, and the ideas that we might associate with Southdale Shopping Center testify to this role.

34 The Zocalo of Oaxaca, Mexico

THE PARTHENON
AND THE CONCEPT OF ORDER IN ARCHITECTURE

Meaning emerging from pattern

Issue

A central purpose of architecture is to bring order to chaos: to create recognizable patterns of material construction that might allow the meaning of habitation to emerge from them.

Order is the word that we use to enunciate our need to find pattern in the world. To not be able to understand patterns in our physical context is to be physically and intellectually lost. We seek to find and to create patterns in the world in order to belong within that world. No one, for instance, really knows if nature is the logical construct often assumed. Who is to say that the heavens move in defined ways or that the evolution of life on earth has really taken place in an orderly progression? People speculate that this is the case because they must. As a species, we cannot imagine that nature is a set of random events because we would find ourselves at the mercy of those events. We are dependent on the sun rising in the east and setting in the west. This pattern of rising and setting structures our lives as the rhythm of day and night with all the associations that this division carries with it. We search for the pattern that led to our own being, whether in science or theology, to find our own existence emerging from a recognizable pattern. Otherwise, as a species, we would represent a random event in time with no past and no future. No one is sure that these patterns exist. If they do, our sense of what they are is conditioned by the period of history in which we attempt to find them. What we are sure about is that all people, from our earliest ancestors with language skills on, have thought about this problem of pattern and have devised answers to it in all facets of their lives.

The following story helps explain our need to find pattern in the world. This was told by Russell Ackoff, a favorite graduate school teacher of mine at the University of

01 The Parthenon atop the Acropolis

Pennsylvania. A psychologist is interested in how people see patterns and how they communicate their perceptions of patterns to others. To test how we create these patterns, the psychologist sets up a condition that is very unlikely to produce an intentional pattern of events. He rents a semi-trailer and installs a light-lock entry at one end and a light-lock exit at the other; these are a double door system that prevents light from entering the trailer when the first door is closed and the second opened. He parks this trailer on a college campus and pays students to walk through the dark trailer with a flashlight that they are instructed to randomly wave around. The psychologist has mounted black and white photographic film in strips on the inside of the trailer. As light from the flashlight randomly strikes these strips, portions of them will be exposed. When this portion of the experiment has been completed, the psychologist develops the film, cuts it into slides, and selects slides from those available using the table of random numbers. Anything that might lead to a pattern of light exposures on the film has been carefully excluded by this process. There is virtually no chance that such a pattern could occur.

To test our ability to find patterns, the psychologist takes this set of randomly exposed slides to a second college campus. Here he pays students to view as many slides as they need to determine if there is, indeed, a pattern that can be found among the flashes of light recorded on the film. Invariably, by the 100th image, the student watching the slides would ring a bell to let the psychologist know that they had discovered a pattern. The psychologist would then come into the slide viewing room and explain to student one that the real challenge of this experiment was not to discover the pattern in question but to explain it to student two. Then he would usher student two into the room with instructions to watch the slides with student one to see if student two observed the same pattern of flashes on light. By the 60th slide, student two would ring the bell to tell the psychologist that there indeed was a pattern of light flashes on the slides but that it was different from that discovered by student one. The psychologist would then explain the entire process that produced the slides to both students. Their reply was always the same. They would always contend that even though the psychologist had not intended to create a pattern of light flashes on the slides, one had come into being, and it was the one that each student discovered.

What an amazing story. It suggests that as Homo sapiens we will discover patterns of events whether or not such patterns exist. It suggests that we are prone to finding these patterns as an innate circumstance of our own mental needs rather than as a condition of the context that surrounds us. It suggests that the ability to understand patterns among events is so central to our ability to think about the world that we are compelled to find such patterns. It suggests that we will arrange the world of our perceptions as a set of patterns in order to give sense to our own existence.

02 The Parthenon

Architectural definitions of order

Architecture is interesting in this regard because its function is less to discover the patterns of nature than to create patterns that order our perceptions of our own domain. The following descriptions of the role of order in architecture, again taken from *The Theory of Architecture: Concepts, Themes, & Practices* by Paul-Alan Johnson, give some indication of the depth and breadth of this word's meaning in contemporary architecture.

> "...it is often stated that the beauty of classical architecture resides in Order. And Order, upon analysis, is found to consist in correspondence, iteration, and the presence of fixed ratios between the parts. Ratio, identity, and correspondence form a necessary web and fabric of our thought. . . . Order is a desire of the mind. . . . What more natural, then, than to say that architectural beauty—the beauty of classic architecture, at any rate —consists in Order."
>
> —*Geoffrey Scott, 1927*

"Order is."

— *Louis Kahn, 1955*

"Design is the conscious effort to impose meaningful order."

— *Victor Papanek, 1977*

"I have come to believe that the problem of physical order — the kind of order that creates quality in architecture — is of so great a stature, that we will have to modify our picture of the whole physical universe in order to see it clearly."

— *Christopher Alexander, 1985*

Scott was an architectural historian with a desire to define the role of order in classical architecture. His definition comes from careful study of Greek, Roman, and Gothic structures. Kahn was an important 20th-century designer and architectural theoretician. To Kahn, the construct of order is a priori in the design of buildings. That is, order is a fixed construct of thought that exists before the act of design commences. It is an ideal that precedes all design thought. Papanek sees order as the result of conscious imposition of the architectural will. For him, order in our constructed environment comes into being because designers make it so. And finally, Christopher Alexander comments that order is central to the idea of quality in architecture. Order, which is so often linked to a measurable identification of pattern, is linked here to an immeasurable idea of the quality of the places we build in which to live. Even this partial list gives some indication of both the centrality of order in design thought and the broad ways in which it may be considered. It might be easier to ask what the world of archi-

03 The plan of the Parthenon

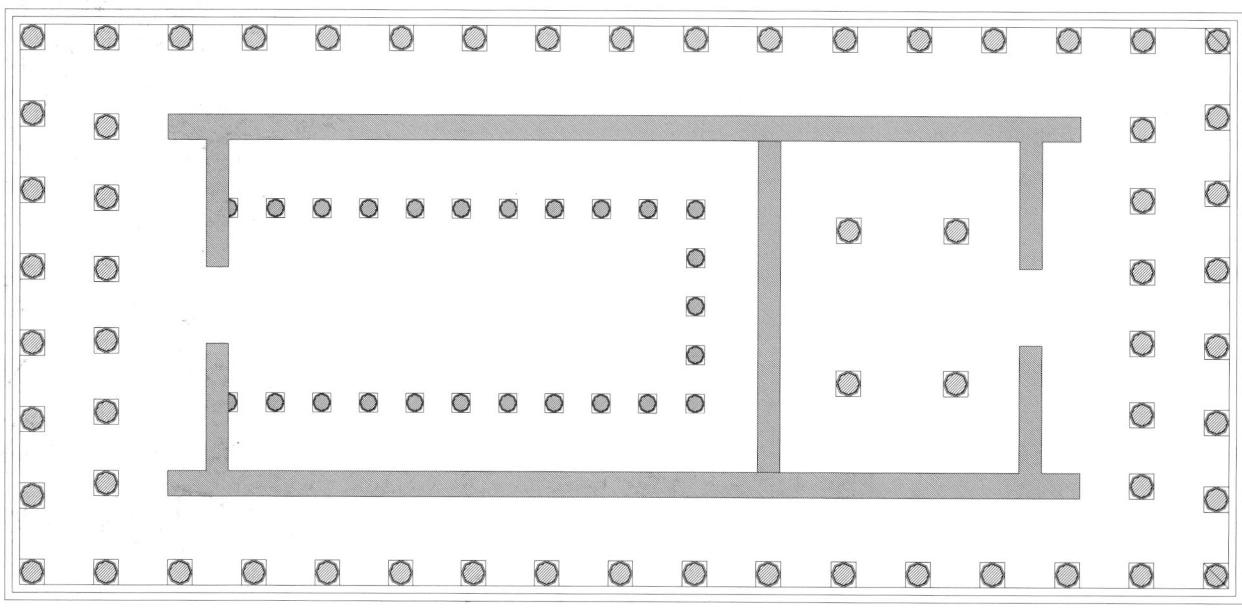

04 Front elevation of the Parthenon

tecture would be without order than it would be to suggest an amalgam of definitions that would bring greater clarity to this issue.

What would there be in our buildings, gardens, and cities if there was not order? How would we recognize such simple constructs as that of room, house, block, path, street, lawn, neighborhood, and city limits? How would we understand the time of the day to have breakfast, lunch, and dinner, or the time of day to be awake and or asleep? How would we keep the social rules of our tribe in our minds if they changed constantly? How would we get to school, work, or shopping without a stable pattern lodged in our minds about where each of these activities was located in relation to the others? How, in fact, could we live at all without a life filled with patterns that allowed us to imagine the future, act in the present, and remember the past? The answer, I believe, is that we would be paralyzed without pattern. It is the ability to perceive and abstractly name patterns that allows human beings to survive and prosper.

Certainly, this ability to create patterns is as true of architecture as it is of other modes of thought. The perception of the forms that comprise buildings is itself a function of our ability to make patterns of those perceptions.

05 Colonnade of the Parthenon

The Parthenon

The Greek culture that reached its peak in the mid-400s BC is called the Golden Age of Greece. This period of history was central to Western thought because it developed many of the fundamental questions that would drive Western philosophy for the next 2,500 years. We remain the children of this culture in many ways.

This era of Greek civilization was preceded by the Minoans beginning about 3000 BC who formed the culture from which Greece would grow. Classical Greek culture as we know it was initiated by the formation of a common Greek language in 1600 BC. Sometime between 800 and 700 BC Homer wrote the *Iliad* and the *Odyssey*, the two books that would provide the core of mythology for this emerging culture. The form of the classic Greek temple was established in 650 BC. The Greek wars with the Persians began in 490 BC and finished in 479 BC. Finally, the Golden Age of Greece emerged from these conditions with the birth of Socrates in approximately 467 BC, the Age of Pericles from 461 to 421 BC, the birth of Plato about 427 BC, and the birth of Aristotle in 384 BC.

Many things make the Greeks of this era stand out against the background of Western history, but chief among them are the development of a democracy and the Greek philosophic tradition of Athens. A series of reformers moved Athens from totalitarian control to a functioning democracy by about 500 BC. This democracy allowed all land-owning males to vote. The body of the whole met monthly to argue and decide matters of policy. Membership in this council and participation in the affairs of the Republic was far more important to these Greeks than were their private lives. A council of 500 coordinated the agenda of the body of the whole, and an administrative council of 50 organized government action. No members of these councils were allowed to serve more than one term. This government was a functioning democracy albeit without the participation of a majority of the Athenian population. What is so important about this democracy to us is that a group of people were given the right and responsibility to decides issues that would affect them. This right differentiated Athenians from other Greek city-states and was a great source of Athenian pride. When the Athenians defeated the Persian army that far outnumbered them in 490 BC, the Athenians thought that their unlikely victory was secured because they were free men fighting for their own country, not mercenaries fighting because of the political power of a despot.

Though democracy was a great legacy of the Athenians, it pales in comparison with the philosophers that this city-state produced. The power of these thinkers reverberates in our thought today. Every subsequent era has had to attempt to rectify its thought with that produced by this little band of Greeks who produced our benchmark philosophical constructs in the 5th century BC.

The evolution of this thought began with the pre-Socratic philosophers. A number of these thinkers asked questions that propelled later Greek and our own thought. Thales of Miletus asked what single element might be the basic stuff of which the universe is composed and answered that it must be water. Anaximander asked how specific things emerged from a source element. His answer was that all things come from an unperceivable stuff (matter) and separate from this primordial ooze to become specific forms. Heraclitus asked what might guide this process of change. His answer was that nothing is because everything is in the process of becoming. The guiding force of this act of becoming is the *logos*, or word, which is a manifestation of a single intelligence. Becoming is guided by the single intelligence of nature. Pythagoras abandoned the proposition that the underlying structure of the universe is matter and proposed instead that it is a set of pure ideas. These ideas are manifest in the human vocabulary of mathematics that specifies the rules of the universe as the geometrically divided lengths of plucked strings creating harmonious sound. The senses are fallible whereas ideas are not. Parmenides could not tolerate that all things were always in a state of flux. His claim was that the real must be permanent. As all material things change, then it follows that only the mind can determine what is real.

These philosophers and their questions set the stage for the three best-known Greek philosophers who remain the guideposts of the Western tradition. The great Greek champion of the examination of issues of human thought through the reason

06 Parthenon columns and Naos wall

of argument was Socrates. No written record of the famous conversations between this philosopher and his students exists because he wrote none. His student, Plato, supplied a record of these conversations as a series of Socratic dialogues. Socrates was concerned with what it meant to lead a good life: virtue. He developed what we know now as the Socratic Method of asking questions to arrive at the truth or falsehood of possible answers to these questions. Socrates believed in the power of reason as the single human capacity that might allow us to find wisdom. Reason made manifest by argument would allow a person to pursue a life of virtue, allowing him to both understand what virtue was and, thus, allowing him to make discretionary judgments based on this understanding. Socrates was put to death by the Athenian Senate in 399 BC for corrupting the youth of the city.

Plato followed his teacher Socrates as the preeminent philosopher of Athens. Plato sided with the idealists and proposed that there were a set of ideal forms that lay outside of human perception as ideas that gave birth to less than ideal manifestations of their forms in the things that we can see and touch. The world of these ideals was thus fundamentally unknowable from our senses and could only be known through inference. In Platonic thought, the mind and human reason are the only avenues to search for knowledge of these forms, as they could exist only as ideas. This contention led to Plato's deep belief in mathematics as a language through which these ideals might be explored

Aristotle was Plato's student. Aristotle reconnected the tangible world with that of the ideal by claiming that ideal forms were housed within tangible objects. He took the path that Plato had rejected by claiming that the only way to know about the ideal world of thought was through the agency of things we could see, feel, touch, and smell. Ideals were the essence of these things that we might search for by understanding them. In contrast to Plato, in Aristotle's formulation, the senses rather than the mind were the origin of this form of thought.

In Plato and Aristotle lie the two ways in which we, as people, still contend that we may know things. Plato privileges thought over material existence by laying emphasis on the mind rather than the senses as our surest way to the truth. Aristotle privileges the senses over the mind by laying emphasis on our power to observe the tangible world around us as the surest way to the truth. The first is a mode of thought we call rationalism. The second is a form of thought we call empiricism. These two ways of understanding ourselves and the world around us structured all succeeding Western thought. Architectural theory was also divided by this distinction.

Greek thought and architectural order

Think of the differences between this line of inquiry and that of the Dogon. In the Dogon myth of origin, a story provides the motive, force, and reason for all things that are. The story can be consulted to understand how the universe works because it defines how that universe came into being. The Greek method is far more skeptical. It begins from the proposition that the world is understandable through reason. When our reason engages the world, it asks questions like: From where did everything come? How are we to understand the relationship between permanence and change? How can we explain the diversity of the world? How might we arrive at the truth? What does it mean to live a good life?

Plato and Aristotle essentially laid out the two ways that over the succeeding 2,500 years we attempted to answer these questions. Plato's realm of ideal forms is the basis of architecture's belief that buildings spring from and deliver immaterial meanings to our society. Underneath the visible form of buildings, there is contended to be an idea that organizes and gives order and significance to its assembly. This immaterial essence is thought to be the commodity that propels the design of great buildings.

Aristotle's empiricism leads architects to examine things that already exist as the basis of design. Material forms of buildings serve as the ground for interpretation of immaterial ideas. We each carry within us a sense of these tangible and observable conditions that can be trusted to serve as the initiation of the design of a building.

07 Corner detail of Parthenon

The Parthenon

It is strange that such a partial ruin as that of the Parthenon atop the Acropolis in Athens should serve as architecture's preeminent guide to the idea of architectural order. The Parthenon was a temple built from 448-432 BC by Pericles to commemorate the victory of the Athenians over the Persians. It was a temple built to the patron goddess of Athens, Athena, to house a large sculpture of this goddess and a treasury. The building was designed by the architects Ictinus and Callicrates and was supervised by the great Greek sculpture, Phidias. It is 228 feet long and 101 feet wide. The temple is surrounded by a row of Doric columns, 8 across the front and back and 17 along each side. Each column is 34 feet high and 1/7 that dimension in diameter. These columns bow out at their midsection 11/16 of an inch to make them appear to be straight. The floor of the temple bows up 2¾ inches at the midpoint of the front and back and 4¾ inches at the midpoints of the sides to make this base appear to be perfectly level. There are, in fact, no straight lines in the elements of the Parthenon. All are distorted to make them appear to be perfect to the senses rather than to be mathematically correct.

Within the ranks of the 8 front and back columns of the Parthenon stand a second rank of columns whose position is determined by the center of the temple rather than from the spacing of the columns they mirror. Within the columns stand four walls that define the *naos* or the rooms of the temple. This naos is divided in two to provide a domain for the statue and a treasury. The art that adorns many of the surfaces of the temple are a celebration of the myth of Athena and a record of the heroic struggle of the Athenians against great forces that would destroy them. The frieze, a band of relief sculpture all the way around the naos, records the events of one of the festivals of ordinary, mortal Athenians. It is thought that this frieze represents the first time citizens of Athens rather than gods were portrayed in the art of a Greek temple.

08 Doric columns of the Parthenon
09 Parthenon elevation as bottom, middle, and top

09

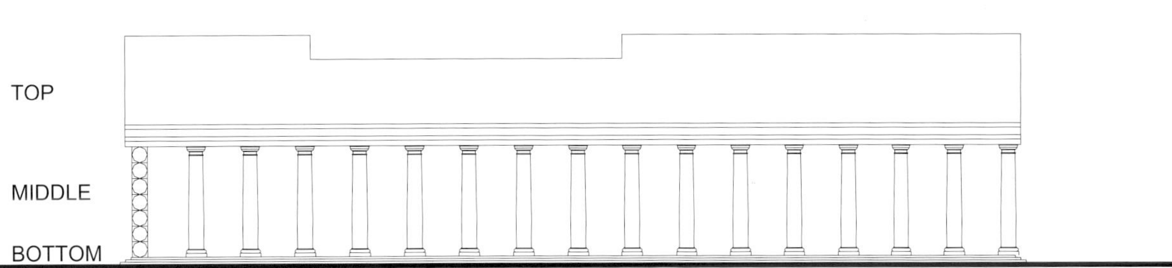

Order in the Parthenon

The Parthenon is architecture's emblem of order because it addresses the issues of order profoundly. There is elegance in the design of this building that parallels the elegance of the Golden Age of Greek philosophy.

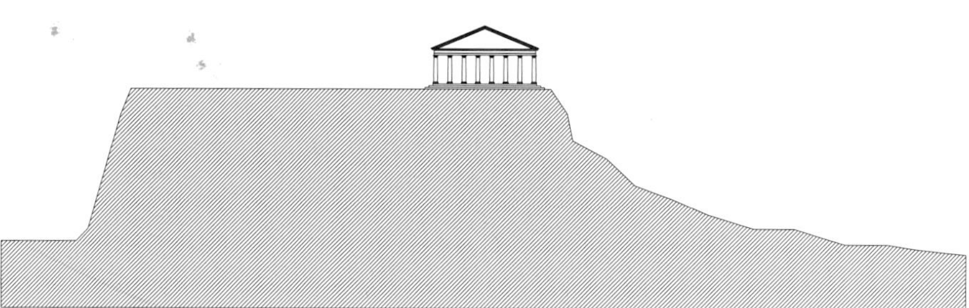

10

Human construction in the landscape

11

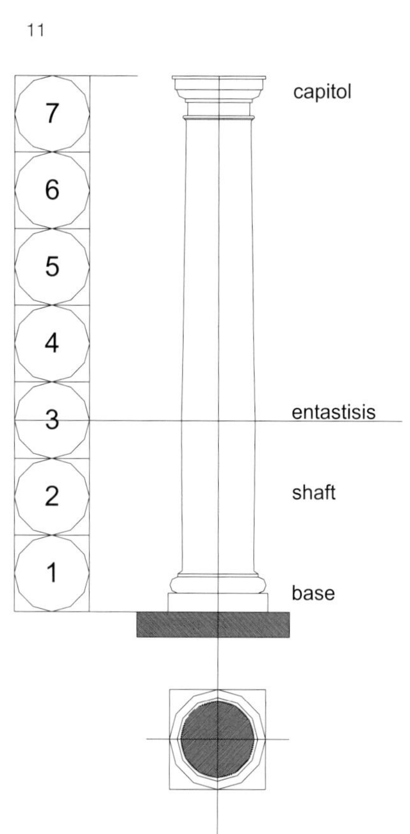

This order begins with the building's placement atop the Acropolis. This placement was typical for Greek temples. By being placed on a rock promontory, this really quite small building is able to gather the surrounding landscape to it. At only 101 by 228 feet, the Parthenon is a tiny assembly of material in contrast to the vast landscape that constitutes its context. Yet through the artifice of design, this tiny building dominates its far more extensive context. The Parthenon is able to do so because of its position, but more so because of the ideas that people ascribe to manmade objects versus the forms of the natural world. The Parthenon, unlike the natural landscape, is a structure that has been crafted by the human mind and hand. A less impressive investment of craft or thought would diminish this temple's ability to loom so large. The Parthenon represents an idea of profound human creation that propels its power over its landscape. This building radiates the beautifully thought out form of its columns creating arcades, arcades creating a place for the naos, and the naos creating a place for the cella of Athena. A less sensitively proportioned column, a less permanent material, or a less worthy representative of the heart of Athenian culture would diminish the power of the structure to dominate its surrounds. Jacob Bronowski said that people "having made something well, strive to make it better." It is the search for making things better that emanates from the precise forms of the Parthenon. The forms of this building approach perfection only because we think they do. But in this thought lies the power of those things that are wrought by human hands over those things that are wrought by natural forces independent of us. The Parthenon stands above the Acropolis as a symbol of the creative power of the human imagination. It is this power that gathers the landscape of the natural world to it.

Architectural elements unto themselves

10 Order in the landscape
11 The Doric column as order in itself
12 The order of element to element

Architectural elements have an order unto themselves, independent of their relationships to other elements. Columns are always tall and slender, upright, and hold something aloft. If lying on their sides they cease to be columns because they have failed to fulfill two of the three characteristics of the pattern that gives them meaning. Floors are flat and relate people standing on them to the ground; roofs are suspended above floors and cover people from the sky; walls are vertical, continuous, and separate domains; and openings connect domains through the passage of people or sunlight. Each architectural element must maintain the substance of this pattern to be what it is.

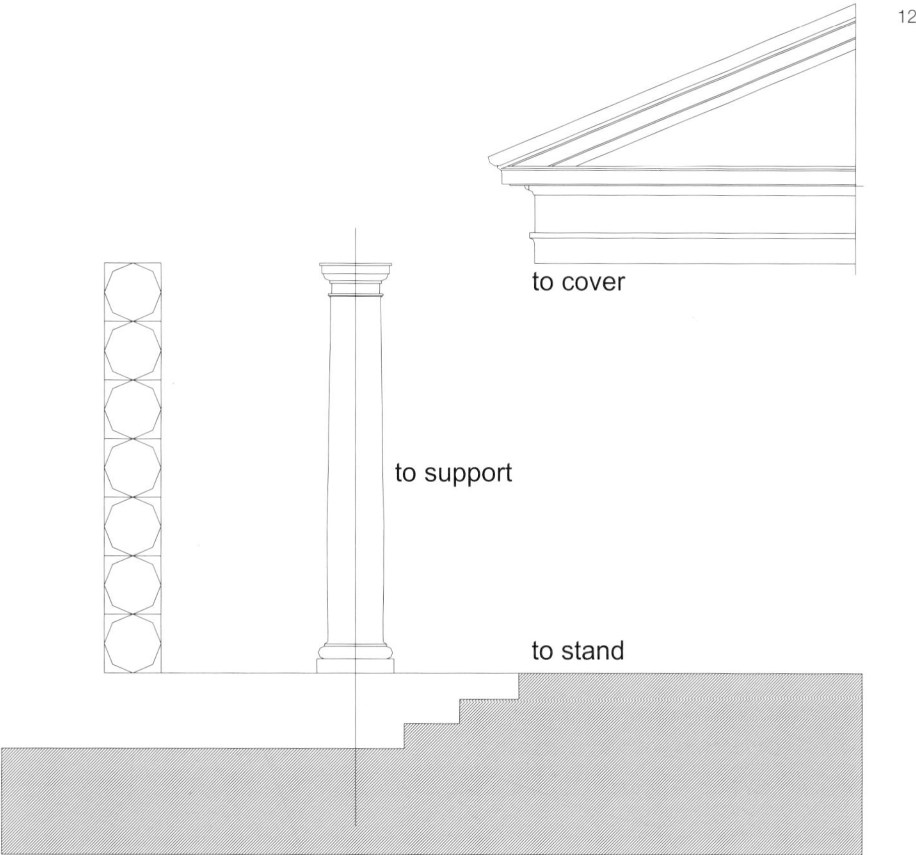

12

Element to element

The creation of a specific architectural idea is relational. People see the grounding of architectural thought as the relation of a particular form of a floor to the particular form of a wall, to the particular form of a column, to the particular form of a doorway, to the particular form of a roof within the particular form of a landscape. These relationships are not random but are controlled by a series of pattern-giving rules. Some of these rules grow from the characteristics of different architectural materials, natural forces, and the human body. These patterns can be manipulated but each is based on limits that lie outside the province of architectural thought. A second set of rules is arbitrarily imposed on architectural thought as a basis for rigorous intellectual craft. The limits of construction materials, natural forces, and the human body are in themselves insufficient grounds for thinking about the shape and organization of architectural material. Architects have always invented sets of rules to fill the void between that which must occur in buildings and that which could occur. This set of rules provides architects with guidelines that organize the millions of discrete decisions that are required of a building design. The outcome of this dual set of organizational patterns is the particular form of a building that allows particular interpretations as to its meaning as opposed to that of all other buildings.

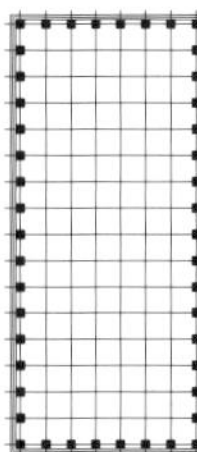

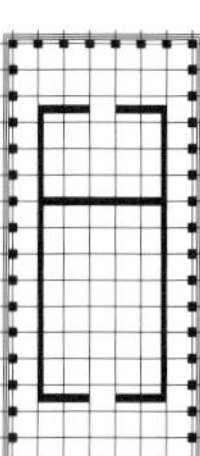

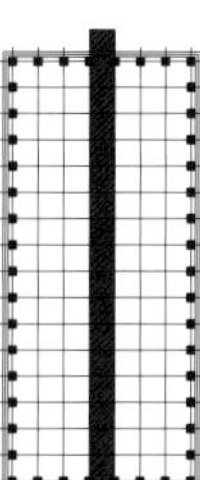

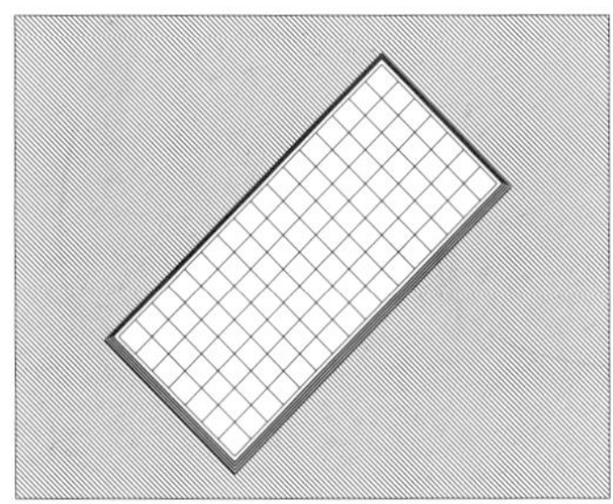

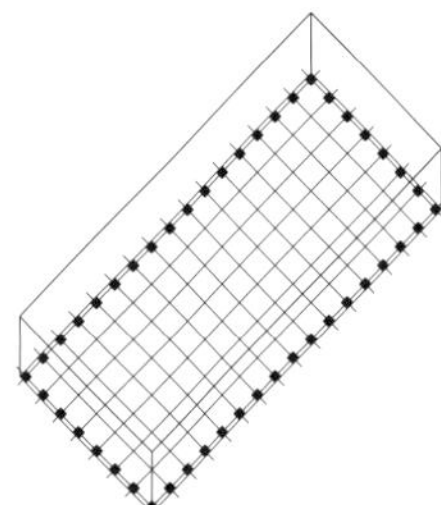

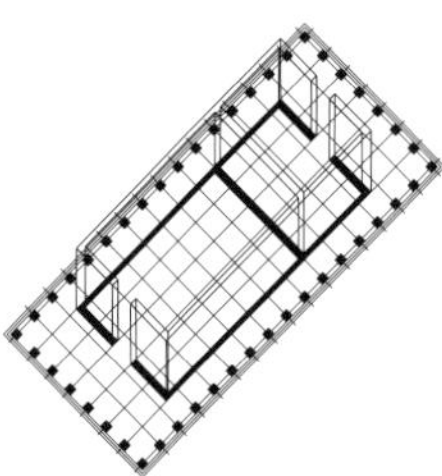

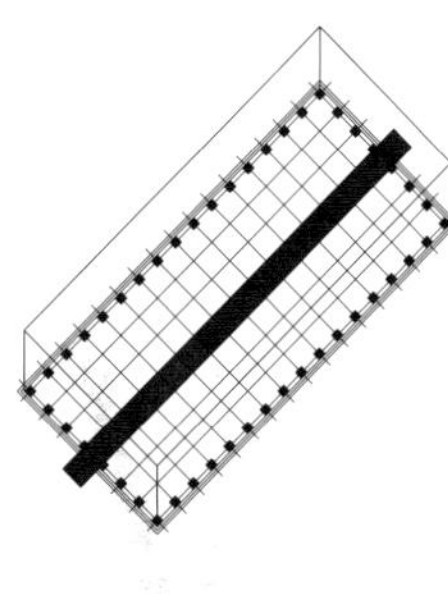

13

Orthogonal organizations

Though none of the lines of the Parthenon are straight, they grow out of the human capacity to order the world around them orthogonally. Lines intersecting at a 90° angle appear to be one of the common ways people produce patterns. People imagine the sun to come up in the east and go down in the west. A line perpendicularly intersecting these produces north and south and creates an orthogonal grid of cardinal directions on the earth. Cities' streets have been often laid out on orthogonal grids, and there seems to be a preference for orthogonal rooms that transcends time and culture. Orthogonal order packs neatly together. It can just as neatly be divided into smaller territories that mirror the geometric properties of an orthogonal progenitor. The floor of the Parthenon forms an orthogonal pattern that will be divided into a finer orthogonal grid.

13 Orthagonal order
14 Proportion
15 Repetition, correspondence, and ratio as order in architecture

Proportion

Proportion is used in architecture to create patterns of relational size. The height of a Doric column like those used in the Parthenon is seven times its diameter. All other dimensions in the Parthenon are, in fact, a function of this column diameter bringing them all to a common source of measure called a module. Relational measures create a set of rules that do not promote capricious design decisions. They provide a framework for rigorous design decisions that complements those of the mechanical limits of material or size of the human body. Proportion creates many such relationships in architecture. There is, for example, something precise about sides of a square being exactly the same length, not simply nearly the same length, that helps create rigor in architectural judgment. The Greeks thought that gods spoke through these patterns. To them, mathematical proportion was the language of perfection. Pythagoras' discovery that the square of the sides of a right triangle equaled the square of the hypotenuse seemed to confirm that mathematical relationships formed the substructure of the intelligible world. The golden mean became representative of this belief. It is a figure that is constructed by bisecting the side of a square, rotating the diagonal of the half square that is formed 90° to become part of the side of a rectangle with the dimensions 1:1 plus the square root of 5. The characteristic of this proportion is that A:B = B:A+B. The form that grows from repeating this process is a lovely spiral not inherent in any of the parts of the golden section but an outcome of the magic formed through their relationship.

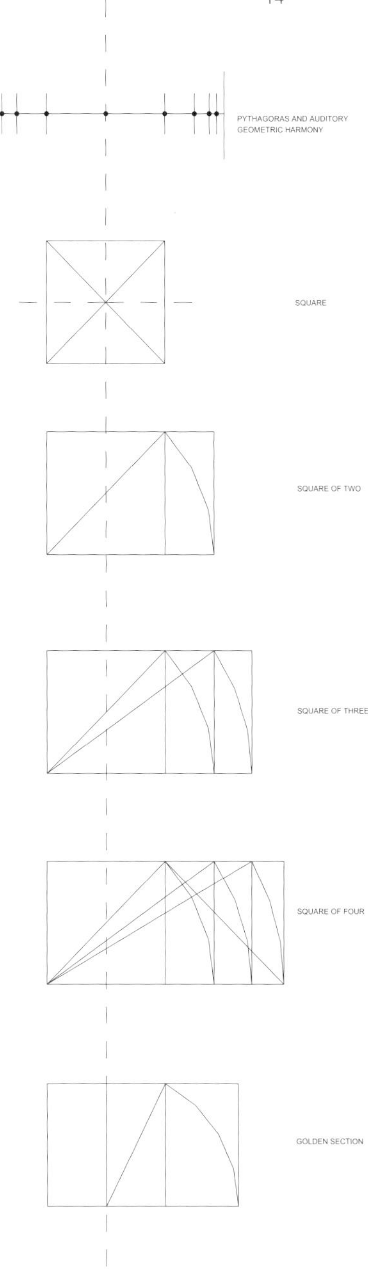

14

15

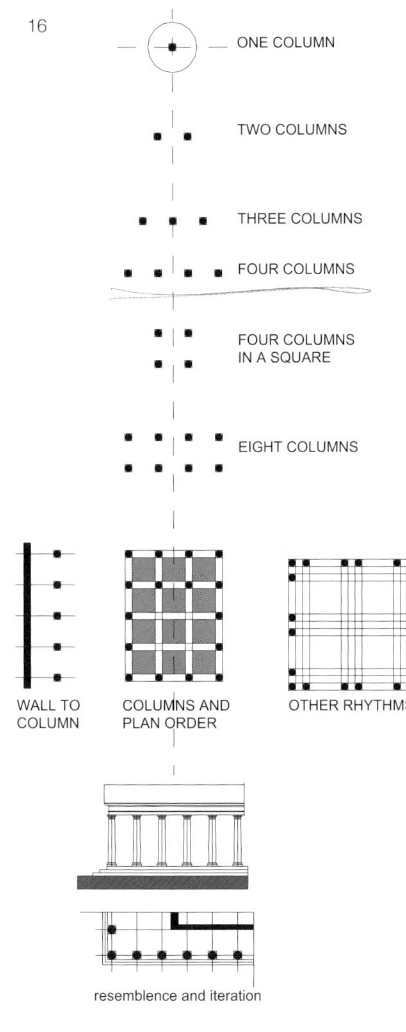

resemblence and iteration

Repetition

Repetition of similar elements gives pattern to much of architecture. Witness the repetition of the columns of the arcade of the Parthenon. A column by itself creates only a singular point in space. Two columns spaced to allow passage between them creates three ideas. Each column represents one of these while the space between them represents the third. If these columns should be placed too far apart or too close together, this idea of passage would disappear. But when placed in an appropriate relation to one another, two columns create two sides with an entry in between. Three columns brought into such a relation create six ideas. First there are the three columns themselves, then the two spaces between them, and finally the idea that the central column marks the middle of this configuration. Four columns might represent themselves plus three spaces, plus one space in the center that might, again, create the meaning of entry. The same four columns arranged in a square now represent the corners of a territory. Adding more columns to this array simply allows more and more complex meanings to be interpreted from their pattern.

Casting them against a wall engages another architectural element in a way that allows the discrete character of the column to be understood against the continuity of the wall. Altering spaces between columns gives rise to major versus minor divisions of space. This list can be expanded indefinitely, but our ability to interpret meaning from architectural elements that are repeated is dependant on our ability to recognize the pattern that binds similar elements together.

Front and side

The Parthenon has 8 columns along one side and 17 along the other. The proportional relation created by these columns is X:2X+1 or 4:9. This mathematical relationship is carried out in other formal proportions that give rise to the temple including the spacing of columns and determination of elevations in the building. But an even number of columns along one side versus an odd number along the other also creates a second level of pattern in the Parthenon. Because we think of symmetry as a prominent ordering device in architecture, people imagine the space at the center of 8 columns to designate entry and, therefore, the front of the building, while 17 columns has a column at the center which prohibits entry and is therefore construed to be the side of the building. Pediments and double ranks of columns creating porches at the 8- versus the 17-column sides of the building reinforce this reading.

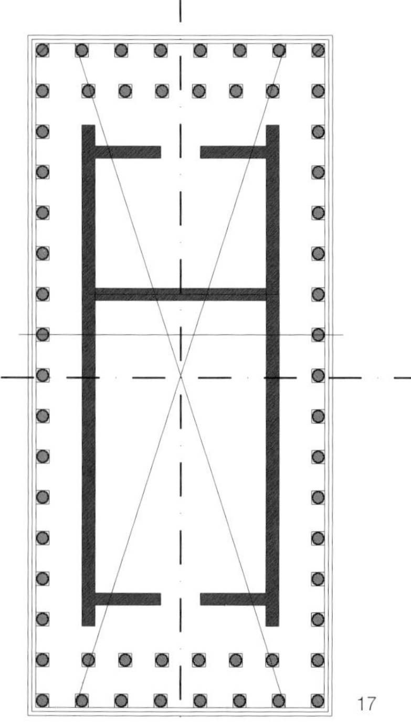

Entry, center, and edge

When we examined domain, we saw that the entry of a building constitutes a special idea that often garners design attention in architecture. The idea of entry is introduced by the space in the middle of the eight-column sides of the Parthenon. It is reinforced by the pediments at each end of the building that sculpturally portray important portions of the myth of Athena. This decoration announces the centrality of the Greek Gods to their culture just as the granary doors of the Dogon announced Amma and the cosmic egg to be the center of their culture. But it is the pattern of columns that stand within this first rank that announce entry as a function of the pattern of architectural elements. These columns are not evenly spaced like the outside columns but rather lie on lines that intersect the center of the outside columns and the center of the statue of Athena at the center of the naos. This subtle transformation of pattern abandons an orthogonal grid in favor of a radial center. In some ways, the placement of these columns, while firmly linked to their exterior colleagues, name an order that is conceptually in opposition to the orthogonal perimeter of the Parthenon. In this manner, edge is wedded to center as the landscape is gathered to Athena.

18

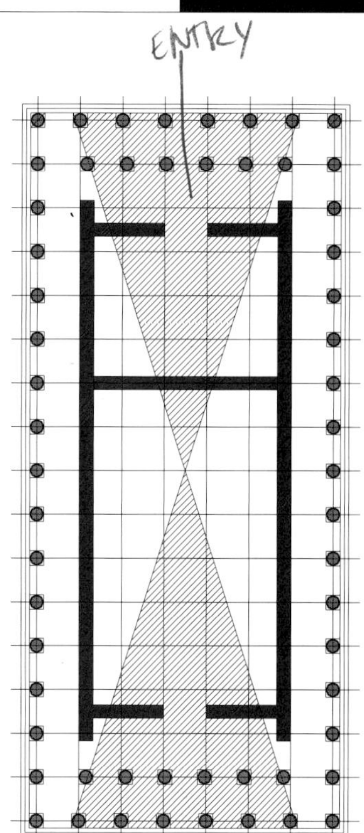

The order of threes

The human mind seems to prefer some organizations of architectural elements over others. The order of threes is such a case. The Parthenon suggests many of these groupings. The elevation of the building can be divided into base, midsection, and roof. The plan can be understood as colonnade, naos, and colonnade in both directions. Columns have a base, a shaft, and a capital. This order of threes can be identified in every facet of this design. Why should an order of nested threes be prominent rather than some other grouping? The order of ones has the problem of being singular. It cannot relate objects except unto themselves. The order of twos is interesting and very prevalent in architecture as bilateral symmetry. In some ways, the plan of the Parthenon could be seen to be divided in two as mirror images. But it is the order of threes that seems to propel many more patterns within this building. The order of threes always has two ends and an intermediate figure. These two ends always bound and give meaning to that figure. Thus, it is far more meaningful to see the axial arrangement of the Parthenon as a central aisle bounded on each side by a space than it

19

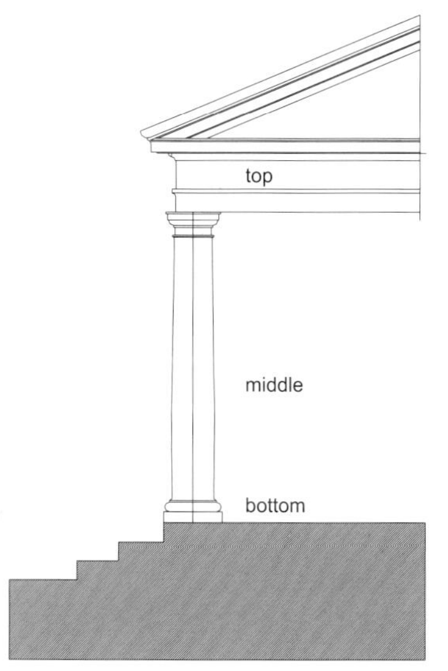

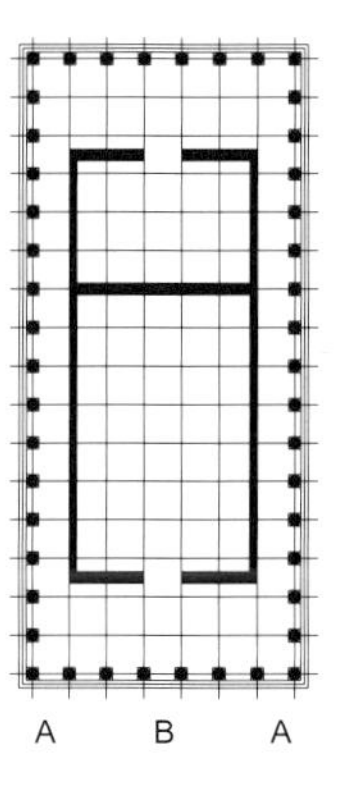

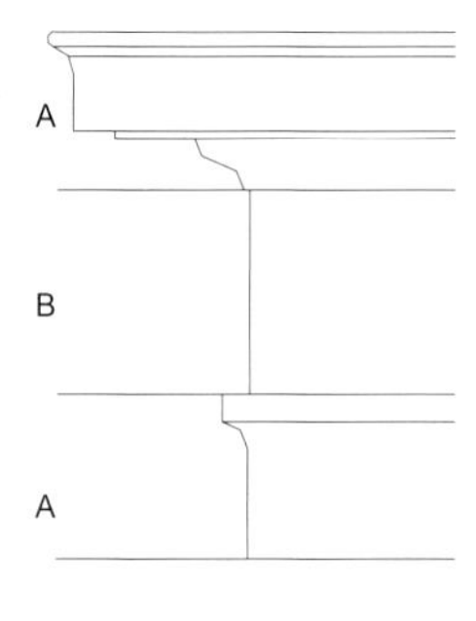

16 Meaning that emerges from patterns of columns
17 Front and side as meaning that emerges from columns
18 Center, entry, and edge as meaning that emerges from columns
19 The order of threes

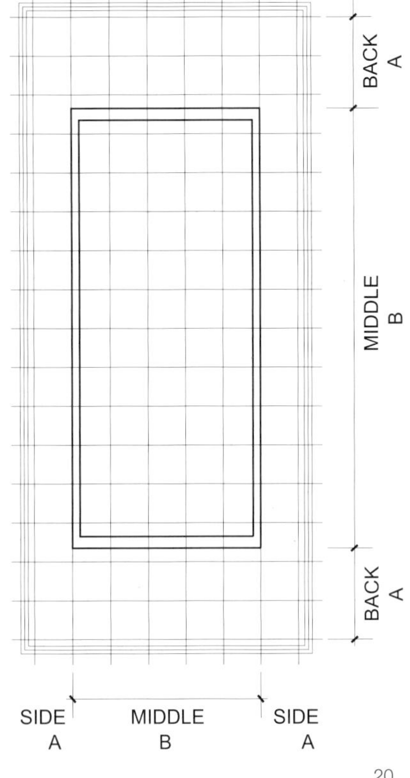

20

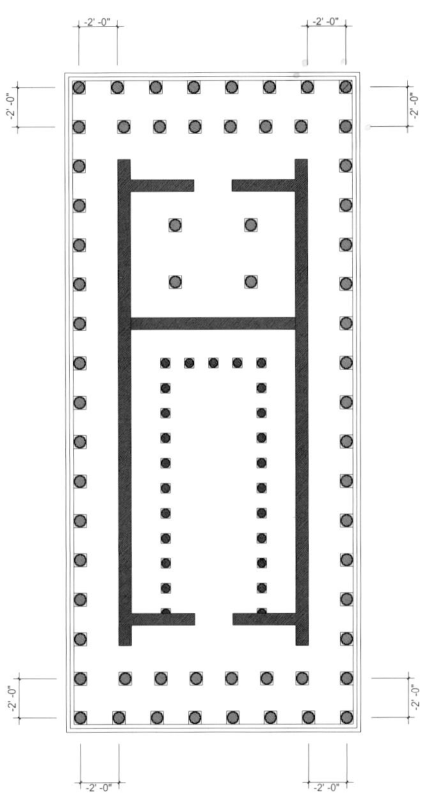

21

is to see the two haves of the plan of the Parthenon fold out from a line. The line is a visual abstraction. The aisle at the center is able to connote central space as entry, entertaining ideas of human habitation as well as of visual pattern. It is this idea of human habitation between two events that seems important to us. We are held between the floor and ceiling of a building. We are held between walls. We are held between the mutable earth and the immutable heavens. Human habitation has frequently been called the middle kingdom to identify our own position within an order of threes. Perhaps this place gave birth to a preference for visual patterns that reflected our own place of being.

Similarity and comparative meanings

The two tiers of Doric columns inside the cella of the naos are similar to but are smaller than the Doric columns in the outside arcade. Their two-tier organization allows them to support the roof of the naos but be smaller than their outdoor counterparts. These Doric columns frame the statue of Athena within the walls of the cella as the similar but larger Doric columns of the arcade frame the naos within the landscape. Their context is formed by the walls of the cella rather than the landscape that surrounds the Acropolis. They are the same proportion as those of the arcade but writ smaller. They relate to the wall of the cella and the statue of Athena as the arcade columns relate to the walls of the naos and to the landscape beyond. Similar elements order both environments but do so with different sizes to correspond to the environment that forms their context.

Deformation and visual versus geometric order

The geometric order of the Parthenon is an order created in the human mind. But the world comes to us through our senses before being interpreted by the mind. These senses tend to see columns as not straight unless they bow out a bit in the middle. They see buildings not standing firmly unless their sides slant in slightly toward the top. They see floors not level unless they bow up slightly toward their midpoint. They desire columns to be visually reinforced at corners where colonnades terminate and no other column exists to define a space between. These are not desires of the mind but of the eye. They correspond to the difference between what we think constitutes geometric perfection and how our eye and mind see perfection of form. This is a troublesome problem for architects. Is architectural order the province of the human mind or of the human body? We will return to this issue in the 20th-century work of Frank Lloyd Wright and Le Corbusier.

Closing thoughts

22

The problem of order in architecture is the problem of the relation of the parts to the whole. How parts constitute wholes and how wholes are made up of related parts is the problem of developing patterns among architectural elements in buildings. Patterns are the way that people intellectually understand these relationships. It matters little if the pattern in question is that of a humanly crafted object or the craft of natural forces in forming the natural landscape. Both are ways that the chaos of unpatterned matter becomes the order of understandable form. In such forms the relation of the part to the whole is understood both as the outcome of a process – human thought versus the organic outcome of competing natural forces – and as a set of formal patterns that emerge to give coherence to the whole. Grains of sand are assembled through the forces of wind and waves to make the comprehensible form of a sand dune that was not inherent in any single grain of sand by itself. The colonnade of the Parthenon only takes shape as stone is carved to become a fluted cylinder (with the entasis bow outward in the middle) and column is set against column, against floor, against architrave, against roof. In this manner, a sand dune is just as much a pattern as the Parthenon colonnade. What sets the patterns of buildings apart is that they reflect organizations of material that are intellectually manipulated to contain us in our daily lives. Simply outlining a domain is insufficient grounds for creating places for people to live. The human mind requires that the elements used to secure our domain be configured in patterns that make these places intellectually as well as socially satisfying. When it is said that the whole is more than the sum of the parts, it is the surplus of meaning created by pattern that is at work. One column standing by itself is able to create only one idea. Two columns set an appropriate distance apart create three ideas. Those are the ideas of column plus column plus entry. Entry is a surplus of meaning of this pattern. It is not inherent in either of the columns by themselves but emerges only through the pattern that two columns are able to produce when placed in relation to one another. Order in architecture is meaning that emerges from perceived patterns among architectural elements.

Creating these patterns is one of the seminal constraints of architectural design. It is a constraint in that it forces design decisions to give birth to understandable relationships that in turn become understandable rules that underlie the shape and placement of architectural forms. Without this constraint, architecture would be lost in a sea of self-expression.

There is good reason at the end of this chapter to return to the Greek philosophers who began it because they were the people who turned order into a question rather than a presumption of fact. Order is given to the Dogon world through their creation story. Order for the Greeks was less a matter of cultural myth than of reasoned conjecture. Order did not exist as a given idea to the Greeks but one that must be formulated

20 Plan as the order of threes
21 Deformation and sensual meaning at the corners of the Parthenon
22 Parthenon corner

by the human intellect. Socrates set the tone of this search when he resisted accepting the dogma of a culture as a satisfying answer to questions regarding truth. Plato identified the source of reason as ideas of immaterial form that preceded the concrete world. Aristotle reversed this process. Their rationalism and empiricism remain the ways we think about order in architecture. Their skepticism should be our own guide to understanding this problem in design. Order is not a given commodity in design but a given question. What should be the base of order of any design is one of the fundamental questions that propels all design thought. Too often this question is set aside for quick, conventional, and un-insightful answers. The results are seen and understood to be the banality of much of our current production of buildings. But beneath this unthinking conformity to the un-understood question of order in architecture stand contemporary works that have taken this problem seriously.

23 Doric columns

*every order has an element [illegible] to itself

order of a greek doric column

7
6
5
4
3
2
1

capitol

entastisis

shaft

base

taller then it is wide

to inhabit

create the order of inhabitation

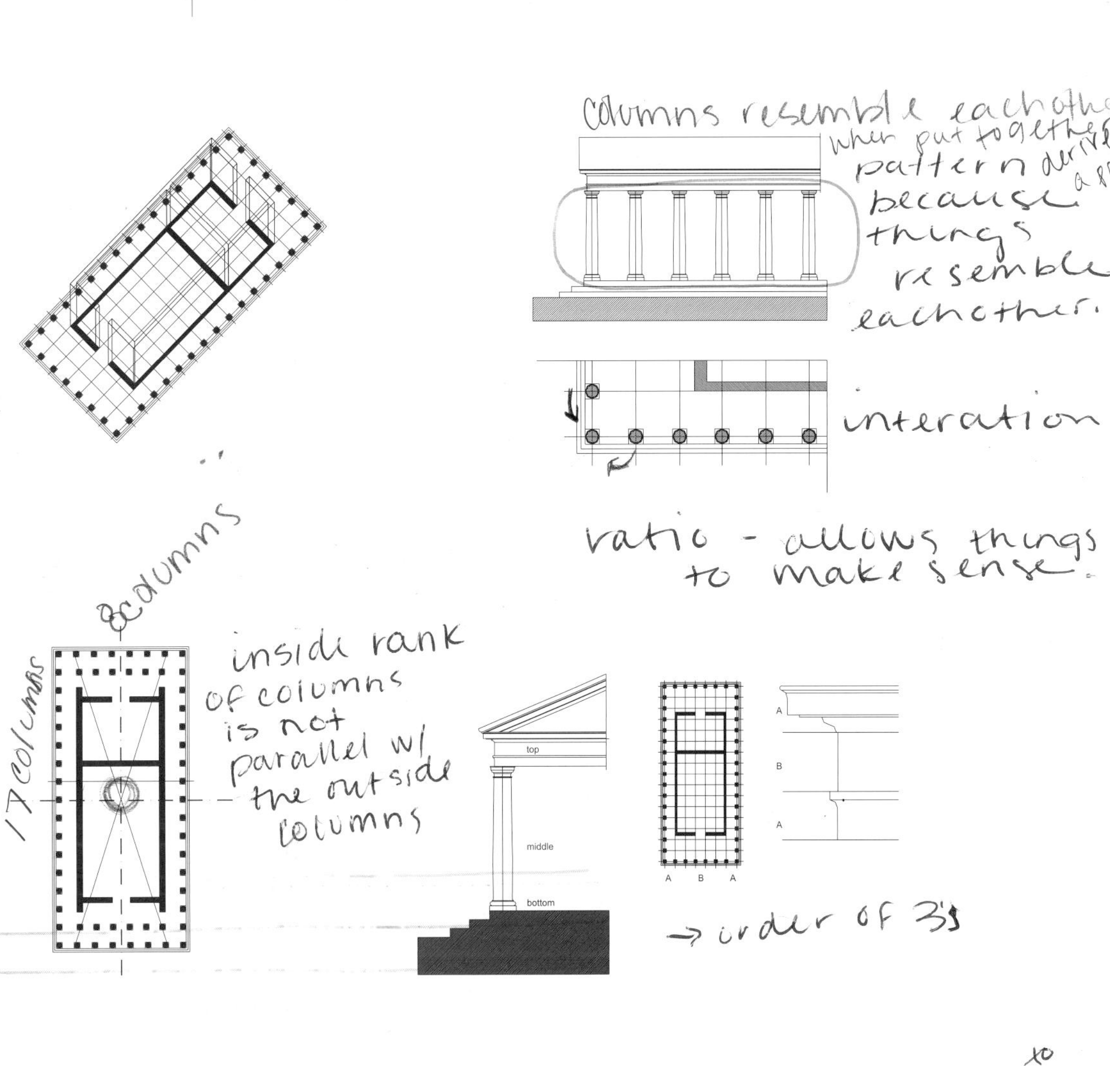

columns resemble eachother

when put together pattern derives because things resemble eachother.

a pattern

interation

ratio - allows things to make sense.

8 columns

17 columns

inside rank of columns is not parallel w/ the outside columns

→ order of 3's

order is central to us - allows us to exist

columns are closer together

gathers the landscape to it — HUMAN attempt to reach perfection

* gathers our attention

notion of order in the landscape

ORDER IN ARCHITECTURE

AFTER 1850

Sensualism, rationalism, elementalism and trasncendentalism in contemporary architecture

Background

The idea of order in architecture changed radically after the Industrial Revolution. Mass production required that parts of buildings be as similar as possible. Columns became standardized shapes and sizes determined solely by the loads that they were required to support. Instead of proposing symbolic order, these columns were placed as far apart as calculations of span might allow. Entries became punched openings in walls that were superficially decorated. All organizations of buildings became systematically orthogonal in support of the standardization that led to economies of construction. Mass produced parts were assembled to fill the functional needs of occupants but mute in terms of the issues of order presented by the Parthenon. A visit to any 20th-century office building or big-box store in the suburbs makes clear the ongoing impact of industrialism on issues of order in architecture.

But beneath this mechanical regularity there persists a perennial search for a humanly satisfying notion of order in architecture. The little channel of water in Kahn's Salk Institute leading the eye to an infinite horizon reinterprets the Pantheon's oculus that defines a symbolic line linking heaven and earth. Both buildings take up the issue that Stonehenge examined in 2000 BC when this observatory connected the regularities of the heavens to the temporariness of life on earth. We remain small in terms of the cosmos. Its mysteries remain shrouded from our insight. Our search for order in this cosmos has changed little over the 4,000 years that separate Stonehenge from the Salk Institute. Each of these buildings attempts to make tangible the intangible order of the cosmos that surrounds us. The reoccurrence of this building type suggests that we remain as concerned about this order now as we were as builders of megalithic monuments.

01 Exeter Library ground floor arcade

Four major strains of thought have characterized 20th-century architecture's approach to the issue of order in design. The first of these might be loosely titled sensualism. Sensualism is meant to signify ideas that emanate from a perceptual understanding of the world. This general category of architectural thought begins with a person as its center. This person is equipped with all of the abilities to perceive the outside word that we associate with our species plus sets of cultural understandings that help convert sensually acquired information into ideas.

The second major strain of this century's architectural thought about order is initiated by an idea that has no necessary sensual underpinnings. This form of architecture might be termed idealism, rationalism, or perhaps rational idealism. Such architecture is initiated by an idea that does not trace its heritage to information interpreted from the senses but from a philosophical tradition that makes the inner working of the human mind the supreme arbitrator of architectural thought. This is a cerebral approach to the problem of order in contemporary architecture

A third movement concerning architectural order might be termed minimalism. Here order is reduced to the organization of a set of primitive, elemental forms that are thought to be the essential foundation of architectural thought. Such a reduction parallels modern science's search for the elemental particles of matter and energy in the universe. Since the time of Greek philosophy, Western intellectual tradition has been concerned with finding the basic ingredients of what exists. Contemporary architecture is just as concerned with a search for the elemental building blocks of constructed environments.

The final strain of a contemporary search for order in architecture is a belief that architecture always has a duty to locate people in the cosmos. The cosmos is not a physical reality but a set of beliefs about what constitutes the largest context of human life. Our myths about the structure of the heavens illustrates that we have always been aware of this larger context. This form of speculation about architectural order might be called transcendentalism, as it cuts across time, place, and culture to seek truths about the core of being human.

Of course, it is often difficult to neatly separate strains of thought in particular architectural works. Sensually conceived projects often contain nuggets of transcendental thought as in Wright's debt to 19th-century American poets and essayists. The reverse is true of the rationalists: Kahn's transcendentalism would mean little to architecture without the rich, sensual nature of the material forms that manifest his ideas. Nonetheless, this distinction is helpful in attempting to look across basic kinds of thought that have driven 20th-century ideas of architectural order.

02 The side of the Robie House
03 Plan of the Robie House
04 Front of the Robie House

The Robie house

The Robie House was designed between 1909 and 1910 by Frank Lloyd Wright for a bicycle manufacturer in Chicago, Illinois. It marked the culmination of the design of a number of houses in Oak Park, Illinois that became known as prairie style houses. These houses became well known because they were organized very differently from the conventional residences of the time. Instead of being square, two-story, gable-roofed houses, prairie houses were low, horizontal structures with shallow pitched roofs and wide overhangs.

02

The Robie House is located on the end of a block. It is organized as two slender tubes of space that stretch along the length of the site to overlap at the center. The living floor of the house is raised up one story while the central portion of the house is centered by a small tower that containes a master bedroom on the third floor. Living and dining rooms are located in the forward shaft of horizontal first floor space with a playroom below. Children's bedrooms, kitchen, and servants' quarters with a garage below are in the shaft behind.

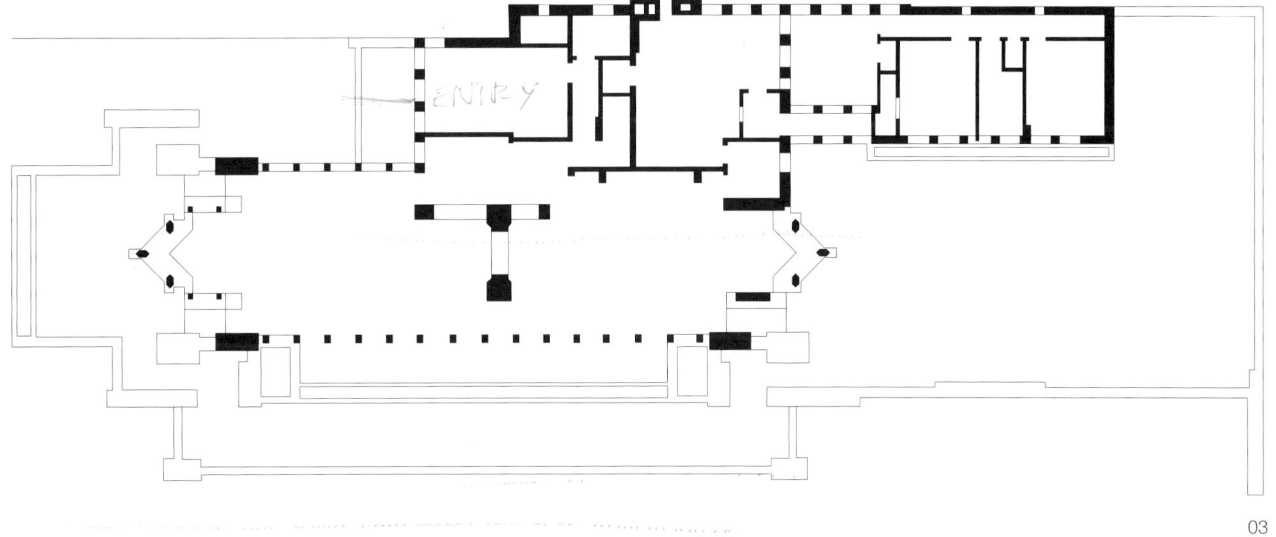

03

04

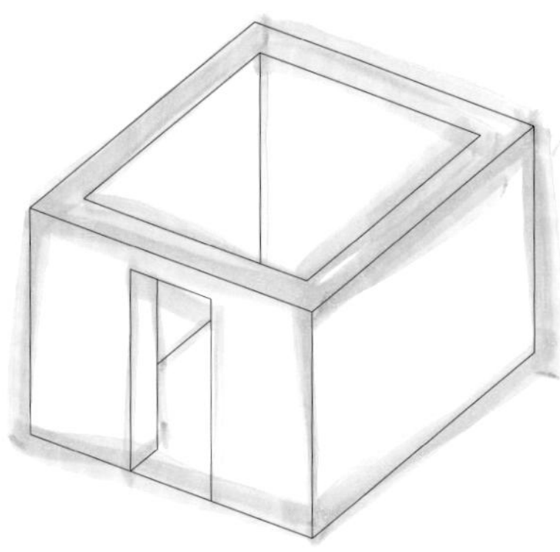

Entry

The entry of the Robie House is composed of a set of form/body/sense relationships that differ from conventional residential entries. In traditional Midwestern entries a sidewalk leads from the larger public walkway to a front porch, then to a front door marked by decoration, and finally into an entry hall that contains a stair to the more private bedroom floor above. In the Robie House these signs are replaced by a set of formal conditions that locate the human body in particular ways along a path. The entry walk of the Robie House leaves the public walkway not to face the front porch of the house but to slide along the back of a tall, brick wall to the center of the site. Here a small, low, plain door identifies an entry into a small, low space. A turn to the right reveals a stairway leading up to the main living area of the house. As a person ascends these stairs the compressed, dim, entry space below gives way to brightly lit spaces of the living and dining rooms above. The stair leads to the back wall of these spaces leaving the process of entry incomplete. To complete the process of entry, entrants again slide along a wall and turn 90° to arrive in open spaces facing the brightly lit side of these rooms. Entry proceeds from the back of these rooms to these windows.

This is a carefully controlled choreography of the human body that replaces the signs of the conventional residential entry with a series of tensions between low and high, back and front, lower and upper, dimly and well-lit spaces. Architectural material and light now position the human body through the human senses in a series of experiences that move through a complex set of horizontal and vertical movements to terminate in entry into the upper living space of the house. It is the feeling of our bodies next to a high brick wall, through a low door, into a compressed room, up a stair, turning to the light that makes this such a memorable experience.

The house one room wide

The Robie House is not a compact organization of eight rooms in a two-story, square envelope as would be found in a traditional Midwestern house of this era. It is rather an organization of tubes of space that are one room wide. The architectural parents of these rooms are Renaissance libraries in which buildings were reduced to narrow rooms so that light could come from both sides so people could see to read the books. The windows on the two sides of this narrow space are close enough together so the light that comes through one side overlaps that from the other side. The wall of one of the spaces containing the living room is punctured by high windows. Along the opposite wall are floor-to-ceiling French doors. The high versus low windows along these two walls suggest the less transparent wall to be the back of the space while the more transparent wall suggests the front. Beyond the French doors along the front edge of this organization, a balcony extends along the entire side of the house creating a narrow veranda that overlooks what was then a meadow. The ceiling of this tube of space is raised in the center identifying an axis that runs from the stair/fireplace at the center of the house to the "prow" termination of each room at either end.

05 Entry room of the Robie House
06 Robie House front door
07 Robie House as one room wide
08 Robie House living room

As the ceiling steps down at the long edges of this room it creates a tripartite division of edge-center-edge within this tube. A tension develops from this organization that pits sunlight against spatial axis. This tension is interesting in that it clouds conventional architectural definitions of front and side. The front of these rooms might be thought of as the French doors that visually connect the living spaces to the landscape outside, or it might be thought of as the doors that lead from the longitudinal axial order of the ceiling to the front porch beyond. This is a complex order that suggests not one but two fronts of this house. One of these fronts is interpreted from the sunlight that passes through the French doors along the long side of these rooms. The other front is interpreted from an axial, elevated ceiling that runs the length of these spaces terminating in the residential street that gives social order to the block.

07

The relationship of these two orders is a bit like a musical sonata in which two themes are introduced and developed in relation to one another. Rhythmic light along one side of the rooms is developed in relation to a special axis that runs counter to it. In the Robie House the formal theme of the axial social order of the block contrasts with the theme of the French doors with the terrace beyond as the natural landscape.

08

Center and edge

09

The entry, stair, and fireplace form a center of the Robie house connected to its edges by the axially raised ceiling of the dining and living rooms. Passing through a portal that signifies a change in domains, rising above the ground to an elevated floor, and gathering around the warmth of a fireplace are all central ideas of home that are tangibly manifested at the center of the Robie House. These three elements are gathered to the center of this design because they also gather us to ideas that center our associations of what a home means. A home means to pass from the domain of the tribe into the domain of the family. Rising up a stairway is a special human event that connotes rising above the fray of the every day world to overlook rather than directly participate in the social world below. Continuing up another floor into the "nest" of the parent's bedroom above signals the special need for privacy. This vertical axis of entry/hearth/master bedroom forms a triumvirate of vertical spaces that is conceptually matched by the horizontal order of the living room/hearth/dining room of the living floor. The fireplace that centers both of these axes is not a necessary source of heat in the Robie House. The house has a hot water boiler to condition air temperature. But the fireplace remains the symbol of the source of warmth that gathered the family to it for thousands of years before the advent of mechanical heating systems. The hearth of the Robie House retains the symbolic capacity to perform this task and in doing so joins the stair and entry as the definition of the center of a home.

The raised portion of the ceiling of the living/dining rooms of the Robie house connects this center to its edges. This ceiling identifies a longitudinal axis that spatially structures these rooms, passes through the hearth, and centers the house. As this axis extends into the spaces on either side of the entry/stair/hearth center it gathers its edges to it. The dropped ceiling at its edge gathers the front of the French doors and the back of the elevated windows to this central axis. It gathers the doors to the front terrace and the roofed terrace beyond them to the hearth as center. It gathers the prow windows of the dining area to the stair that it bisects.

09 Robie House French doors
10 Robie House as center and edge
11 Robie House ceiling detail
12 Robie House exterior massing as heavy base, floating roof, and horizontal and vertical axes

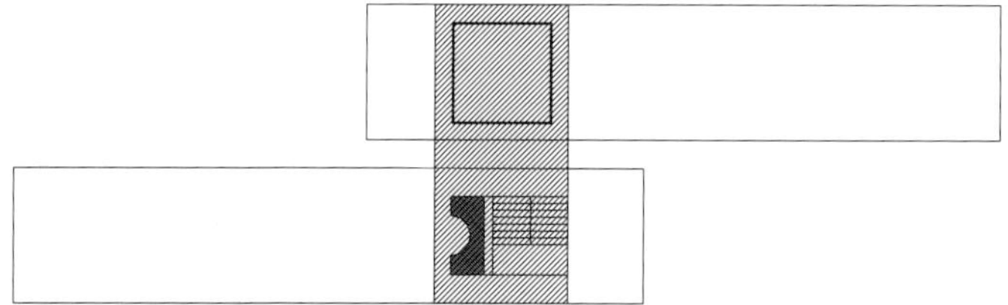

10

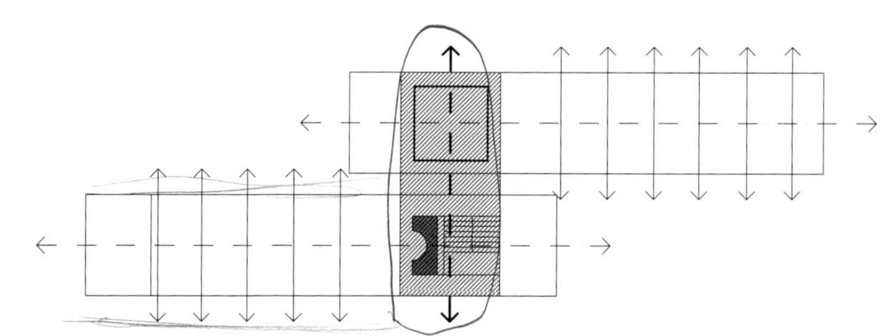

The house reconfigures the site

The base of the Robie House is perceived to be a solid mass in relation to its context. The roof that hovers above this base is made to appear light in relation to the heaviness of the base of the building. Living occurs in the middle domain between the hovering roof and the stability of the base. At each end of the living space this middle domain is modified to create a specific kind of juncture with the outside world. At the front of the house the floor of the porch is lowered, altering the horizontally compressed vision of outside from the interior living space. The heightened ceiling and descending stair of this front porch connote a partial opening up to the public world of the block. At the other end of the house this floor descends to the back yard. The side of the house is protected from the public sidewalk by a brick kneewall that encloses the outdoor terrace adjacent to the playroom located on the ground level of the house. The entry is formed by a path that runs along the non-public side/back of the house to the center of the site where it intersects the stair that rises through the center of the house to the master bedroom "nest." The vertical order of the entry/hearth/ master bedroom is made visible from the exterior of this domain as it intersects the horizontal order of the living spaces. The second, service tube of space and a wall at the edge of the site enclose the back, service portion of the yard. The prow of the living room terrace juts into its front yard without suggesting access through it.

11

Each of these formal contrivances alters the way the Robie House site might be perceived. An entry at the center rather than addressing the normal front of this house sets in motion a whole set of formal circumstances that remove the Robie House from the social rules of the neighborhood. The site has neither a true front yard nor a true back yard. Living above ground level behind fortress-like walls reorganizes the relation of this house to the social rules of the block that forms its context. Entry in the middle of the site, first floor raised a full level above grade, and enclosing walls surrounding the house all remind us that house, site, and social neighborhood go together as a piece. Altering one of these components must also generate change in the others.

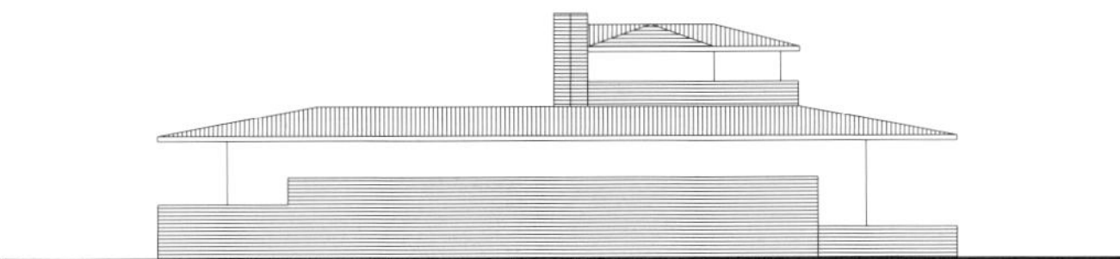

12

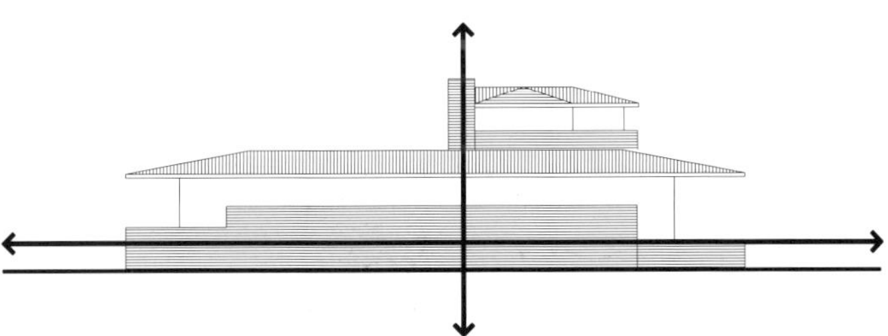

13

The significance of this analysis relative to architectural notions of order is that it always indicates the central position held by the human body in developing architectural ideas. Each of the design maneuvers that make this house an exceptional piece of architecture are initiated by how a human body would feel inside the house. The material forms of this house also create a series of special ways that occupants are held in relation to themselves, to one another, to the public world, and to nature. The origin of this set of ideas is the human capacity to sense the specific conditions of their physical surroundings. Sensual data are interpreted to become architectural ideas in the Robie House with no division between emotional and intellectual thought. Sensations give pattern to human experience in this house as the grounding of architectural order.

13 Robie House side façade
14 Villa Savoye

Villa Savoye

Villa Savoye is a vacation house designed by Le Corbusier and constructed outside of Paris from 1929 to 1931. It culminated a series of residential projects in which Le Corbusier developed a cerebral interpretation of order in contemporary architecture. The underlying structure of architecture in this mode of thought lies in the permanent and unchanging realm of ideas. These ideas might be called rational because their origin is found in our mind rather than in our body. Villa Savoye is a wonderful example of this kind of rationalism in architecture. As a building it sets out to define the ideas of architecture that are central to conveying meaning. It does this by making explicit the vocabulary of these ideas and their grammar.

The house consists of three floors. The first or ground floor contains an entry, garage, and servants' quarters. A central ramp connects the ground, second living floor, and the third floor roof terrace. The second, living floor contains two light courts, a living room, kitchen, bedroom, master bedroom, and master bath. The third floor roof garden is bounded only by a single curvilinear wall with a window in it, and a stairway.

14

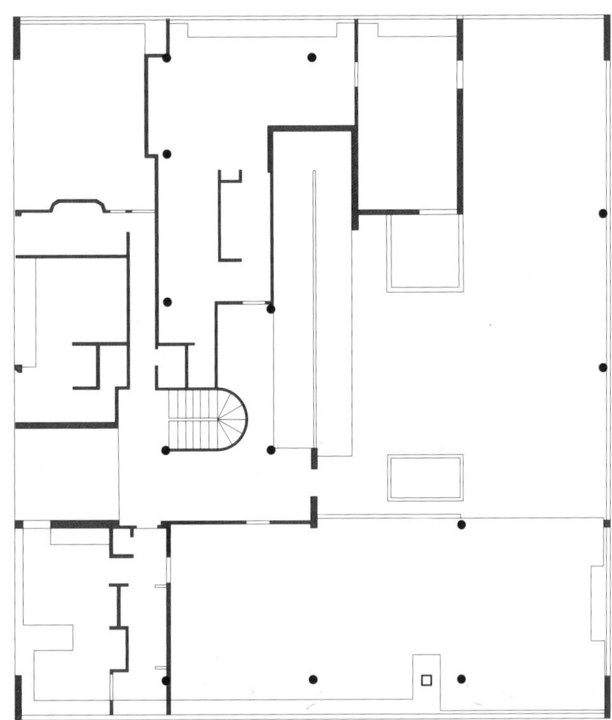

15

Two slabs and three domains

The order of Villa Savoye begins by placing two square slabs, one above the other at equal distances. The first slab creates a domain between the underside of that slab and the earth. This domain physically and figuratively connects house inhabitants to the world around them. The second slab creates a domain between its upper side and the sky. The heavens are the source of life in sunlight and the home of the mythology of the gods. This is the space of the imagination and intangible aspirations. The space between the two slabs forms the middle kingdom. It is the place that people create to live between the ever-changing earth and the stability of the heavens. It is the place of transactions of the family: the social and physical locus of events that we call home.

16

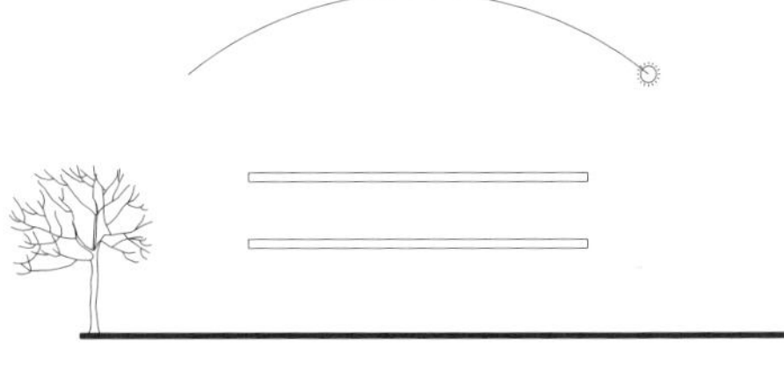

The 16 perimeter columns

These square slabs are bounded by five evenly spaced columns on each side. The five columns divide the square into four spaces per side or the whole square into 16 smaller squares. The corners and midpoint of the square are marked by these columns revisiting the role of the columns of the colonnade of the Parthenon but without the central space of entry formed by the even number of columns at the front and back of the temple. These 16 evenly spaced perimeter columns translate the unique geometric characteristics of a square plan into the vertical dimension. They now parse space into a series of identical forms as they divide the space created by slabs first into quarter spaces then into sixteenths. There is no subversion of this intellectual order in either the shape or the placement of these columns as there was in the Parthenon. The mind rather than the eye is given first place in this order.

One-way beams atop the perimeter columns

The beams that rest on these columns are not developed as one might expect. If they were to be consistent with the formal instincts of the square slab and the organization of the perimeter columns, they would form a two-way system that again would subdivide the square slab into a series of similar forms. Instead the 16 columns are spanned by 5 one-way beams. These beams are extended at each end of the square. This extension elongates two sides of the square slab making it a rectangle. These one-way beams and the rectangle that they create initiate a dialogue between the perfect form of the square and the imperfect form of the rectangle. This is a cerebral dialogue between pure geometry of the mind and the mechanical ability of one-way beams to cantilever beyond their supports.

17

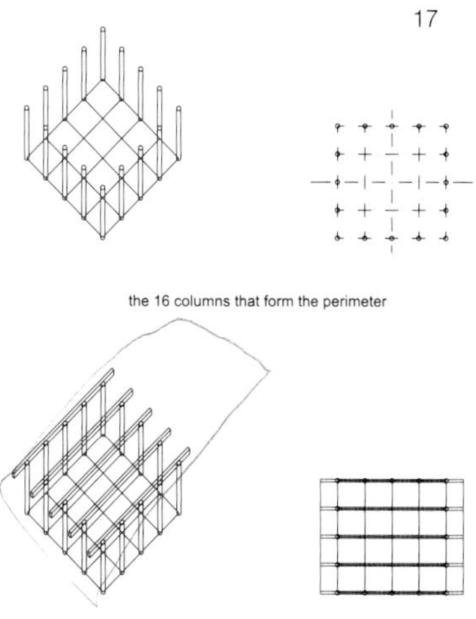

the 16 columns that form the perimeter

one way beams sit on top

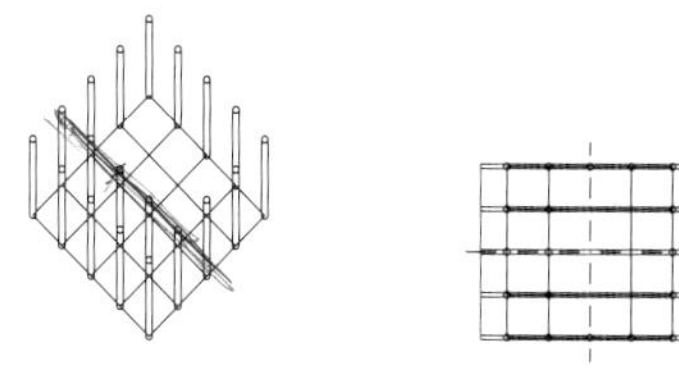

signifying the front with parallel rows

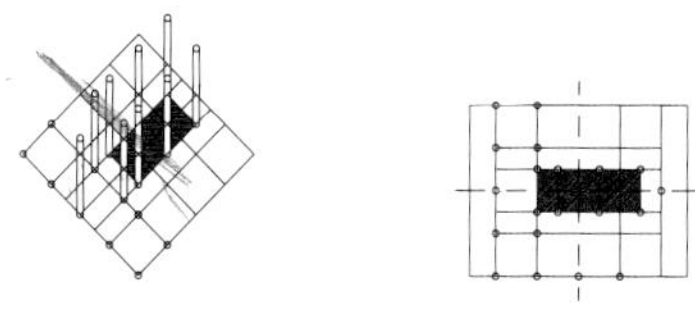

signifying the front with parallel rows

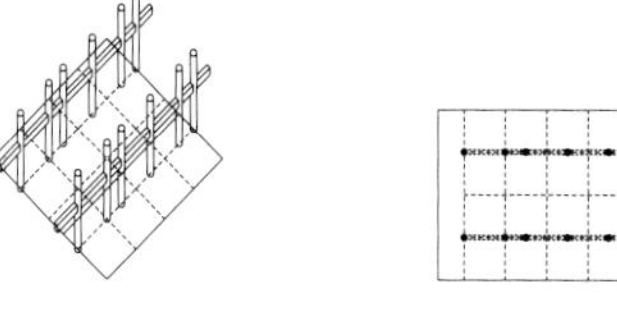

one way beams an circumstantial columns

18

15 Living floor plan of Villa Savoye
16 Villa Savoye as rational square plan and two slabs creating three domains
17 The columns of Villa Savoye as a rational perimeter, topped by one way beams, restated rational order of columns at the front, bifurcation of columns to create the center, and the conditional columns of the interior
18 Side elevation of Villa Savoye

Geometrically consistent columns as the symbolic front of the house

19

The front of Villa Savoye is located on the side opposite the public street that provides access to this residence. On this side of the house the idea of front is restated by a second row of columns inside the first that maintains the order of the perimeter columns. This set of columns rises through the first slab of the house to the second slab containing the living room. The living room reverses its orientation on the living floor, looking in at a courtyard rather than out at the landscape as does the ground level of the house. This second, evenly spaced rank of columns within the first allows this reversal of orientation to take place while maintaining the idea of front as a formal order that faces an outside domain.

Entry and ramp at the center

The square grid of perimeter columns makes no provision for a void at the center of the plan that might indicate a space of entry. If the center is to be recognized as a place of transition from the community of the tribe to that of the family, then an opening, rather than the point of a central column needs to be carved out from an architectural order that would seem to resist such an intrusion. The middle column of the second or front defining row of columns of Villa Savoye is divided in two to create this space. This division makes the center a more special event than if it were able to organically grow from the initial order of the columns as in the entry to a Greek temple. The need to intentionally reconfigure the order of columns gives the entry a special status as not simply growing from the perimeter order of the columns, but from superimposing a new order on them. The division of the central column of the second rank of front columns creates a space where there originally was none, and houses the ramp at the center of the house that connects the earth to the sky as it rises through the floors of the house. This entry is a special social distinction in a home and, thus, requires a special formal order to represent it. While a sensual experience formed the order of entry in the Robie House, a cerebral set of symbols form the entry to Villa Savoye.

19 Living room of Villa Savoye
20 Ramp of Villa Savoye
21 Exterior view and interior view of the entry of Villa Savoye

20

21

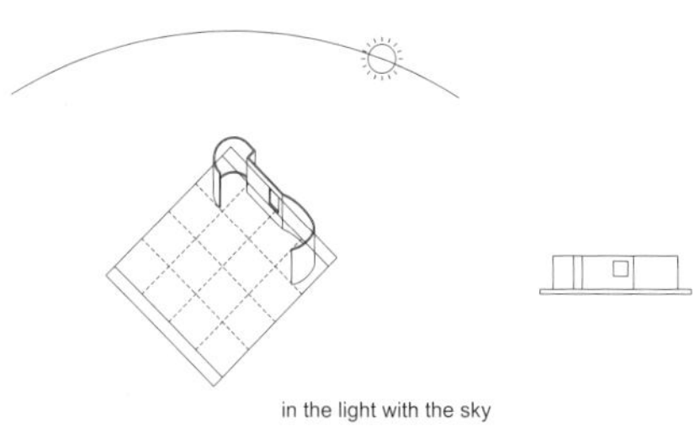
in the light with the sky

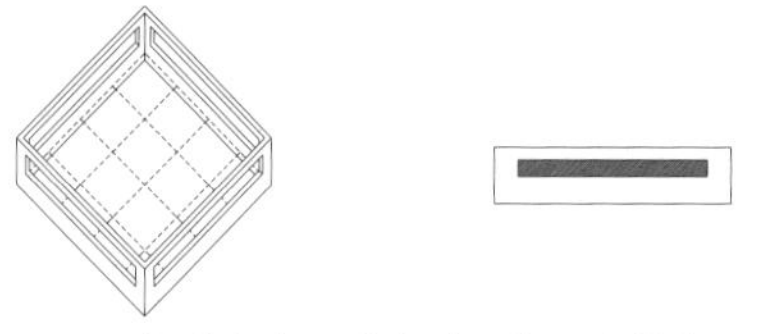
making the horizon as the boudary of human habitation

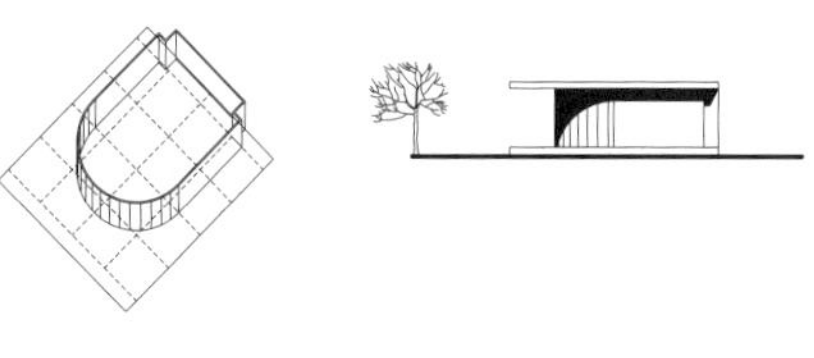
on the ground in the shadow

22

The conditional column

Those columns not making the edge, front, entry, or center of the house (all fundamental formal/existential issues in architecture) are allowed to slide along the interior one-way beams of the house and come to rest as required by the pragmatic needs of the house plan. The conditional and pragmatic use of these columns, whose shape and location is determined only by local circumstance, stands in bright contrast to the rational placement of the perimeter columns of Villa Savoye. In this comparison the possibilities and duties of the column in architecture are relatively defined. On one hand the column is purely utilitarian. Its sole duty is to hold the roof up. On the other hand the column is one of architecture's central means of stating the order of a building. Placing one use of the column directly against the other makes this distinction clear.

The sun and the order of domains

The forms of the third, garden floor of Villa Savoye thrust up into the sky and into the sunlight. They directly mirror all the time and place changes in the light of the sky. The horizontal slit in the perimeter wall of the second, living floor of Villa Savoye suggests a manmade horizon. The light and images carried through this slit refer to the natural horizon as where the sky meets the earth to form the largest boundary of our domain. The walls of the ground floor of the house are removed by 15 feet from the edges of the slab above. As a consequence this domain does not receive direct light but only the reflected light of the forms that surround the house and connect it to the surrounding landscape. The direct sun of the roof garden, and indirect sunlight as landscape image of the ground floor become both the direct light of the open courtyards and the symbolic horizon of the horizontal opening around the middle, living floor of Villa Savoye.

23

24

The two courtyards as definition of the manmade outside

The two courtyards of the living floor of Villa Savoye accept the light of the sky into a new, middle kingdom, manmade earth. The first and larger of these courtyards is surrounded by a series of openings that catalogue the ways that an architectural opening is able to connect the inside with the outside. The first of these is the master bedroom terrace that is open to the courtyard. The second is the living room that is separated from the terrace by floor-to-ceiling glazing. The third is the glazing of the ramp that is separated from the terrace by translucent glass block. The fourth is the punched opening of the master bedroom that allows visual connection with the terrace but does not allow physical passage. Conversely, the kitchen courtyard is opaque to its surroundings except for the horizontal slit of the manmade horizon. It links the new earth of the terrace floor with the sky. As in the difference between the geometrically ordered perimeter columns and the interior conditionally ordered columns, the contrasting organizations of the same architectural element in each courtyard signify a different kind of connection to environments beyond. The potential meaning of the openings surrounding the larger courtyard is one of horizontal communication; it is the purpose of these openings to connect people to all things on the earth. The smaller courtyard connects only the earth to the sky, fulfilling the other purpose of architectural openings: to connect people to the cosmos.

22 Villa Savoye as a garden under the sky, a horizontal extension of the landscape on the ground, and a living domain in between
23 The central courtyard of Villa Savoye
24 The roof garden wall and window
25 The two courtyards of Villa Savoye as a complementary pair

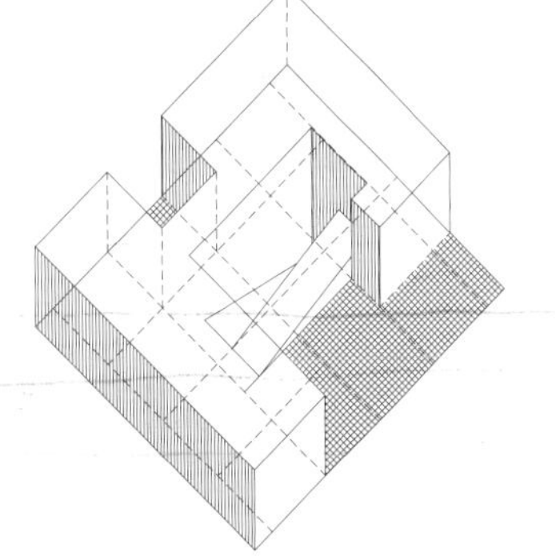

25

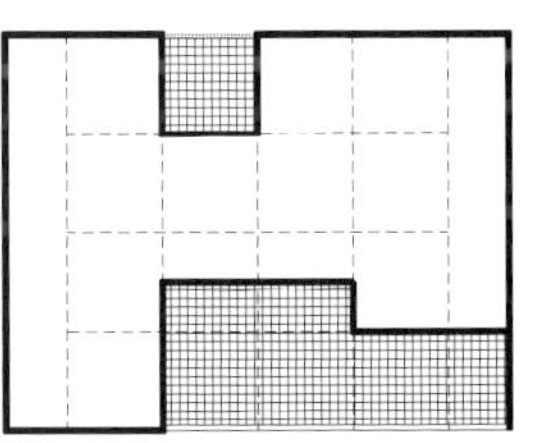

26

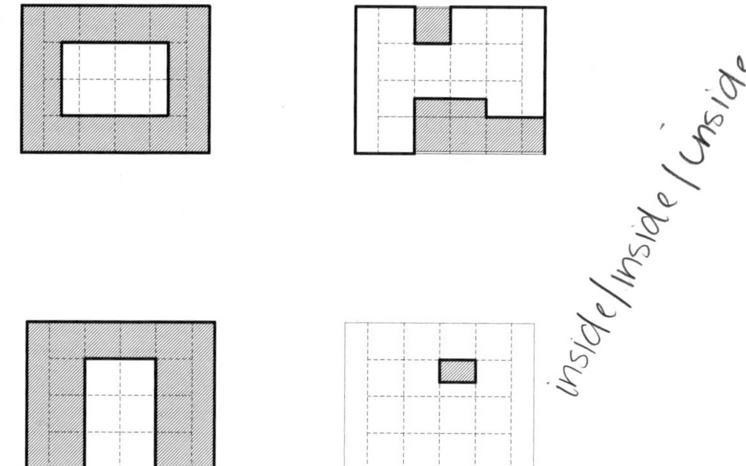

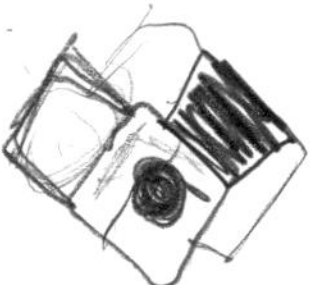

Definitions of inside and outside

Inside and outside seem to be such easily understood constructs in architecture. Either inhabitants are inside a domain or they are outside of it. But beneath this simplistic dichotomy lies what we all perceive to be a range of these conditions. In Villa Savoye this range is identified by the ways in which the light and air of nature are allowed to touch and be seen by inhabitants. Outside of the perimeter walls of the house is the place not under the control of people but under the control of natural forces. This is the outside/outside of Villa Savoye. The courtyards of the house are an outside/inside. Each of these spaces is directly available to sunlight and climate yet exists within the manmade boundary of the surrounding horizon wall of the living floor, and is thereby transformed to be within the symbolic control of the house. The master bedroom terrace is covered from the sky by a roof but is otherwise open to climate. This is an inside/outside space.

The living spaces of the house are all connected to the courtyards or the exterior of the house through glazed openings in walls. These spaces are the inside/inside of the house. They exist within the symbolic boundaries of the horizon wall of the house and within its shell that separates the inside from the outside climate. The master bath receives light only from a skylight in its ceiling. It exists within the boundary wall of the house, and again within the flesh of the inside/inside of the spaces that adjoin it. This space is the inside/inside/inside of the house. It is that place of protection that is guarded from all that surrounds it allowing only the sense of time that is bequeathed it by the light from the skylight above.

This series of spaces, as more and less exposed to the sunlight and climate of nature, represents an intellectual view of the common, but rarely noted, range of ways and associations with which people actually navigate a complex set of ideas about how the inside of a domain might be separated from and connected to its outside context.

26 Inside and outside as defined by Villa Savoye
27 The master bathroom as the inside/inside/inside of Villa Savoye

Front and back as the outcome of columns and walls

front and back

side

28

The ground floor façade of Villa Savoye is composed only of columns. The façade of the roof garden is composed only of walls. In the middle domain the columns and walls are woven together to form the façade of the house. This restatement of the necessity of column as order and wall as domain becomes the front/back of the house when it restates the original square that initiated the design of Villa Savoye. This is the representation of a regular geometric figure that might be recognized by a community. Think of the front of suburban or urban houses and how the elements of this façade are composed symmetrically or in a careful balance as opposed to the sides or back where they are not. The side façades of Villa Savoye have walls that extend beyond the original square. This form is circumstantial or arbitrary in that this cantilever could be any length as long as it could sustain the force of gravity. This surface becomes the side of the house as the intersection of wall and column as a consequence of this arbitrariness. The geometrically precise form of the square becomes the formal front/back of the house in contrast to the arbitrary form of its rectangular side.

Villa Savoye is a building that is best thought rather than felt. It appeals less to the senses than to the mind. Each foundational idea of architecture – initiation of domain from the ideal pattern of the square, column spacing determining front and entry, the conditional column and one-way beams, sun and climate as definitions of nature's outside versus the symbolic inside constructed by people, and the symbolic analysis of the distinction between front and side – are all argued out in this design with an intellectual rigor rarely achieved in modernism.

This analysis makes clear the very abstract, cerebral nature of Villa Savoye. Its forms become a symbolic language that can be used to explore the fundamental issues of architecture as their grammatical order is manipulated. As architectural element is set against architectural element, new architectural sentences are formed. As these sentences are assembled, new architectural paragraphs of relational form are writ that may be interpreted as new architectural ideas. Order in architecture emerges through this rational process. Villa Savoye is the dream of the Age of Enlightenment come true in architecture. Its rational order represents one of the great triumphs of reason in design.

28 Columns and walls woven together to define front and side in Villa Savoye
29 Entry façade of Villa Savoye
30 The German Pavilion at Barcelona
31 Plan of the German Pavilion

29

The German Pavilion in Barcelona

30

Architecture returns periodically to a search for its roots. This search normally centers on ways to reduce design to elements found in the first constructed buildings. As in many other modes of thought, there is in architecture the sense that this return is a search for an authentic basis for design thought. The primal elements of a building are thought to be those that are most necessary for ideas of human habitation to emerge, and thus those that form the elemental foundation for all subsequent elaborations of thought. The modern source of this kind of thought is the ideas put forth by modern science in the late 19th and early 20th centuries. The elementalism of modern particle physics has created a powerful model for all modern thought. The German Pavilion designed by Ludwig Mies van der Rohe for the 1929 International Exposition in Barcelona, represents architecture's attempt to reduce its constructions to similar elemental principles.

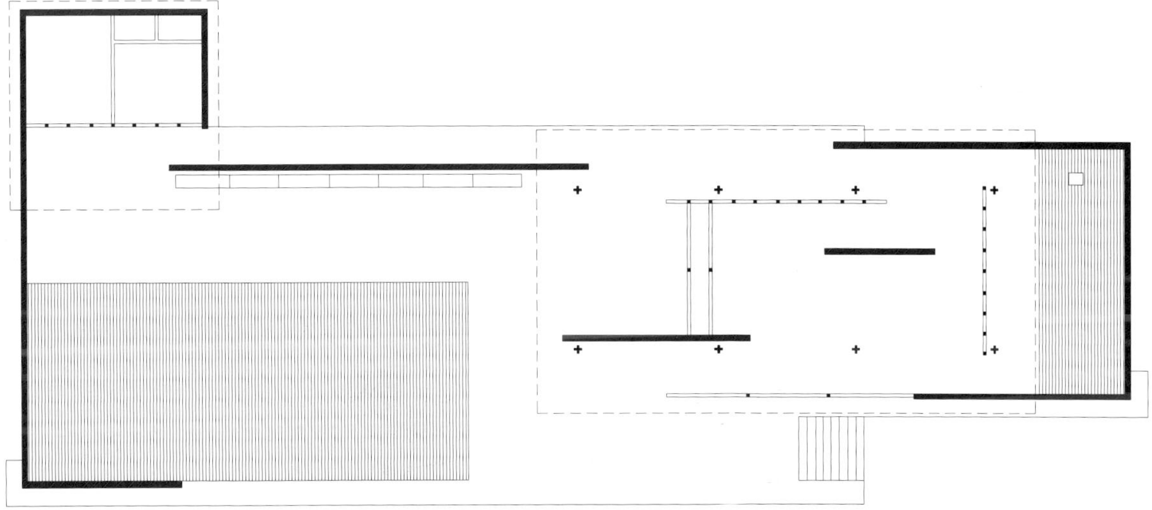

31

Reduction to essential horizontal planes

32 Wall extending from under the roof into the front courtyard of the German Pavilion
33 Spatial complexity of the German Pavilion

The German Pavilion reduces buildings to two planes with a space between them that is high enough to accommodate human beings. The first of these is the floor. The second parallels the form of the first with the exception that it is overhead not underfoot. These two planes are held apart by two ranks of four chrome-plated columns. Each four-column rank develops three spaces as opposed to the single space between pairs of columns perpendicular to this rank. This distinction might be said to give birth to architectural ideas like proportion, side, and front that grow from elemental patterns of column placement.

32

33

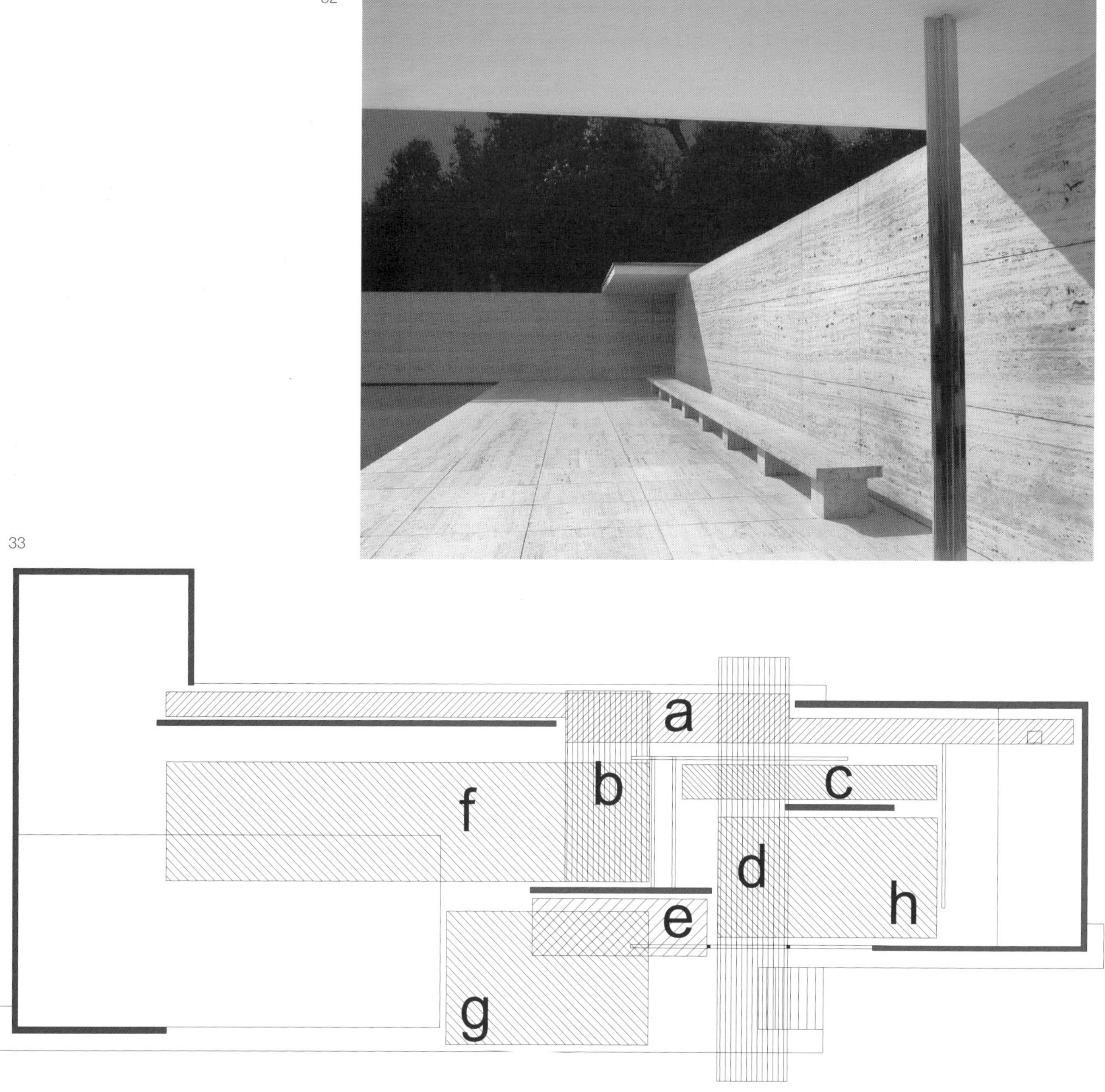

34

35

Reduction to essential vertical planes

Walls designed to separate domains are also treated as planes in this design. The outermost of these walls contain not the building but its site within their confines. This walling off of the natural world allows the forms of the natural landscape to be represented as manmade abstractions within them. These representations of the natural landscape carry the meaning of natural material like water, earth, and vegetation as architectural abstractions. Such abstractions loosen nature's grip on the manipulation of these natural materials so that they might be reconfigured to have uniquely human meanings. The natural landscape of water, earth, vegetation, and sky retain their natural form but are captured within the domain of human thought by the framing walls of the site.

The second set of three walls is opaque stone separating areas within the house into distinct domains, or suggesting domains that overlap bordering areas.

The third set of walls in the German Pavilion connects the interior of this domain with its site. They accomplish this either by transparently allowing light and image to pass freely between the two, or by extending beyond the roof to invade the site beyond. This sensual continuity reunites what opaque walls of rooms had separated. In doing so, these walls of continuation restate the essential character of the wall as a vertical plane with two sides. It is only when this elemental particle of architecture is joined at a corner that the idea of enclosure is initiated. Before the corner came the wall as a

36

34 The German Pavilion as an idealized landscape
35 Column and wall as fundamental architectural symbols in the German Pavilion
36 The wall enclosing the site of the German Pavilion

37

neutral device. Its only inherent characteristic is that of two sides formed by vertical continuity.

In this design, these primary architectural building blocks are universalized by being reduced to a geometric abstraction of plane. Regardless of the material, at the heart of any floor is a horizontal plane that symbolically lifts human existence from the uneven terrain of the natural landscape. Regardless of shape or material, at the heart of every ceiling is a plane that covers our existence from the sky as it holds us with the floor. Regardless of its configuration or material, at the heart of every wall is a vertical plane with two sides that differentiates one domain from another.

38

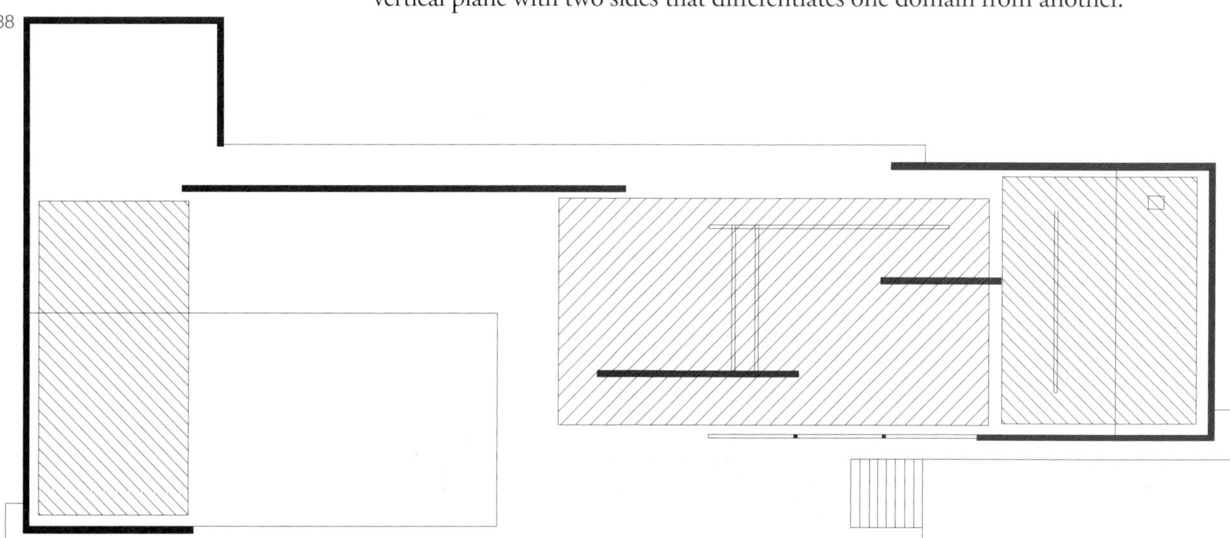

Spatial organization

Much of the rhetoric of the modern movement focused on spatial organization but few of its buildings developed complex statements of spatial order. The German Pavilion in Barcelona develops a surprising complexity of order with few elements within a highly constrained context. The floor-ceiling paired planes indicate the difference between site and interior domain. The site becomes both water and earth as two pools of water are carved from it. Three sets of walls bound this site. Two cup the ends of the site while the third defines an opening that might be construed to create the front of the site by linking it to a park and major walkway beyond. The eight columns that hold the roof aloft order four tubes of space. The first runs along the longitudinal axis of the site connecting the front and back pools of water to the interior of the domain. The three tubes of space between the four columns arranged in two ranks organize the space under the roof of the building perpendicular to the first tube of space. Walls within this structure begin to outline the complex array of spaces that might emerge from this order. The three transparent and three opaque walls combine with columns to create a plethora of possible spatial readings. The sculpture located in the rear corner of the site combines with these walls to create another set of spatial readings. Rarely in architecture have so few elements arranged in such a constrained fashion produced such complex spatial organizations. To be in the German Pavilion in Barcelona is like listening to a Bach two-part piano invention. In each, the most basic rules produce a profusion of meaning.

It is wonderful to see these abstractions in the Pavilion, each writ in the precious material that such a search for origins might warrant, set against the lifelike 19th-century sculpture in the building's rear courtyard. Here one imitation of nature confronts another. Sculpture's representation of the sensuousness of the female body is confronted by the intellectual sensuousness of architectural form reduced to elemental abstraction. Both search for the heart of nature, one in an imitation of form and the other in an intellectual imitation of nature's structure. This confrontation of form as image and as underlying rational order restates the question asked by the Parthenon: Is our world what we perceive or an underlying structure of ideas?

39

40

37 Front elevation of the German Pavilion
38 Site enclosing walls plus three opaque and three transparent walls within
39 Sculpture in the rear courtyard
40 Sculpture through the window

Phillips Exeter library

41 Exeter Library as a rational square form placed in an unsymmetrical, empirical nature
42 Phillips Exeter Library
43 Plan of Exeter Library

Phillips Exeter library was designed by Louis Kahn between 1966 and 1968 for a preparatory high school in New Hampshire. It is a modest building packed with ideas about the nature of order in architecture. In an era when most architects were interested in innovation and the opportunities presented by new technologies, Louis Kahn retreated to studies of classical architecture to form the base of his work. At the center of this quest lies the notion that there are questions and issues in architecture that are perennial. To Kahn the central issues of architecture emanate from a core of human being that does not vary by time or place. These transcendental notions of purpose are wedded to a similar set of means. In this view, the implements of architecture are seen to be the plan as a mental conception of order; the opening as the time of sunlight; the role of the column and the wall as vertical order in buildings; the arch or beam's ability to span as a testament to the natural force of gravity; and brick and concrete masonry joints as emblematic of the material nature of architecture. Returning to these ideas is to attempt to reconstruct an architectural logic from its Western intellectual foundations. Kahn's interest in classicism stems from the kinds of problems that Greek and Roman architecture considered. These problems might include the issue of order, the relationship between rational and empirical thought, and the reconciliation of sensation and reason.

Plan as a square: implications in terms of rational and empirical architecture

The square plan of the Phillips Exeter library is the product of rationalism in architecture. It is an ideal geometry of the mind as opposed to order that grows from an empirical understanding of nature. It mirrors the changes of the natural world not by directly responding to them, but rather by remaining unchanged as a complement to nature's ever-changing empirical context. As the sun moves and the climate changes, the library's plan with its four identical walls remains the same. These walls do not respond differently to the sunlight of the south versus the sunlight of the north, east, or west but remain unchanged as the sun moves across the sky. They likewise do not respond to the northwest winds of winter versus the southeast breezes of summer or the changes in temperature associated with each of these seasons. Similarly, the square plan gives little credence to gravity's desire to span a short side. The plan of the library is the product of a human mind that sees ideal forms in buildings to stand in opposition to the tangible changes that characterize its natural context.

41

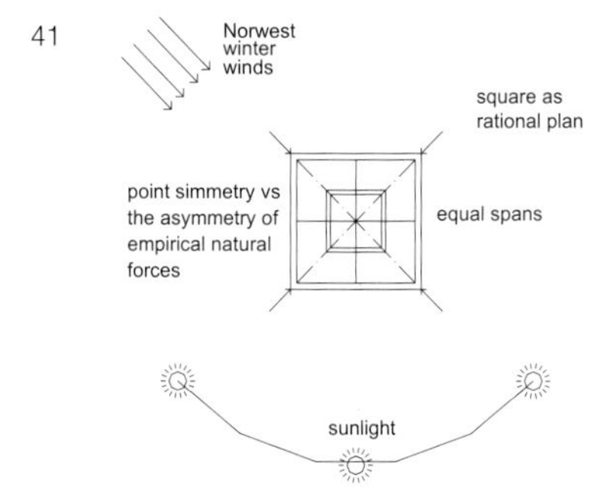

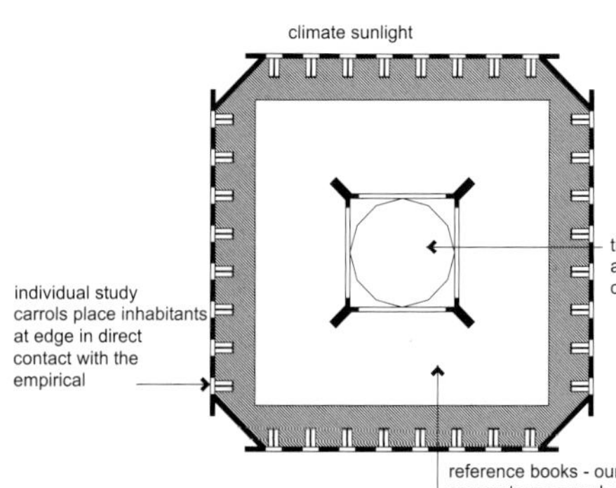

42

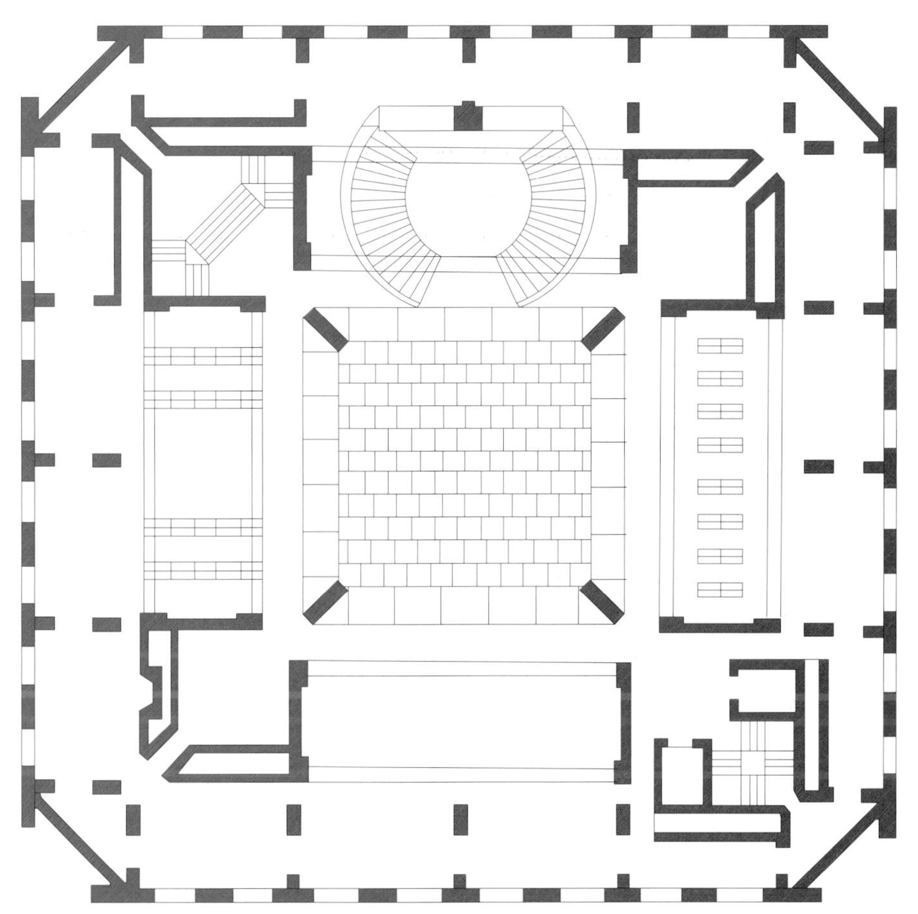

43

* thick brick wall on the outside.

* light comes in from the side and not the top.

Arcade going all the way around.

The column/arch resolution of the problem of order proposed by the Coliseum in Rome

44

The four exterior walls of the Phillips Exeter library are treated in a very special manner. First, they are disconnected at their corners so that their thickness is revealed and their independence as an architectural construct enunciated as a part of the building's form. Each wall is then developed as the intersection of the column and the arch. The order produced by these two gravity-redirecting forms in architecture is classically stated in the Roman Coliseum where the horizontal order of brick arches is paired with the vertical order of columns. Arches inherently create a horizontal order. Rows of arches do not comfortably pile atop one another to create multistoried buildings. To rectify this problem in the Coliseum, columns are embedded in the surfaces between arch openings at each level of the building. Stout Doric columns at the bottom support all the weight above them while slender, Corinthian columns at the top need to support only themselves. Ionic columns vertically order the space between these two. The result is a somewhat awkward juncture of arch and column where pilasters (columns embedded in walls) create vertical order as their appointed meaning attempts to forge a vertical formal unity that complements the strong horizontal unity of ranks of arches.

Kahn solves this problem by allowing both the arch and the column to arise from the same source: the spring line of the arch. At each level of the library, the openings in the wall increase by the width of the brick arch's spring line as it intersects the brick column of the wall. The width of the brick column diminishes as it rises by this same dimension. In this resolution the differences between column and arch are reduced to a single principle stated in a single material and in a single form. In this way the wall solves the problems of rational order (the problem of the pattern of horizontal and vertical elements in the façade of a building) at the same time that it fulfills the empirical requirements of gravity that call for more slender column sections as the column supports less weight. The façades of the Phillips Exeter library are walls made of the intersection of columns and arches regulated by the spring line formed by the bricks of these arches. This is a truly elegant contemporary solution to an architectural problem posed by the elevation of the Coliseum.

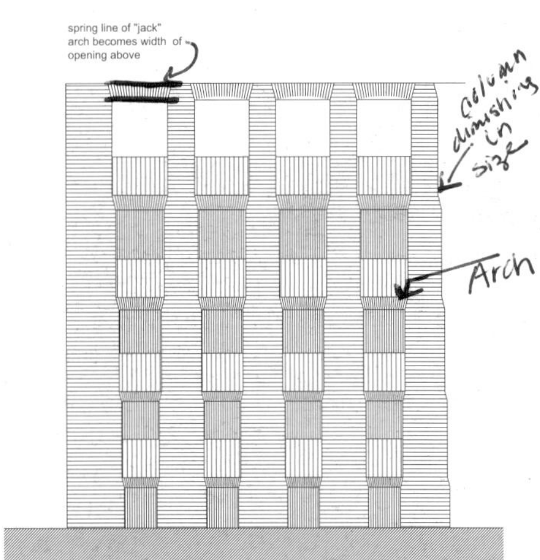

45

46

44 Exterior wall of Exeter Library
45 Spring line of arches creating the diminishing dimension of columns in the wall of Exeter Library
46 Spring line of the arch
47 Opening plus arch plus column

Arcaded top and bottom

The ground floor of the Phillips Exeter library is ringed by an arcade that gathers the campus of this preparatory school to it from all directions. Rather than a single front, this building has four fronts. None is more important than another in elevation; all are equal. Like a Greek temple, the building gathers the surrounding landscape to it. The top of the building mirrors the bottom as it too is an arcade, but twice the height of the lower arcade. It thrusts into the sky instead of being compressed by the weight above it. It logically terminates the wall of the building façade but gives that wall the depth of a path as does the ground floor arcade. The top is architecturally writ in the same formal vocabulary as is bottom but with modifications that make clear the differences as well as the similarities between the two.

49

The exterior edge as the place of change

The Phillips Exeter library is a dialogue between building as center and edge. Order is produced at the edge of the building from an interpretation of nature. The brick of the walls is assembled in conformance with the demands of gravity to produce wall, column, arch, and opening. The light on each of these walls reflects the position of the sun as orientation and as time. The climate is controlled by a mechanical system that is made manifest in the duct work at the perimeter of the building. Occupants of study carrels see the world beyond their individual windows as seasonal vegetation changes color. The building at its edge responds to each of these conditions of nature in a clear, empirical way. Architecture is, at the edge of the library, the way that empirically constructed material places people in a natural context by making the activities of that context manifest and explicit.

48 Roof top arcade of Exeter Library
49 Column
50 Interior courtyard of Exeter Library

The skylit interior volume as the place of permanence

If the exterior of the library is about the natural context of architecture as empiricism, then the interior of the building gathers around a center that manifests a nonempirical, rational vision of buildings. The central courtyard is framed by four large concrete circular openings that have neither top nor bottom. These openings have centers that meet in a point at the very center of the central courtyard space that cannot be occupied by the human body. This point is a mental abstraction as center: it is an idea that can be thought but not experienced. The sunlight from above is baffled by deep beams that disperse it evenly around the edges of this space, taking notions of time or orientation from this sunlight. This center is made of concrete in which responses to gravity (metal reinforcing bars) are hidden from view. It is placeless, timeless, and uninhabitable. It is constant and universal. The center of the Phillips Exeter library is a product of the human mind.

50

Study carrels at the edge and reference books at the center

51

Individual reading areas are at the edge of the building. Reference books ring the center of the library. Normal texts lie in plan between these two ways of learning. Reference books gather us together as a common culture. Nonreference books proclaim our individual proclivities. Reference books attempt to find universals in our culture. Nonreference books present different views of knowledge. Culture holds us together in common values but the quest of each individual in terms of this knowledge remains singular. The individual study carrels at the edge of the library form a complement to the common knowledge of reference books that rings its center.

The contention that each era of architecture simply reinterprets the core of human being in new material form makes architecture the province of perennial questions. The issues of architecture are thought to remain constant in this viewpoint because the human condition is based on abilities and needs that do not change. The human need to be with others, to understand through knowledge that is transmitted from one to another, and to commonly wonder about our place in the universe have always characterized our need for institutions, and it is these institutions that bind us into groups.

Form in the Phillips Exeter library is the Platonic property of buildings that reflects the unchanging core condition of humanity. Order always has been a fundamental constituent of this form. Searching for the order of a design is a search that therefore links architecture to its history and to the fundamental human need to find distinctly human patterns that separate us from those of the natural world.

52

51 Reading desk next to the window of Exeter Library
52 Ceiling of the central courtyard

Closing thoughts

The uses of order in architecture have always been a means to codify architectural knowledge. Order acts as a reasoned constraint in the process of design. After 1850 this role was challenged anew by the mass production of building components. The formal order of classical architecture no longer had the power to communicate what people held to be significant about order in buildings. New approaches to this old issue were necessary to rectify architectural history with the new context of building and living generated by industrialization. Frank Lloyd Wright found this order by retreating to a more fundamental definition of order than that presented by classical architectural thought. At the heart of contemporary order he placed the human body with its capacity for sensation and association that such sensation might engender. By contrast, Le Corbusier picked up the strains of the Enlightenment that initiated modernism and made our intellect the center of this order. The order of Villa Savoye in contrast to that of the Robie House is one of cerebral distinctions. Ludwig Mies van der Rohe attempted to find order in architecture in its origins as a vocabulary of irreducible architectural elements. This elementalism is presented in terms of the modern materials of glass and steel but retains a sense of connection to all other architectural creations as a vocabulary of architectural order reduced to essentials. Finally, Louis Kahn attempts to rectify modernism with classical architectural thought through forms that reinterpret classical architectural problems of order in contemporary terms.

Order is not, as some have claimed, a dead issue in architecture. We have not been overwhelmed by the banal commonalities produced by mass production and mass consumption. Order remains a central search for contemporary architecture because it must. People require the meanings that emerge from these patterns to locate themselves in the world just as they always have.

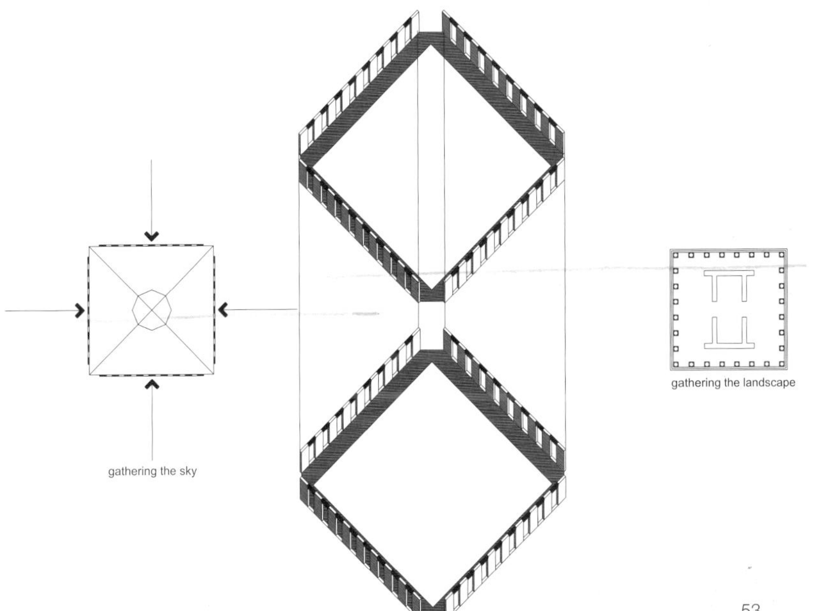

53

54

53 Arcades of Exeter Library drawing the campus, the landscape, and the sky to the building
54 Exterior wall of Exeter Library

CHARTRES CATHEDRAL
AND ARCHITECTURAL TECHNOLOGY
Symbolic form that redirects natural force

Issue

When people think about the word *technology,* they generally have in mind the kinds of tools that facilitate a specific task. A hammer is a technology for driving a nail. A computer is a technology for managing information. A car is a technology for transportation. Buildings are required to redirect the natural forces of climate, gravity, and sunlight. The frame of a building is a tool to redirect the forces of wind and gravity. The weather envelope of a building is a tool to separate comfortable from uncomfortable climatic conditions. The opening in a wall or roof is a tool to transmit sunlight into the interior of a structure. It is the engineer who uses calculations to determine how big structural members need to be, appropriate sizes for air conditioning systems, and artificial lighting levels. How well each task is performed by these tools is a measure of their efficiency. An efficient tool performs the most work with the least energy or material. The ability to find more efficient solutions to technological problems over time is called technological progress. Hammers have not changed much in this regard but both computers and automobiles continue to increase the efficiency with which they perform their respective tasks.

This 19th-century definition of the role of technology as the efficient performance of a task is insufficient to describe the role of technology in buildings. The problem with architectural technologies is that they assume material forms in buildings that we inhabit. Because we are inside of these forms rather than understanding them as objects that we manipulate, architectural technologies bear a special responsibility.

01 Chartres in the city

They cannot simply redirect natural forces efficiently because they also house us and we interpret their tangible forms to have meaning over and above those of the efficient accomplishment of a task. Columns support the weight of a roof, but they also order the space of our residence in a building. To support weight is a calculable task. To give order to a place of habitation is not. Walls separate outside from inside climates. In attempting to separate one measurable climatic condition from another, these walls also create the social distinctions of inside and outside. Openings that allow sunlight to pass through can be measured in lumens or footcandles. The way in which this light gathers images from outside a wall to the space within or the way that variations in natural light set one architectural form against another are not measurable characteristics of natural illumination.

The use of technology in architecture presents a special kind of problem. Buildings cannot deny the importance of measurable, empirical performance because they must stand up in the face of gravity, keep us comfortable in the face of sometimes harsh climatic conditions, and bring us light so that we can see well enough to perform tasks. Accomplishing these tasks with the least possible material or energy identifies only a portion of the architectural problem of technology. The material forms that these technologies take are asked to accomplish much more in buildings. They are asked to create ideas of domain and order as they relate us to the natural world that they modify. This is not a calculable task but one born of interpretation of architectural form. Technological forms in architecture thus bear symbolic as well as mechanical responsibilities.

What makes this particular set of architectural forms different from other architectural elements is their need to redirect natural force. Each of these forces is a manifestation of an empirical natural world that always serves as a context for buildings.

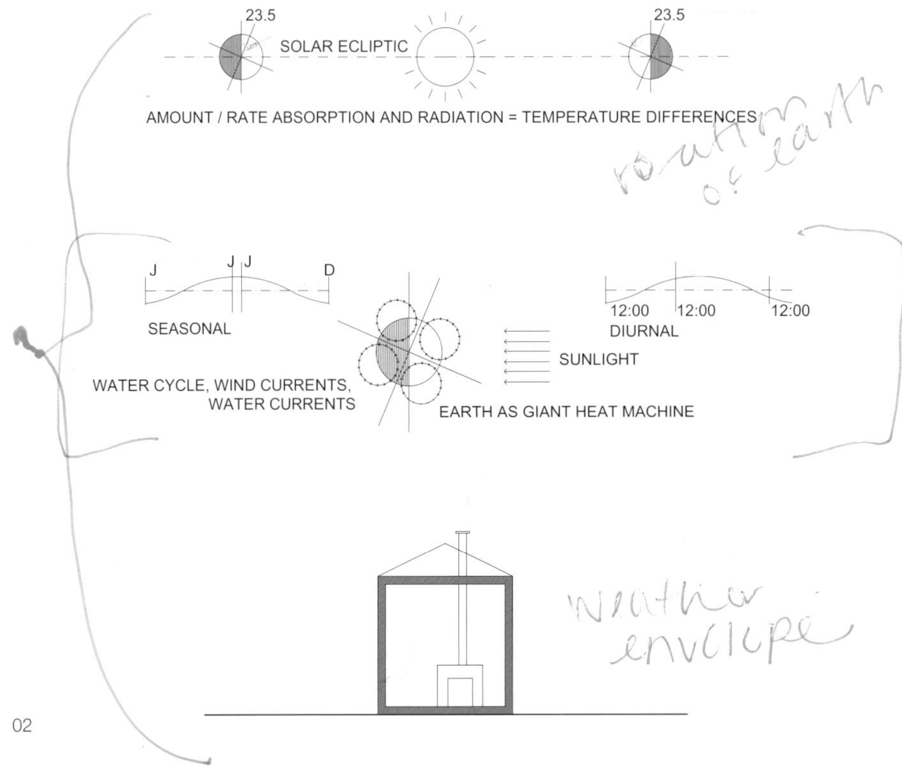

Climate is a result of the tilt of the earth's axis with respect to the solar ecliptic and the natural equalization of temperature and pressure across the earth. The sun heats the earth unevenly as solar radiation is absorbed or reflected by the earth's surface as a function of angle of incidence and the absorptive characteristics of that surface. Different temperature regions emerge as the earth reradiates this energy. The air and oceans at the equator are warm; at the poles, they are cold. As the warm fluids of air and water attempt to equalize energies with cold regions, air and water currents develop to transmit these energies. The air absorbs water vapor as the sun heats the surface of water to become the source of a hydrologic cycle of rain and snow redelivered to oceans by rivers. We feel these natural events as the touch of temperature, wind, and moisture.

The building technology that redirects the natural force of climate in architecture is called the weather envelope. The technical duty of the weather envelope is to create a thermal barrier that allows the temperature, wind, and moisture conditions within a building to be different from those outside this envelope. It is composed of the walls, floors, and roofs that separate these climatic conditions from each other at the boundary of the building. Moisture is shed, wind blocked, and the desire of thermal energy to migrate from higher to lower states is retarded by a building's weather envelope.

03

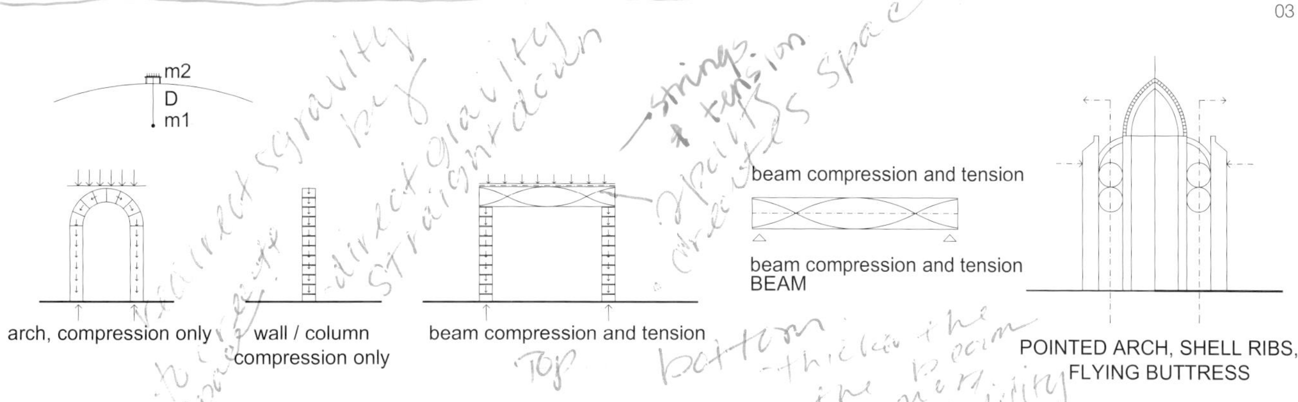

Gravity is the most unusual of these three forces. Newton's classic definition of gravity as directly proportional to the masses of two bodies and inversely proportional to the square of the distance between them is useful when considering building structures. Building frames create hollow spaces within gravitational forces that would like to pull all material to the surface of the earth. Gravity does not change over time or place. It is the most regular of all human experiences. Because of this, the structures of buildings throughout time and in all places must respond in the same way to this natural force. This requirement of permanence and regularity has given birth to conceptions of order that are associated with the gravitational frame of buildings.

The architectural technology that redirects the natural force of gravity is called the building frame. A number of forces need to be resisted by this frame. The first of these is the weight of building materials themselves. These are called the dead loads of buildings because they do not change over time. Dead loads present two kinds of technological problems for the building frame. The first are the loads that are generated by the need to span a space. This need is created by the roof of the weather

02 Climate as the outcome of uneven absorption of solar energy redirected by the weather envelope of a building

03 Gravity as the pull of the mass of the earth as redirected by the frame of a building

04

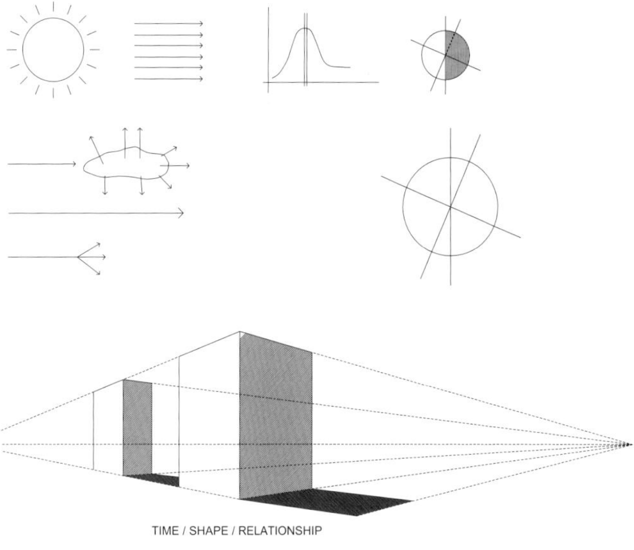
TIME / SHAPE / RELATIONSHIP

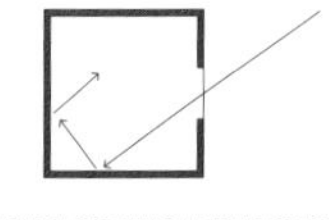
SUNLIGHT / OPENING / REFLECTION

envelope as it shields inhabitants from the moisture and thermal conditions of the sky. The roof collects all the vertical loads of gravity along its length and transfers them to columns or walls that carry these loads to the earth. The forces gathered by beams that perform this task push down and out along spanning members. These spanning members may be arches, beams, or trusses. Each of these material configurations must resist compressive, tensile, and rotational forces as they span space. Once they are brought to columns or bearing walls, both the vertical and lateral thrusts developed by a building frame must be transferred to the earth.

Sunlight is the product of a thermonuclear reaction 93 million miles from the earth. As the sun fuses hydrogen into helium, energy is released as radiation. Our eyes are sensitive to particular wavelengths of this radiation. As surfaces on the earth reflect this radiation, the world of form is born. Surfaces of objects each reflect this radiation in their own particular way to become three-dimensional objects in our vision. Each object is given a place in relation to all other objects in this light. Our domain is often defined at the farthest extent of this vision: the horizon. Here, the reflected light of the earth meets the reflected light of the atmosphere to enclose us in a domain of sight. Sunlight orchestrates a profusion of relationships within these limits to become our image of the world in which we live. The tilt of the earth's axis and its rotation on this axis creates uneven periods of light and dark that order our lives as day, night, and seasons. We measure the longevity of our own lives in terms of the number of times the earth has revolved around the sun.

This sunlight is brought into buildings through openings in walls and roofs. The openings transmit solar radiation, but this radiation does not become visible until it is reflected from a material surface. We do not see the air in a room because the atmosphere is transparent to visible solar radiation. Material surfaces are opaque to sunlight, however, creating a world of visible forms. Sunlight places building inhabitants within a larger domain as it brings the images it collects through a window to announce the formal context of a room and the time of day.

These three forces form a natural fabric that houses the development of all buildings. Whatever else technological constructions in buildings accomplish, they must respond to these natural forces in particular ways or they will not be able to perform the tasks required of them by empirical natural forces.

Why shouldn't an effective and efficient response to these forces be sufficient in buildings? Why do we ask more of building technologies than we ask of other technologies that perform useful tasks?

Perhaps a story about the musings of a great early modern scientist, Johannes Kepler, can shed some light on this issue. Kepler was the German scientist who demonstrated that the planets revolve around the sun in an ellipse rather than in a perfect circle. This was a monumental discovery in modern science. Just 60 years earlier, Polish astronomer Nicholas Copernicus had proposed that the planets revolve around the sun rather than the earth. This was a potentially elegant resolution to a Ptolemaic solar system in which all celestial bodies revolved around the earth. Over the course of 1,400 years, Ptolemy's model had been elaborated upon with epicycles and retrograde motion until it very accurately predicted the position of planets and stars in the sky. The map of the solar system had become, within this Ptolemaic scheme, a mass of small independent circular motions within large orbits and reversed, retrograde direction of movement as necessary. Copernicus' theory called only for singular, one-directional orbits of planets around the sun. The problem was that this model, though elegant, did not predict the position of the planets in the sky as well as did the more awkward Ptolemaic system. From 1600 to 1609, Kepler used very accurate observations of Mars to work out the path of planets around the sun. This path had two centers rather than one, forming an ellipse.

Kepler's predictions were worked out with a mathematical rigor unknown before his time. Kepler had both solved the problem of the path of the planets and simultaneously set standards for modern science that continue to hold today. His work was an enormous intellectual triumph. Mathematically calculating the elliptical orbits of planets as they revolve around the sun constituted a very elegant mechanical solution to a problem of how the natural world operates. The scientific method and rigor with which Kepler applied it proposed a new and effective way for people to probe how nature works.

It seems strange, then, that Johannes Kepler spent the rest of his life attempting to demonstrate that five Platonic solids fit between the orbits of the six known planets of his day. Nearly 2,000 years earlier, Greek philosopher Plato proposed this special category of geometric solids because all their faces and angles of intersection were identical. There still are only five of these figures. Plato thought that God spoke to people through the perfection of geometry. Kepler agreed with him and contended that since God had created the solar system, that system ought to manifest itself as a geometric

04 Sunlight as visible wavelengths of radiation reflected by architectural surfaces to produce form

perfection analogous to that of God's. Johannes Kepler identified that perfection as the Platonic solids; and thus, those solids must be part of the underlying structure of the solar system as the outcome of God's labor.

How could such a search, considered by a scientific era to be a step backwards, be so important to Kepler? How could a person with the courage, tenacity, and intelligence to demonstrate with great mathematical rigor that planets traveled in ellipses fall back into the trap of metaphysical thought?

A different approach to Kepler's problem might focus less on what science professes to constitute the truth about the natural world than it would on why we are interested in defining the structure of our solar system in the first place. Such knowledge is really not very useful to us. We will do little of real consequence in our lives based on our conception of the order of the cosmos. Yet, all eras of history have proposed a structure for the heavens. Kepler was not different from all of his thoughtful ancestors in this regard.

The issue of this quest would seem to be less one of mechanical accuracy than one of suggesting a pattern that allows people to see the natural world as orderly rather than chaotic. If nature is chaos, then we are lost in events that have no pattern. If the patterns that we propose to structure the universe are purely mechanical, like Kepler's elliptical orbits of the planets, then we are part of that pattern as purely mechanical parts of a larger mechanical scheme. People do not want to think of themselves as mechanisms. To us, we are richer than the mechanical ways in which our bodies operate. If the solar system is to be a projection of us as human richness rather than people a projection of its mechanical fact, then the solar system must manifest more humanly satisfying patterns than that of an ellipse based on calculation of gravitational versus centripetal forces. Kepler's Platonic solids represented this need for a humanly satisfying structure of the universe as the perfection of God. A solar system that was equally structured by calculable mechanics and by perfection represented by Platonic solids constituted a structure of the natural world rich enough to allow people to belong within it in all the ways they chose to think of themselves. Kepler's quest for the place of Platonic solids between the elliptical orbits of planets around the sun is an understandable quest to define nature as patterns that reflect the richness of our perception of ourselves, and thus a pattern within which we might belong.

This rather long and complicated story makes a single point. Buildings are no different than Kepler's solar system. They contain us just as the solar system holds the earth. We require of their mechanics the same richness that Kepler sought by placing Platonic solids within the mathematical definition of the paths of planets. This structure must be symbolically satisfying as well as empirically accurate. We need to accurately calculate the weight a column must bear but the shape of that column in a building needs to create a form that symbolically places us in our environment. The problem of the role of technology in architecture is only partially solved by efficiently performing its appointed task. The second portion of this task is to ask how the material form of that technology might be interpreted within the material form of the building to constitute a symbolic meaning that reflects the richness of being human.

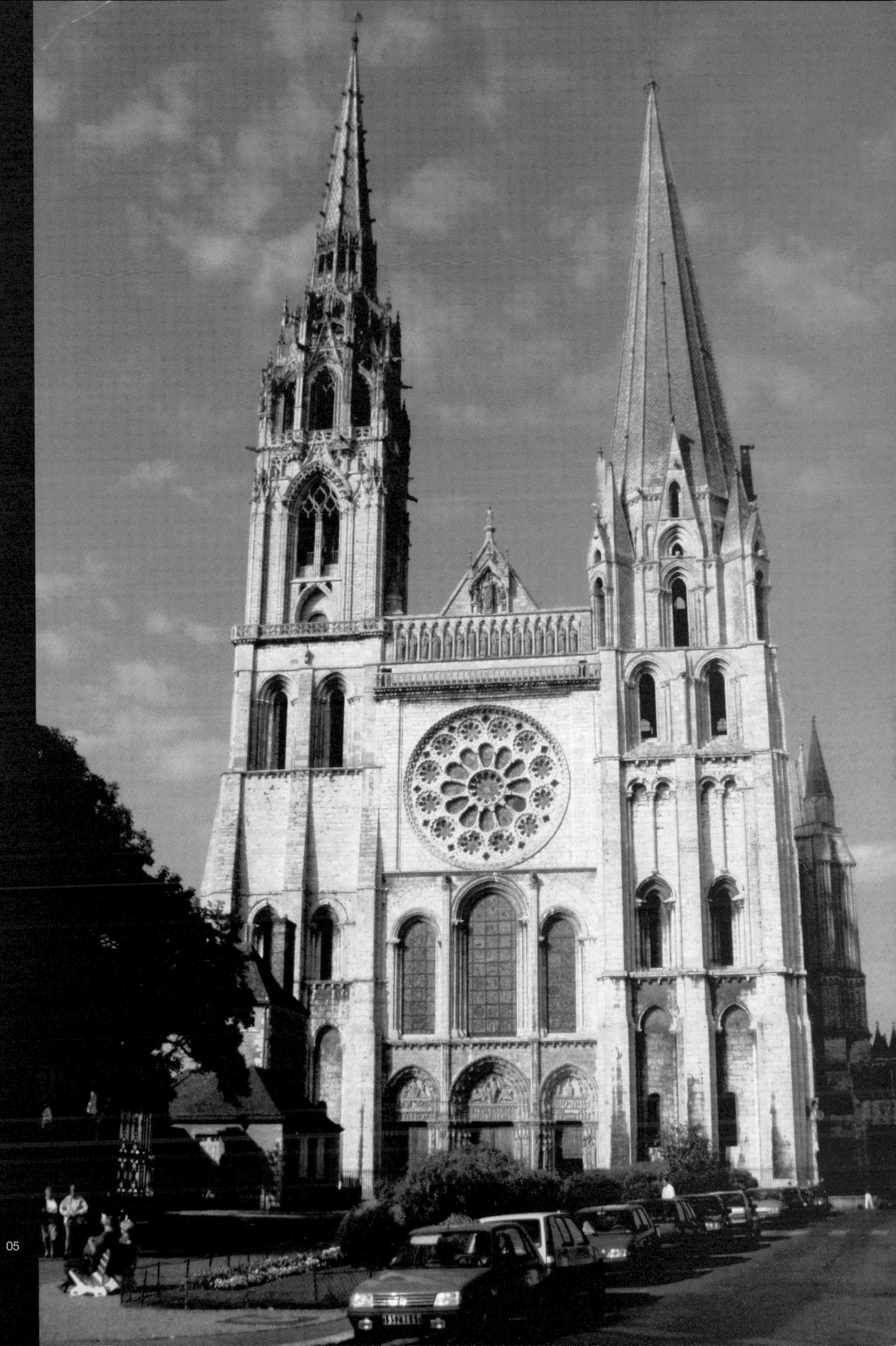

05

Cathedral at Chartres

The major sections of Notre-Dame de Chartres (Cathedral of Our Lady of Chartres) were constructed from 1194 to 1220, at the height of medievalism. To some critics, the Gothic cathedrals of the medieval period represent the pinnacle of architectural production. The intellectual world would never again be as "whole" as it was at this time. The Renaissance would begin to cleave thought into faith versus reason, feeling versus intellect, interpretation versus fact, and art versus science. The Age of Enlightenment and modern science would complete this separation of the way we think about ourselves into two distinct camps represented by the sciences and by the arts. The chasm between these two modes of thought has persisted to become the foundation of contemporary thought. The medieval European world was not bifurcated into feeling and intellect, science and art, fact and interpretation but found the Christian Bible to be a singular source of knowledge. Today, we do not even attempt to solve a similar problem in thought. The arts and the sciences have no common ground. They divide our existence into two parts just as they divide our thought into two irreconcilable modes of understanding ourselves and our place in the universe.

Erwin Panofsky eloquently links medieval thought to the design of Gothic cathedrals in his 1948 Wimmer Lecture on Gothic Architecture and Scholasticism. There he contended that Christian philosophical problems are reflected in the design of Gothic cathedrals. The medieval thought that was central to the design of French Gothic cathedrals was called Scholasticism. In Scholasticism, the Christian Bible was considered the base of all knowledge. Irish philosopher John the Scot summarized the intellectual problem of this era by claiming that reason and faith both come from God; and thus, there can be no conflict between them. The goal of Scholastic thought was to establish the unity of truth. This unity was to be found by creating a bridge between faith and reason, between Christian theology and Greek philosophy. Philosopher and theologian Thomas Aquinas summarized the Scholastic position on this issue by claiming that the goal of human reason was to make clear what was set forth in Christian doctrine. The goal of the Gothic cathedral was, therefore, a reasoned exposition of the grounds of Christian doctrine.

Scholastic argument was characterized by its intellectual rigor. Arguments were broken down into their logical parts just as the Scholastics were the first to subdivide books into chapters, headings, and subheadings. The goal of these subdivisions was logical transparency: the ability to know the whole from the parts. Richness of outcomes should be demonstrated to grow from elaboration of a few initial parts. There ought to be a clear and cogent argument that traces the development of these foundational parts to become the complex whole that their elaborations construct.

Architectural technology in cathedral at Chartres

We will examine the Gothic cathedral as an exemplar of architectural technology by dividing our investigation into two parts. In the first, we will ask how a Gothic cathedral mechanically overcomes the force of gravity to produce its vaulted and light-filled interior space. In the second, we will ask how the forms used to accomplish this mechanical task are shaped to reflect the ideas put forth by Scholasticism.

A Gothic cathedral differs from its predecessors because its interior space is much higher and more filled with natural light than were the interiors of Romanesque churches. This shift is not a difference in degree but in kind. The technical problem of the Gothic cathedral was to become a soaring and light filled space in comparison to the relatively squat and dimly lit space in a Romanesque church. This shift in spatial intent could not be produced by simply making the Romanesque church larger. A new technical system was required to meet the spatial and symbolic demands posed by the Gothic cathedral.

One way to think about these technical demands is to envision the Gothic cathedral first as a triangular tube of solid stone. Technically, this tube of stone would be much like an Egyptian pyramid. Pyramids achieved great height by piling up a solid mass of stone. Just as sand falling through a funnel forms a cone-shaped pile of individual grains, pyramids piled up individual pieces of stone in a form that grew progressively smaller in area with height. This form mimics the funnel-formed sand pebbles because gravity is naturally resisted in this form. Progressive layers of stone always rest on larger layers assuring their stability as they rise away from the surface of the earth into the air. The interior opening in an Egyptian pyramid is a tiny deep cell. The Gothic cathedral, conversely, is a stone structure that achieves great height but is required to create a soaring, light-filled, interior space.

06

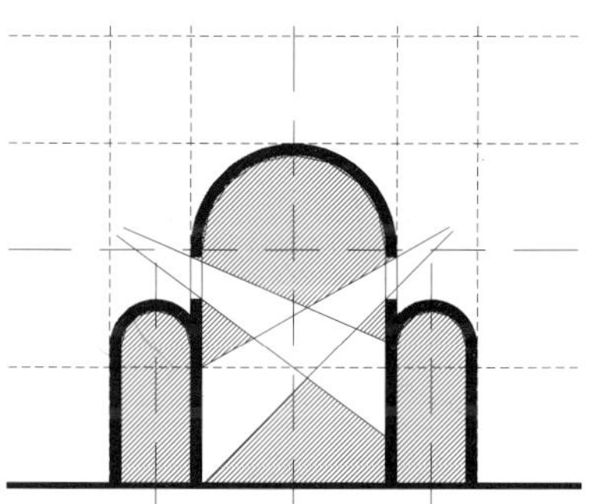

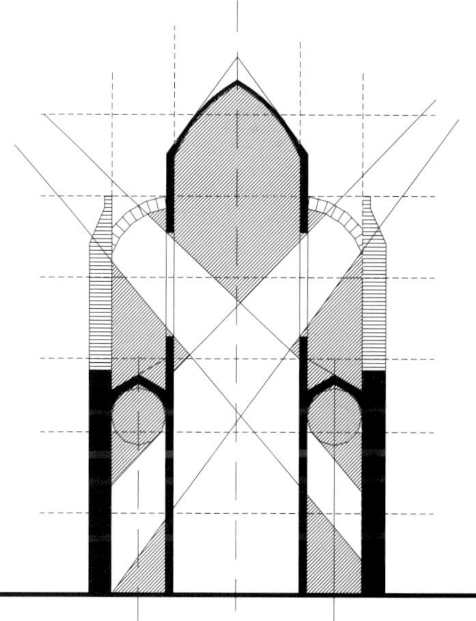

The transformation of the pyramid-like tubular triangle of solid stone into the Gothic cathedral is achieved by carving away all unnecessary material until only a stone skeleton remains. This carving away of excess material is the technical triumph of Gothic cathedrals. The Pyramid as a replication of nature's gravitational form of a sand cone of pebbles requires little human ingenuity. It is an imitation of a gravity-resisting structure that occurs in the natural world without human intervention. Removing unnecessary material from this structure is a function of the human intellect. Nature's solution is not good enough in these terms. The human brain and hand intervenes in the natural world to produce material forms that nature could not produce by herself.

This desire to carve away redundant technical material so that tasks are performed with fewer resources is called elegance. The drive of elegance is to do the most with the least. All that is left at the end of this uniquely human act is what is essential to the performance of the task at hand. Eliminating any more would result in the failure of the construction to redirect natural forces. In terms of the structural system of a building, such a failure means that the building would collapse under stresses created by gravity.

The key technical discovery of Gothic architects was the flying buttress. Spanning an architectural space produces forces that thrust both down and out. Both of these forces must be resisted by the structure if it is to be covered by a roof. A second force on buildings is created not by gravity but by the wind. Buildings as large as a Gothic cathedral produce large surfaces that must resist the power of the wind to bend them. The tendency of a building is to rotate along one of its edges to lessen the structure's wind resistance. Thus, two lateral forces are at work in a Gothic cathedral. Pyramids resist these two forces by having a broader base than top and by being solid. A Gothic cathedral solves these problems by creating a series of lateral braces outside the structure of the building that periodically broaden its base. This periodic resistance of lateral gravitational and wind forces is called a buttress.

07 The nave of the Cathedral
08 Flying buttresses
09 A solid pyramid hollowed out to become a gothic cathedral

08

09

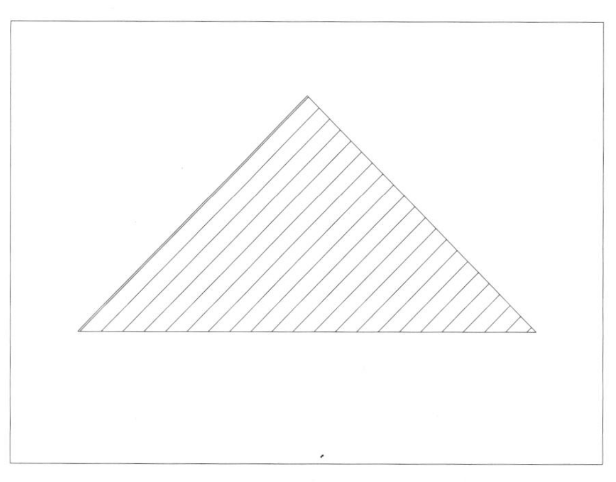

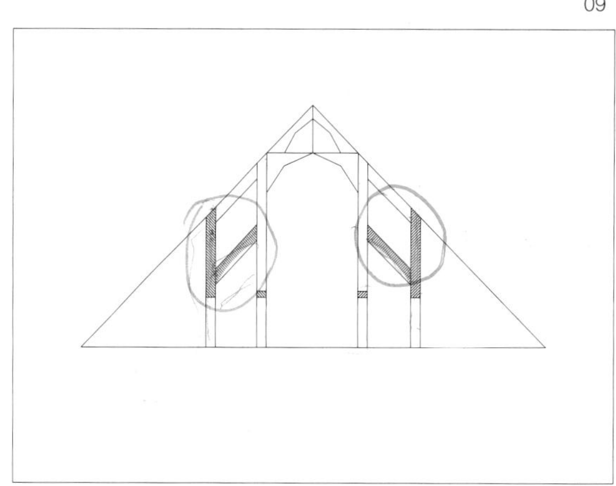

10

Buttresses are normally solid masses of stone located at intervals along building walls to take up the relatively modest lateral thrusts of buildings that were not very tall like those of Romanesque churches. The interior vault of the cathedral at Chartres, however, is 125 feet tall. This is not a modest height, and it does not produce modest gravitational and wind loads. These loads might be redirected by solid stone buttresses that broadened the base of the cathedral's structural system but much of this material would be doing no more work than holding the stone above it aloft. If the intermediate space could be spanned with a stone arch then this unnecessary material might be removed. What would remain of the buttresses would be only the material essential to resist the lateral loads created by spanning the interior space of the cathedral's nave and wind pressure on its side.

These same intellectual processes were applied to each part of the Gothic cathedral until only an essential stone skeleton remained. Surfaces between stone frame members could then be filled with light-admitting glass or opaque stone as called for by nontechnical requirements of the building.

The hallmarks of these processes are the human desire and ability to reshape the natural world to fit human purpose. This reshaping requires the natural forces of gravity, climate, and sunlight to be redirected by material shaped by the human hand. As people reshaped natural resources within this context of natural force, they learned how the intersection of constructed material and natural force worked. Failures of technological form in buildings were made clear by collapse, discomfort, and darkness. Trial and error led to solutions that effectively redirected natural force. But simply finding workable solutions seems not to satisfy the human imagination. Once started down the path of reshaping natural resources in the context of natural forces, people often attempt to extend their technological prowess. This is such a common phenomenon today in the midst of a technologically driven era that we give it little thought. The progenitor of our current technological inventiveness lies in inventions like the Gothic cathedral. It is this apparent human need to test our intellect and ingenuity against the forces of nature that drives our inquisitiveness about the limits of human thought in the face of natural constraints.

Architectural technology as metaphorical thought

This technological need to push against the constraints of nature is necessary but not sufficient to understand the use of technology in architecture. If it were, architectural technology would become engineering. Forms that performed their technological tasks most effectively would become the technological forms of design choice. The only criteria that these forms would be required to fulfill would be those of technological elegance. Technical elements of buildings that performed their assigned tasks with the fewest resources would always be selected as the technological solutions to building problems created by gravity, climate, and sunlight.

Why are such solutions less than what are called for by architecture?

A Gothic cathedral is a wonderful place to examine this question. Without a doubt, this structure is a masterpiece of technological elegance. But if it were that alone, the place of the cathedral at Chartres in architectural thought would be much different than it is. We would now be comparing it to a computer that is twice as fast and has twice the memory of an older model or the environmental benefits of hydrogen as a source of energy. Comparing a Gothic cathedral to the capabilities of a computer or the environmental benefits of the hydrogen-driven fuel cell is inadequate because we ask different questions of machines than we do of buildings. The technologies of buildings house us with all our values. The ability to elegantly push nature around is only one of those values. The Gothic cathedral asks that this technological elegance be used to promote a nontechnological human need. The medieval European mind was preoccupied with the meaning of life as defined by Christian theology. Central to that theology was the idea that a well-lived life on earth led to an ideal life after death in heaven. Heaven was a Christian idea without reference in the natural world. Heaven had to be different from earthly existence because it eliminated the struggle of life on earth. The Gothic cathedral was the source of knowledge to a Christian populace in an era before the invention of the printing press. If people were to begin to sense the perfect world of the Christian God then they would need a metaphor that could begin to manifest the qualities of an ideal vision of heaven as the kingdom of God. The Gothic cathedral served as that metaphor.

What, then, were the metaphorical characteristics of heaven that the Gothic cathedral was asked to explore? First, heaven was an extraordinary place, a place not normally found on the earth. Heaven is an ideal construct within Christian thought, thus its metaphor must convey a sense of what such perfection might be. This perfection was certainly not manifest in the low and dim space of a Romanesque church. Instead, it was thought to be a triumphant, luminescent place in the heavens. Heaven

10 The vaulted ceiling of the Cathedral

was the house of God; and therefore, its metaphor was required to manifest the majesty that such a residence would require.

As the Scholastic mind sought to rectify faith with reason, the Gothic cathedral was required to present heaven both as the reward for faith and as the outcome of God's gift to humankind of our ability to think about the world and our place in it. God's world was thought to be an orderly world, one in which reason could be as firmly satisfied as was faith. The technical forms of the Gothic cathedral could not stand independent of these symbolic requirements. The Gothic cathedral as a metaphor of the Christian idea of heaven required technological ingenuity to create the soaring, light-filled space that was competent to form the base of this metaphor. In this conception, there is no difference between the technological capacity to create this place in the context of gravity and wind and the symbolic values it was thought to manifest.

All building technologies serve this dual purpose because we live within them. And because we live within them, these technologies are asked to mediate between the empirical constraints of natural force and our human need to be symbolically as well as physically housed by buildings. A Gothic cathedral as a metaphor for heaven on earth requires that building technologies fulfill both of these human needs. Entry into this cathedral was not the simple act of entering an earthly domain. Going through cathedral doors was to leave the secular world behind on the way to the ideal Christian world of heaven that was the reward for a devout life on earth. The light-filled stone cage of a Gothic cathedral is unlike a computer or fuel cell because these technologies are not often asked to represent symbolic ideas independent of measurable performance. Entering the triumphant and orderly world of heaven made possible by the technology of carving away nonessential stone is therefore a unique kind of technology.

11

11 Gothic bays and the development of bundled columns
12 Bundled column plus vault of the Cathedral

Architectural technology as the intersection of empirical and metaphorical thought

The two worlds of empirical force and symbolic form merge in the technology of the Gothic cathedral. This intersection is accomplished in what is called the homologous form of the cathedral columns, meaning having a single stem form from which variations might emerge. In homologous forms, variations can always be formally traced back to their common root. Some people identify this thought as the base of modern science in that science is always attempting to trace the variety of natural phenomena back to as few initial conditions as is possible. Our contemporary conception of quantum mechanics might be seen to be the outcome of a search for the homologous form of the universe.

The homologous form of a Gothic cathedral begins with the core of a column. If that column were not supporting any other spanning members it would remain unadorned. Now imagine that this column is placed at the intersection of four spaces that require arches to span them. First, place this column between two arches that span an area to each of its sides. These arches might be identified by adding a small column, or colonnette, to each of the sides that trace the arch that extended from each side of the core. If this process were to be rotated 90°, tracing arches that frame an orthogonal space, then the core column would have four colonnettes attached to it identifying the four spanning arches adjacent to the column. If the bays of space suggested by these four colonnettes were to be completed and spanned by diagonal arch ribs, then four more colonnettes would be required to trace the four arches that would extend from the column. Such a column would identify its location within a Gothic cathedral to be the intersection of four bays of space, and thus, a nave column. Were the same logic to be followed for a column embedded in a wall along the outside edge of the cathedral, the core would only have three colonnettes that would identify one 90° and two diagonal arches emanating from it. If the special structure were not orthogonal but radial, then the location of the colonnettes around the core would also not be orthogonal but would identify appropriate radial geometries of bays surrounding the column. If the distances to be spanned were increased, the diameter of the column would be asked to grow proportionally as in transept columns of Gothic cathedrals.

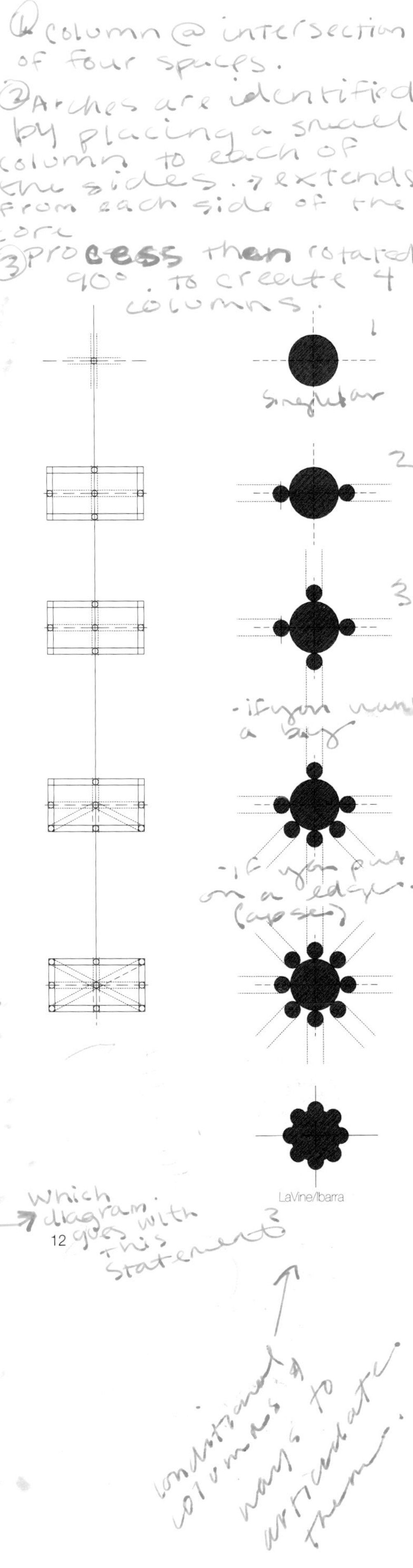
LaVine/Ibarra

12

In each of these cases, root technological form and rules for variations remain constant. What is important is that the place of a column within the spatial structure of a Gothic cathedral can always be identified by the column's section. By reversing this analytical process, the spatial structure of a Gothic cathedral can be built up from its columns. A single, rectangular, nave bay initiates the cathedral. This bay has a

13

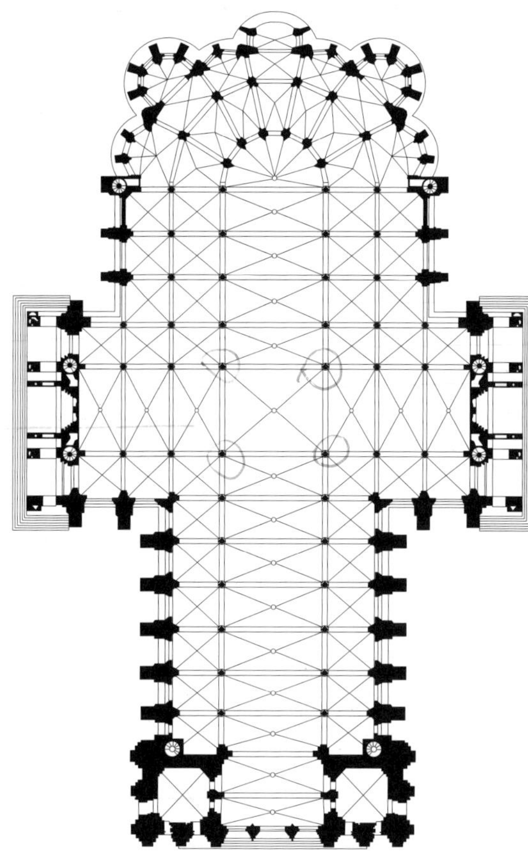

13 Plan of the Cathedral at Chartres
14 The Cathedral as an accretion of bays
15 The clearstory of the Cathedral

14

column at each corner and each column would have three colonnettes. Two of these colonnettes would trace the perpendicular arches of the sides of the bay, and one would trace the diagonal arched rib that extends to the diagonal corner column. The nave of a church is generated by attaching a series of these rectangular bays along their long side. A column between two of these bays now would have five colonnettes. Three of these would trace the same arches as did those of a singular bay. The additional two colonnettes trace the short side arch and the diagonal arch of the attached bay. Most Gothic cathedrals have what are called side aisles. These spaces are smaller than nave bays and run along the sides of the cathedral's nave. If these squarer bays were added to the short sides of nave bay columns at the intersection of these bays, columns at this intersection would have eight colonnettes. The first five of these trace arches are already described. The sixth traces the arch that extends the long side of the nave bay, attaching the side aisle to the exterior wall of the cathedral. The two additional colonnettes trace the diagonal ribs of the two flanking side aisle bays. The edge column that receives side aisle bar arches at the wall has only three colonnettes because they trace only the orthogonal arch that extends the nave aisle to the wall and the two diagonal ribs that trace the midpoints of arched side aisle bays. At the transept of a Gothic cathedral, four nave bays form a square central space in the cathedral. This central space has the same spatial order as that of a normal nave bay with the exception that it spans twice the area. To bring these increased loads to the earth, this column must have a larger section.

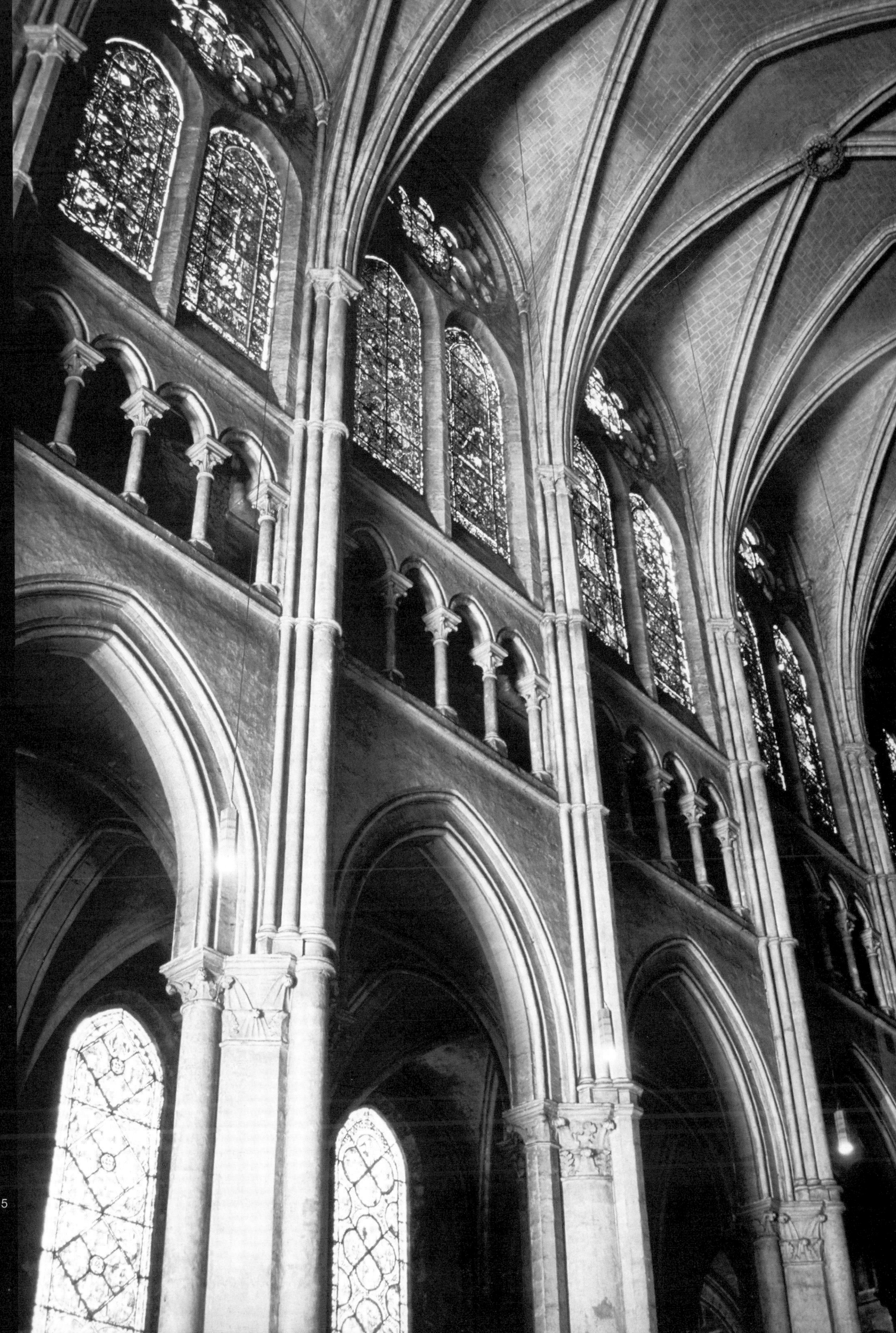

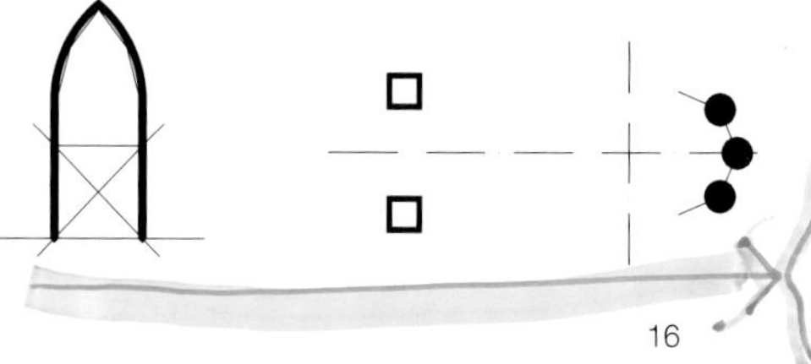

16

Finally, the procession of the nave is terminated by a spatial configuration called the apse of the cathedral. The apse is a radial rather than a rectilinear form. It often has a series of semicircular bays at its edge that are considered to be portals to heaven. Worshipers enter a Gothic cathedral through entries that proclaim a transition from a secular to a religious world, worship in the procession of nave spaces that lead to an altar, and symbolically leave the church through its apse to encounter the kingdom of God. The columns of this similar but slightly different spatial bay configuration must formally proclaim their new spatial duty. They do so by allowing colonnettes that identify adjoining bays to emanate from their central shaft that trace the new geometry of this radial organization.

This long description of the sectional form of Gothic bundled columns makes a simple point: the entire spatial structure of the cathedral might be explained by examining the section of only four of these columns. These four columns would be generated from a single root and follow a uniform set of rules to develop the spatial structure of a Gothic cathedral. Why is it important to go through such a long explanation to make such a simple point? Because what might be taken from this description is far from simple. The primary technological duty of a column is to support the weight of a spanned space. A cylindrical steel column could support the weight of Gothic spanning vaults with fewer resources than these stone columns. In this sense, they would be a more technologically elegant solution to the problem of a Gothic cathedral. But such a column would mechanically perform its task efficiently by excluding the spatial articulateness of the colonnettes that are attached to Gothic stone core columns. The idea of an orderly heaven in which all variety emanates from a single source would be lost. The articulateness of spatial organization as manifested in the section of each of its parts would be lost. Elegant engineering would be detached from the metaphor of the Gothic cathedral as a manifestation of the Scholastic conception of heaven.

This use of technology in a Gothic cathedral is unusual because it does not conform to the 19th-century's definition of technology as a manifestation of progress. Progress in this sense is measured by the utilitarian values of economy of means or size of accomplishment. To be the tallest building or the longest bridge or to do the most with the fewest resources are all manifestations of this point of view. In some ways, the Gothic cathedral is an illustration of this vision of technological goodness. These buildings were the tallest structures of their era. But in another and more profound interpretation of the technology of Chartres, size serves only to promote ideas that lie outside of those based on measurement: the height of the interior of Chartres serves to manifest the idea of heaven on earth. Two issues thus come together in this structure. What we think of as science and engineering make possible an idea that we might categorize as spiritual or concerning the humanities. The boundary between these interpretations is seamless. Faith has been reconciled with reason. Engineering has become the source of thought in the humanities. Mechanics have become meaning.

17

Closing thoughts

All buildings are constructed within a natural context of the forces of climate, gravity, and sunlight. All buildings must redirect these forces if they are to exist. Architectural technology is based on the ability of material assemblies to effectively redirect these natural forces as a necessary but not sufficient definition of its responsibilities. The ability of architectural material to perform tasks is seen not as an end in itself but as a vehicle to create architectural meaning in this use of technology. Each of the elements of architecture that modifies a natural force – floors, walls, and roofs of the weather envelope, windows in walls and roofs, and columns and beams of gravitational frames – must perform its appointed empirical task; but in doing so, it does much more. Each of these elements has ideas associated with it that grow from these empirical responses but are not themselves empirical. In this way the weather envelope separates, the opening connects, and the frame orders our experience of the natural world. These are symbolic rather than empirical distinctions. They are immeasurable ideas that grow from empirical responses of architecture to natural forces, yet are distinct from them.

This distinction emanates from our need to inhabit these technologies. We do not use them as objects as we might a computer, camera, or hammer; we reside within them. As places of residence, these technologies are required to become parts of our domain. As such they are required to reflect the values of this domain. As in the structure that holds up the floor of a Dogon granary – nine sticks representing the four original parents of tribes and the god of water – technology in architecture is never devoid of the values represented within our domains.

The cathedral at Chartres is a wonderful exemplar of architectural technology. This 13th-century structure is a marvel of engineering and of the symbolic potential of architectural technologies. The goal of these Gothic cathedrals was to produce an image of heaven on earth. The Scholastic mind that gave birth to them sought to rectify faith with reason. Faith gave birth to a vision of heaven as a towering space filled with light. Reason gave birth to the material means to accomplish this vision. The technological key to this possibility was the Gothic invention of the flying buttress.

The flying buttress is the result of this carving away of unnecessary material. What remains is a cage, a skeleton of stone columns connected by arcaded walls. The result in Chartres is an interior space 125 feet high that is illuminated from above by the very large clearstory windows that this cage of stone makes possible.

Reason is rectified with faith in the order of Chartre's column sections. The triumphant light-filled cage made possible by the intellectual triumph of the flying buttress over the force of gravity becomes a portion of a frame that marks the spatial order of a cathedral as a metaphor for the orderliness of a Christian heaven.

16 Homologous parts and the Cathedral as an entry to heaven as Scholastic thought
17 Entry of the Cathedral

This description of the use of technology in a building is surely different from what other disciplines might put forward. While it is true that Gothic cathedrals of the Middle Ages were triumphs of engineering, it is equally true that these triumphs of material form over natural force are manifestations of architectural ideas that are not empirical. They are architectural thoughts that, as Erwin Panofsky said, represent a medieval "mentality which deemed it necessary to make faith clearer by an appeal to the imagination (and) also felt bound to make imagination clearer by an appeal to the senses."

Technology, as the ability to push nature around, is thus a double-edged sword in architecture. It must work in an empirical world of natural forces or a building cannot exist. If the empirical forces of gravity, climate, and sunlight are not effectively redirected by technological elements of buildings, habitable space will not be formed. At the same time, simply working well is not sufficient to express human values. This same technology must therefore be arranged in such a manner that it expresses cultural values. No better example of such a marriage of physics and metaphysics exists than in the use of technology in a Gothic cathedral.

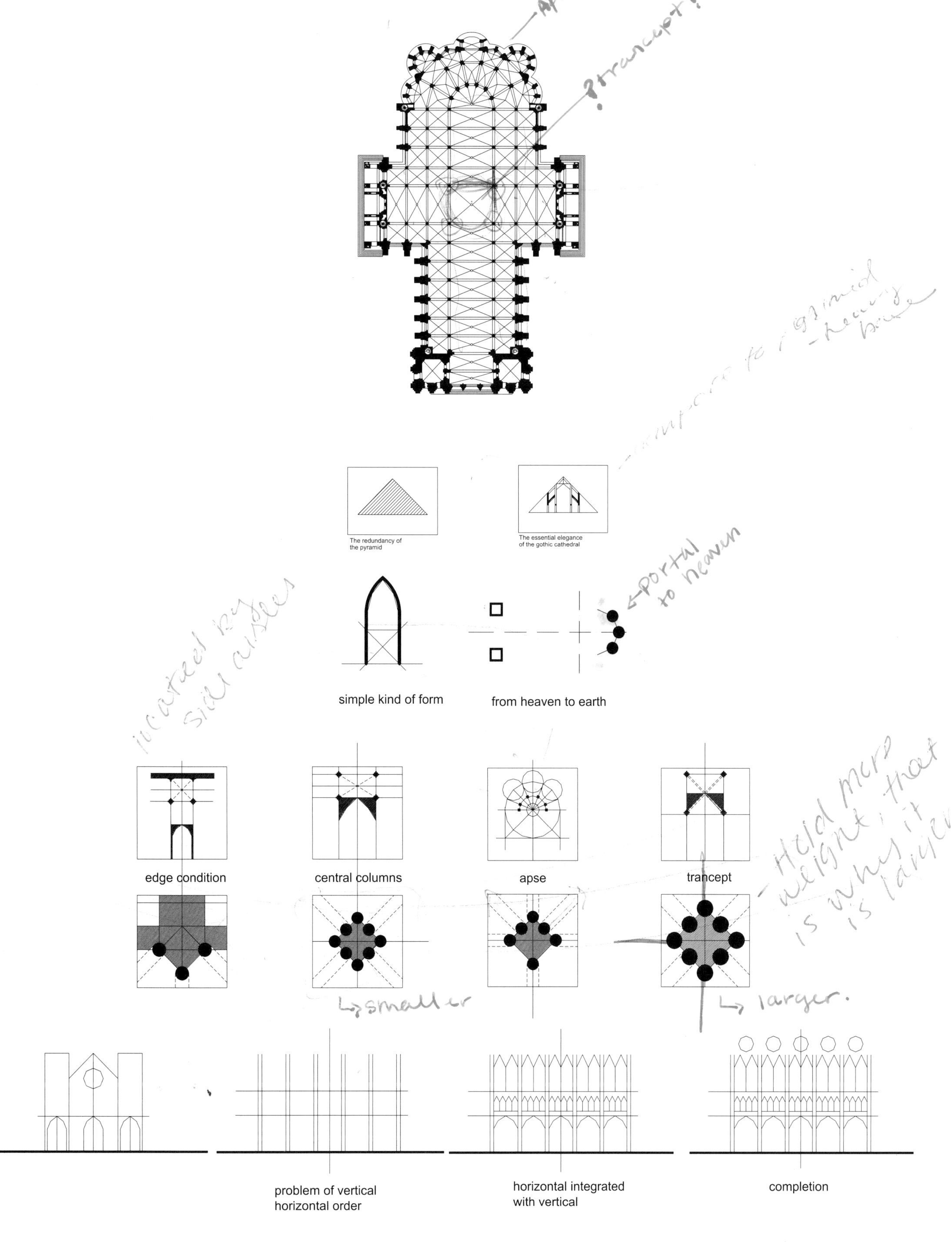

Apse
?trancept?
The redundancy of the pyramid
The essential elegance of the gothic cathedral
portal to heaven
simple kind of form
from heaven to earth
edge condition
central columns
apse
trancept
smaller
larger.
problem of vertical horizontal order
horizontal integrated with vertical
completion

TECHNOLOGY
IN ARCHITECTURE AFTER 1850

01

Background

The Western post-1850 world differed markedly from its predecessors. These differences are sometimes thought to be so great as to constitute a break in history. A series of shifts in the way we think about the world and ourselves dramatically altered 20th-century perceptions of the constructed environment and the issues that it ought to address.

Modern physics

The late 19th and early 20th centuries produced a spectacular array of discoveries concerning the structure of the universe. Rutherford, Thomson, and Bohr defined subatomic particles and their organization as atoms. This set of discoveries offered a lens directly into the fundamental structure of nature, creating a working theory of natural operations that was empirically testable. Max Planck, Werner Heisenberg, and Albert Einstein were to continue this work as a revision of Newtonian mechanics. Together this band of physicists changed how we envisioned nature. There was little need for the "hand of God" in this vision. The workings of the physical universe could now be explained as the empirical interactions of force and matter.

01 Structural detail of Centre Pompidou

What it means to be human

Two people transformed the way we think of ourselves in the middle and late 19th century. Charles Darwin proposed that human beings were the outcome of a mechanical process of natural selection. Under this theory, shifts in genetic material created mutations in living organisms. These mutations either gave the new organism a survival advantage in its specific environmental context or did not. Positive mutations created more successful adaptations in the competition for scarce resources and hence the genetic pattern for succeeding generations of an organism. Human beings could be explained as the latest of these mutations.

As Darwin explained the physical landscape of human beings, so Freud explained the psychological landscape of this relatively new organism. Freud's view of the human psyche was that there was a hidden mechanism underlying human thought and feeling called the unconscious. The unconscious stored a nucleus of human experience that conditioned how future experience would be understood by an individual without that individual being aware of its influence. Both the origin and the behavior of people could now be explained without retreating to concepts like the gods or fate.

Technology and the industrial revolution

The Industrial Revolution began in the middle of the 18th century, but it did not become a force with major consequences until it matured in the early 20th century. Assembly line production such as for Winchester rifles and Ford automobiles allowed goods to be standardized and produced at a vastly accelerated rate. The outcome was both the creation of the middle class and the use of natural resources at a scale that dwarfed that of previous eras. After World War II, 75% of the U.S. population belonged to the middle class, a historically unparalleled development of community wealth. Technology was to become the business of the 20th century, producing an ever-expanding array of new machines to produce goods, transport people, and convey and store information. These new machines transformed the social and physical context of 20th-century lives. The levels of global wealth, resource requirements, and pollution that have resulted have become central problems of the 20th century.

Population growth, urbanization, and democracy

In the 5,000 years of recorded history before 1850, the population of the world had changed little. Historically, the vast majority of people were farmers so there was little question of urban development. At the beginning of the 20th century, about 20% of the U.S. population were urban dwellers while 80% lived on farms. The population of the world has increased exponentially since 1850, as modern sanitation and medical care created a population explosion that continues unabated. Today, the proportion of urban versus rural dwellers is almost exactly opposite what it was 100 years ago.

With a few exceptions, historic populations were governed primarily through structures of fiscal or physical coercion. The democratic revolutions in the United States and France built on a British tradition of individual freedoms changed the political landscape of the Western world in the 19th century. Women were granted the right to vote in most of these countries in the early 20th century, doubling the potential number of participants in these democracies

The rate of change

For thousands of years, the conditions of the world remained essentially stable. The agrarian revolution in 10,000 BC changed forever how people and nature would interact but not our general numbers. The industrial revolution and vision of nature created by modern science had quite another effect. Beginning in 1850, world population began doubling approximately every 35 years. This growth coupled with technological innovation that promoted ever-larger human capacities to push nature around has created a civilization that now challenges the capacity of natural systems to sustain us.

These shifts in philosophy, technology, and economics may have begun earlier, but their impact is dramatic after 1850. Those who argue that these changes constitute a break with history suggest that people never before faced the problems that these transitions have created. Never before has the lens of science allowed people to understand and transform the physical structure of the nature that provided their context as is possible today. This habit of thought has invaded even our sense of selves. The alienation felt by much of 20th-century culture suggests that the secularization of our sense of self has been both fruitful and displacing. The technology of today that has followed in the wake of modern science is capable of transforming natural conditions at a global scale. Our concerns about the ecology of the planet under the stress of industrialized societies attest to the seriousness of these issues. Finally, the scale if not the kind of our social issues has been transformed by the size and concentration of populations who have all the aspirations that a representative government might promote.

These are not easy issues. They have left modern architecture with sets of problems with few precedents. Housing the six billion people of the world in communities that both accommodate the technologies of the 21st century and provide for the continuity of our social and cultural lives is central to the problems that contemporary architecture faces.

The development of modern architectural technology

The development of technology in architecture after 1850 is part of this larger shift in the ways in which people are able to think about and to transform their surroundings. The problems faced by building technology will not, after 1850, be defined as they were in the cathedral at Chartres as creating a bridge between faith and reason but as the problems that grow from mass production to meet the needs of a rapidly expanding and urbanizing population.

A number of inventions provide the base for the rapid evolution of technology after 1850. Lewis Mumford contends that these began in the 9th century with the invention of the horseshoe and in the 10th century with the invention of the mechanical clock. Horse hooves are too soft to walk on hard road surfaces for long without wearing down. The horseshoe allowed horses to pull carts of produce along roads to markets by placing a metal protection between road and hoof. In this invention lies the driving force of modern markets. Cities depend on the ability to bring large amounts of produce from rural areas to population centers just as they must disperse the wastes these population concentrations produce.

The mechanical clock generated a different kind of a change. Until the invention of the clock, people followed the rhythms of the solar day. They rose to work with the dawn and retired with sunset. Daylight hours were long in the summer and short in the winter. The mechanical clock was invented by religious orders that needed to pray at specific times of the day independent of solar fluctuations. This liberation of time from changes in sunlight made each hour the same in the rotation of the hands of the mechanical clock. Saying prayers or going to work could now be standardized independent of the position of the sun in the sky. Human rhythms were now those of the machine rather than those of the natural world.

Two other inventions spur those that form the base of technology in contemporary architecture. The first of these is the reinvention of the process for making glass. The Romans knew how to make glass, but the ability of Europeans to replicate this process was not rediscovered until the mid-16th century. Open windows in buildings allow light to come in but also allow heat to flow out, constituting a thermal wound in the weather envelope of a building. This is an especially pressing problem in northern countries where winter weather can be severe. One solution to this problem is to eliminate windows in harsh climates, but doing so severs all ties between the inside and the outside of a structure. Openings can be made to be very small and covered in the winter with an oilcloth, which is translucent but retards the flow of heat through an opening, but the amount of illumination garnered from such openings is necessarily small. Glass provides a wonderful solution to this problem. It is transparent to visible radiation while retarding the flow of precious heat from the inside to the outside of a building. The rediscovery of the method to make glass helped to produce a new generation of buildings in which windows grew in size.

Coupled with this rediscovery of glass production was the invention of the chimney. In the medieval manor house, all farm laborers slept together in one large room around an open fire. Smoke from this fire was allowed to wander up to the ceiling where it exited the room through a smoke hole in the ceiling. Only one such fireplace was possible per manor house because the inefficient means of exhausting the byproducts of wood combustion required a large, high space to distance smoke from room occupants. The chimney gathered smoke into a small, vertical channel effectively reducing levels of contamination. The result was the ability to produce heat more effectively within dwellings. This source of heat could be distributed because the efficiencies of the chimney allowed small as well as large fireplaces to be built. The lord and his lady could now have their own bedroom because they could have their own fireplace.

These two inventions come together in "Hardwick Hall more glass than wall" built in the midlands of England in the late 16th century. In this manor house, a profusion of windows is accompanied by a profusion of chimneys. The chimney produced an efficient heating system that allowed the glass area in structures to increase even though such an increase meant a proportional increase in the amount of heat that would be lost through them.

02 Hardwick Hall, more glass than wall

02

In the 19th century, the invention of the steam engine produced the steam locomotive. Few technological changes in history have had the power of the railway locomotive to propel both images of the power of technology to effect change and the consequences that such changes might produce. The steam locomotive was a large and noisy technology that was visible to all. It was not locked within the walls of mills or diminutive in size like a clock. The steam locomotive cut through previously quiet farmlands with a speed and power unknown to people before the 19th century. But it also had its limitations. It required a steel track to guide it that could not climb slopes greater than 3 percent because the friction of steel wheels on steel rails would not tolerate steeper inclines. Relatively level rail track beds meant that hills and valleys would have to be made level by tunnels and bridges. The speed and capacity of the railway as a passenger delivery system would become the base of modern transportation systems that would allow cities to grow beyond historic limits. The need for railway bridges propelled the understanding of the use of iron for structures that would become the base of modern steel frame technology.

The bridges developed later in the 19th century spanned ever greater distances with less material. Steel enlarged these technological capacities finally producing the modern suspension bridge. The Brooklyn Bridge became a powerful icon of its time. Designer John Roebling was an American engineer who thought that his discipline was the wave of the future. Engineers were to create utopian social worlds by rationally applying engineering principles to produce goods and create communities. The Brooklyn Bridge was the longest span of its era yet cost the least amount of money per foot of span. Its goal was not only to connect Brooklyn to Manhattan but to put Brooklyn and the United States on the map as technological leaders of the world.

In 1878, Thomas Alva Edison invented the electric light bulb. Two years later, a generating plant provided enough electricity to illuminate a city block in New York. For hundreds of years before this invention, illumination had been provided by burning oil. The problem was that this source of light also generated large amounts of heat and air pollution. Like the chimney-less fireplace, gas lamps contaminated the air in rooms. So much pollution was created by these lamps that they posed a significant health hazard to building occupants. The electric light bulb solved both these problems. It burned cleanly and, particularly in the form of luminescent tubes, coolly. As a result, the artificial illumination of buildings became a matter of a flick of a switch and large areas of floor space could now be illuminated independent of the sun.

These major inventions powered the forms of new technologies that emerged in buildings after 1850. They changed the limitations that had constrained building construction for thousands of years. In doing so, these new technologies created new opportunities and new problems for architecture. A number of buildings remain icons of these changes.

03 The Crystal Palace
04 Construction of the Crystal Palace

The Crystal Palace

© Hulton-Deutsch Collection/Corbis

03

Few structures more powerfully illustrate post-1850 changes in building technology than the Crystal Palace in London. The Crystal Palace was designed and built for an 1851 industrial exposition by Joseph Paxton with help from railroad engineers. The building was 1,848 feet long and 456 feet wide, dwarfing contemporary structures of the time. The design of this enormous exposition space was the product of the failure of architects to produce large and cheap structures that could be built in a short period of time. Joseph Paxton was not an architect. He was an English botanist who had developed his building skills by designing and constructing palm houses that provided appropriate climatic conditions for the plants that English explorers brought home from distant lands. These exotic plants often came from regions of the world with different climatic conditions than are found in northern England. Paxton solved this problem by designing ingenious iron and glass conservatories for these special plants. Plant conservatories provided the model for the Crystal Palace.

The goal of the Crystal Palace was to house technological inventions that would impress other countries in a building that would do the same. A competition was held for the design of this structure yielding a series of masonry proposals that recognized architecture's technological past more than they did its future. Paxton was invited to submit a design for the exposition hall after it was deemed that none of the competition entries were acceptable. It is noteworthy that Paxton and the railway engineers

04

© Hulton-Deutsch Collection/Corbis

05

that he worked with were members of professions other than architecture who sought pragmatic solutions to empirical problems because their training promoted such a perspective. The Crystal Palace is less a product of architecture than it is of the pragmatic and empirical point of view that modern engineering would bring to architecture.

There were 3,300 iron columns in the Crystal Palace of only 17 different shapes. Its large, open space was spanned by 2,224 iron girders that resembled trusses common to railroad bridges. The building was clad by 900,000 square feet of glass. The exhibition hall contained 33,000,000 cubic feet of space interrupted only by the slender shafts of iron columns that held spanning girders aloft. Materials for the Crystal Palace were fabricated and assembled in only nine months. The Crystal Palace was completely disassembled and reassembled twice after its original construction before a fire destroyed it.

06

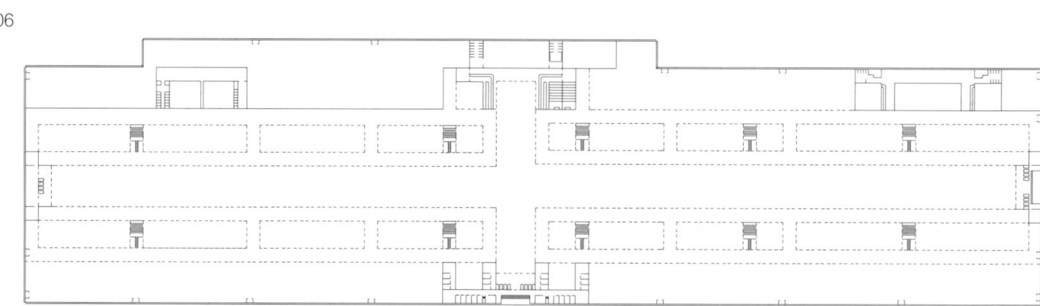

Each of these characteristics represents a startling shift in technological perspectives about building construction. All would have been impossible without the technological prowess generated by the industrial revolution. The manufacture of 3,300 iron columns or 2,224 iron girders in nine months in a handcraft-based society was unimaginable. The production of 900,000 square feet of glass would have baffled even the great technical minds of the Romans. Only a fundamental shift in human productive capacity could make such a building possible.

The characteristics of this shift are those born of engineering as it emerged from the 18th century to become the driving force of 19th- and 20th-century modes of production. Machines fabricated building components just as they fabricated other commodities. These components were required to be of similar shape because machines were not capable of making the same distinctions as human hands. The shape that building elements took after this was a negotiation between the requirement of machines to create identical shapes and the specific technological requirements of building components in particular contexts. Industrially manufactured building components that were able to accomplish constructions that could only be imagined before 1850 generated standardized building forms that fueled 19th- and 20th-century fears about the impact of industrialization on environments.

The technical characteristics of the Crystal Palace can be seen projected forward in the manufacture of building components like the steel frames and curtain wall systems that dominate contemporary office and commercial space throughout the world. Components of these frames and cladding systems are available in standardized shapes that are assembled to become the buildings that dominate every urban skyline. These buildings vary only in detail. Economy of means has been purchased with a rigidly enforced regularity.

The dimensions of the Crystal Palace also announced a central technical goal of 20th-century architecture. This destination was first pointed to in bridge design. The small, single-span bridges of the 18th century became iron truss bridges in the early 19th century and then transformed into the grand suspension bridges of the 20th century. These structures demonstrated the power of modern engineering to push back empirical limits. The romantic images of suspension bridges became symbols of the technological prowess of those who built them.

 07

 08

09

05 Erecting the Crystal Palace
06 Plan of the Crystal Palace
07 Great Hall of the Crystal Palace
08 Crystal Palace under construction
09 Interior of the Crystal Palace

10 John Hancock Building in Chicago
11 Façade of the John Hancock

10

© Joseph Sohm;ChromoSohm Inc./Corbis

Size became synonymous with power in the late 19th- and early 20th-century construction of environments. Bridges and towers were known by name as indications that the cities in which they were located were where players in the 20th-century rush to technological progress. The Brooklyn Bridge was joined by the likes of the Golden Gate Bridge, the Empire State Building, and the Chrysler Building in announcing that the United States would lead this charge.

A powerful example of this urge to extend empirical limits is the John Hancock Center in Chicago. Fazlur Kahn, a structural engineer employed by Skidmore, Owings & Merrill (SOM), used the newfound power of computer-based computation to develop elegant ways to build skyscrapers. The structural problem of skyscrapers is that they are giant cantilevers rising from the earth. As the wind strikes the vertical surfaces of skyscrapers, it attempts, as in the Gothic cathedral, to bend this lever to the ground. Before Kahn's engineering work on these structures, this force was resisted by concrete elevator cores at the center of these buildings. Kahn reasoned that the most effective place to resist wind loads on tall buildings was at their perimeter where the dimensions of its base were greatest. He redesigned each face of the Hancock building to be a giant steel truss. The truss was made of triangulated steel members so that a change in its shape required a change in the length of one of its sides. The truss was anchored to the earth so that the tower's desire to rotate on one of its edges in a strong wind was resisted in a technically efficient manner. The result was four façades of a building made of four steel trusses thrust 110 stories into the air. This design greatly reduced the amount of structural material required to counteract wind forces in tall buildings. Because these trusses were exposed on the façade of the Hancock Building, they left their imprint on this building and on future buildings in the elegant engineering thought that they exemplified.

11

© G.E. Kidder Smith/Corbis

This same kind of technical prowess was demonstrated in a different way by the Lever House in New York, another SOM design. The Lever House was not a particularly tall building, but it was one of the first sealed buildings in the United States. A sealed building is a technological achievement because it requires that all of the air within the structure be mechanically conditioned. This does not seem like a major technological achievement today when most large buildings depend on mechanical air heating, cooling, and humidification; but in 1950, it represented a significant accomplishment. Large amounts of energy, relatively sophisticated machines, and new control systems were required in buildings in which windows could not be opened for natural ventilation. Lighting systems were required that did not produce so much heat that structures with large artificially lit areas would overwhelm the capacity of air conditioning systems to keep them climatically comfortable. The Lever House demonstrated all of these capacities. Its sealed exterior of transparent and opaque glass hung from a structural frame became the model for all the curtain wall buildings that followed. Its ventilation louvers and ceiling bay system of florescent lights, which produced one-third the heat of incandescent lights, became the industry standard. The image of the Lever House as a means to technically control interior climatic and luminescent conditions became a symbol of American business ingenuity and power. The design of the Lever House has been imitated thousands of times in the ubiquitous office buildings that seem to populate every urban landscape and climate in the world.

© Angelo Hornak/Corbis 12

Finally, there is a tiny building that takes issue with the premise put forth by the Crystal Palace. Many designers have argued that standardization of building components need not lead to standardization of building design. Their argument is that industrially produced building components are really conceptually no different than their preindustrial counterparts. As trees and stone quarries once produced the raw material of architectural design, factories now did the same. The issue was less one of how these components were produced than it was the creativity with which they were assembled to create original designs. Charles and Ray (Kaiser) Eames were important American industrial designers who took on this problem. They designed a house for themselves in Santa Monica, California, that was made completely of off-the-shelf industrial components. Their first design for this house was a bridge. After they had ordered the materials for this design, they decided to rethink their position.

13

The conception of house as bridge grew more from picturesque images than from the kind of pragmatic problem-solving that typified industrial design. The couple responded to this observation by using the same kit of parts they had ordered for the bridge to construct the largest volume of space that these parts would allow. The addition of one 8-foot girder allowed the creation of their now famous house. This house is a two-story rectangular shell in three parts arranged in series along a rise on the site. The first of these is a living area, the second a central courtyard, the third a studio. The materials of this house are clearly factory made. The design impetus to create the largest volume possible with a limited set of parts is akin to the engineering impulse to strive for an elegant use of resources. The outcome is a unique residence, one that is particularly suited to its site and to the needs of its inhabitants. The counterpoint of industrially assembled components in the Eames House played off against the natural landscape of the seashore is a particularly powerful visual reminder that

12 Lever House
13 Eames House

all architecture is composed of human fabrication within a natural context. The beauty of the building is the beauty of a 12-meter sailing yacht or a fine camera. Its parts are designed to elegantly perform a task and in this conscious reduction of resources to the essentials lies a kind of human joy that accompanies profound resourcefulness.

The Crystal Palace, like significant buildings before it, gave birth to a new range of architectural design speculation. It represented an exploration of the possibilities of industrialization and mass production that marked a new importance of engineering in architecture. It became the model of contemporary buildings as containers to be filled with changing contents. Its size and speed of construction shifted architecture's conception of buildings from handcrafted products to an assembly of manufactured components. The Crystal Palace became architecture's icon of the new industrial era and its ability to take on problems of a scale that were impossible to conceive in preindustrial eras. Its thought gave birth to a range of architectural ideas. One hundred years later, the Hancock Building, Lever House, and Charles and Ray Eames House emerged as the progeny of the architectural thought propelled by the Crystal Palace.

14

14 Interior of the Eames House
15 Front façade of Centre Pompidou
16 Structural joint of Centre Pompidou
17 Plan of Centre Pompidou

Centre Pompidou

Centre Pompidou differs from the Crystal Palace in that it is less the product of industrial production than a conceptual model of how the machines that underlie that production might become buildings. Centre National d'Art et de Culture Georges Pompidou in Paris was designed by Renzo Piano and Richard Rogers with the engineering firm of Ove Arup and opened to the public in 1977. Machines are not the source of building components in this design: they have become the model for the building itself. The structural skeleton of the building, its mechanical system to condition the building's climate, and the means to move people and goods vertically become the visual form of Centre Pompidou.

15

The plan of Centre Pompidou is a simple, uninterrupted rectangle. All technical elements required to hold these floors aloft, to illuminate them, to condition the climate within their boundaries, and to move people or goods through them have been moved to the edge of the building. The result is a clear division of architectural responsibility. Each architectural element is given the form of the task that it accomplishes. Each of these sets of forms is joined to others with connections that clarify the intersections of functional systems. The result is like looking into the back of a mechanical watch in which the propulsion spring is connected to the hands of the watch by a series of gears that make explicit the mechanical motion of the watch. There is a kind of beauty manifested in the precise functional forms, arrangements, and connections of these gears that has become the design model of Centre Pompidou.

16

The structural scaffolding of Centre Pompidou is made of stainless steel tubes connected by iron fittings. Steel frames in conventional buildings are covered by concrete fire protection and then by the building's cladding system. In Centre Pompidou, the steel frame is exposed to become the façade of the building. Building façades have traditionally enunciated the public face of a building with front doors, porches, arrangement of windows, and fine materials that proclaimed this surface to have different social responsibilities than do the other exterior walls of a building. In Centre

17

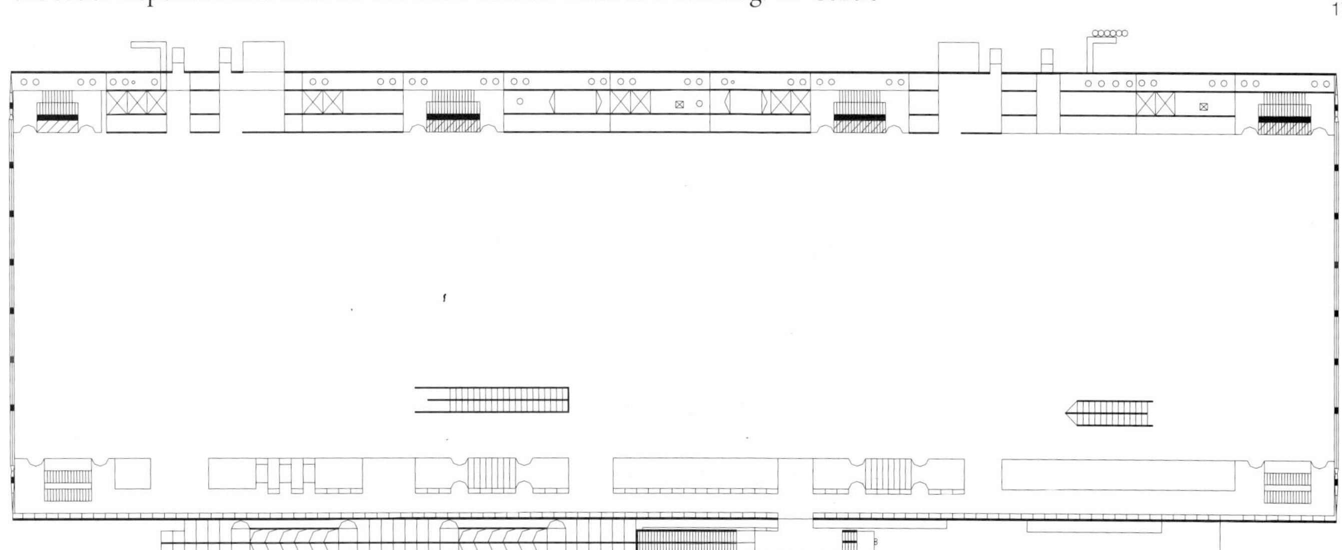

Pompidou, this distinction is done away with. It is replaced with elements that proclaim their mechanical function as the symbolic material of the building's façade. No apology is made in these forms for their lack of cultural symbols that might link them to façades of the past. Each face of Centre Pompidou unapologetically proclaims its mechanical duty as translated into forms symbolic of machines to become rational building form.

Each of the connections of the frame of Centre Pompidou is a sensuous, sand-cast, iron fitting that reflects its mechanical requirements much as a beautiful sailboat reflects forms required to propel a boat with the wind. There is in these forms an imagined pattern of the way in which nature accomplishes her tasks. This is not the rectilinear world of orthogonal architectural form because gravity is imagined to be a liquid force that flows toward the earth just as wind fills sails to become gentle curves. Connections of the stainless steel tubes that form the trusses and columns that support the floors of this building manifest this liquid sense of gravity in their rounded shapes as they attach one frame member to the other. Each is molded to reflect the special conditions of gravitational force that it is asked to redirect. Corner connections differ from those at edges, which differ from connections within this frame as each is asked to redirect different amounts of gravitational force in different ways. The joint has always been recognized in architecture to pose a different design problem than that of the material it connects. The frame of Centre Pompidou becomes an object of art as it attempts to precisely trace its mechanical duty.

The pipes, ducts, escalators, and elevators housed within this structural scaffolding take form in a similar manner. Each is like wearing the internal organs of a human body outside rather than inside its skin. The flow of liquids, air, electricity, and people become no different than the flow of blood, air, waste, and neural impulse in the human body. These functions are now exposed in Centre Pompidou instead of hidden below a surface that masks their operation. Manifesting their form on the outside of the building visually declares their importance. The mechanical function becomes the whole of the building's meaning in the design of Centre Pompidou.

19

20

18 Detail of rear elevation of Centre Pompidou
19 Ventilation tubes of Centre Pompidou
20 Rear elevation of Centre Pompidou

22

21 Sagrada Familia in Barcelona
22 Park Güell in Barcelona
23 Empirical model used by Antoni Gaudi to understand loading conditions in Sagrada Familia

23

Making mechanical function explicit in building form has propelled a good deal of architectural design throughout its history. More attention has been placed on the structural frame of buildings in this history than on other systems because illumination, waste, and climate-control systems are relatively recent inventions. The modern roots of the form of the frame of Centre Pompidou might be found in work like that of Antoni Gaudí.

Gaudí was a Catalan architect of the late 19th and early 20th centuries who was interested in how the forces of gravity were actually carried to the earth by members of a building's frame. To understand how this redirection of gravity occurred, he built empirical models of how these forces were transferred from structural element to structural element. This model began with an organization of strings hung from the ceiling that mimicked the form of the structural members of the structure being designed. Each member was then weighted with little sandbags in proportion to the gravitational loads on that member.
21 All were connected by strings as they would be in a

24

25

building. The result was an upside down diagram of how gravitational forces would actually be carried to the earth by the structural frame of a building. If inverted, this model could serve as a means to rationally shape structural frames. The result is often portrayed as formal fantasy but in fact is a much more accurate reflection of gravitational force than are the rectilinear frames that architecture so often constructs.

Gaudí's Colònia Güell chapel in Santa Coloma de Cervello, Park Güell buildings, and Sagrada Familia all use this technique to organize their stone frames. Park Güell was intended to be a utopian community on the outskirts of Barcelona. Its houses, marketplace, gardens, and plazas never accomplished the intended social goals, but the tilted columns of the stone passageways that connect places within this site suggest a primitive past absent the alienation of industrial eras. The beautiful sensual form of the columns in these passageways is a graphic reminder that the earth they retain pushes out as the roofs that they support push down.

The columns of Sagrada Familia register the same combination of vertical and lateral forces. Unlike the frame of the cathedral at Chartres, lateral loads on these columns are not taken up by flying buttresses but by the tilted axes of column members themselves. The visual outcome is more akin to the form of the trunk and branches of a tree than to that of conventional building frames because trees must also resist lateral and vertical loads without the help of buttresses. Like the great Gothic building projects of the past, Sagrada Familia will take many years to complete.

The Colònia Güell chapel represents a smaller version of the same set of principles found in Park Güell and Sagrada Familia. This building is a complete testament to Gaudí's preoccupation with rational stone frames. The tilted columns of this small chapel support ribbed ceilings that trace the flow of gravitational energy from spanning a volume to the earth. There is a particular formal power of Gaudí's research here because it is concentrated in a small space.

24 Collonade at Park Güell
25 Vaults of the Chapel at Coloma
26 Collonade at Park Güell
27 Entry of the Chapel at Coloma
28 Interior of Chapel at Coloma entry

26

27

29 Lisbon Olympic City train station
30 Tracks and roof of the train station
31 Detail of the roof structure of the train station

The work of Santiago Calatrava in the Lisbon train station is a more recent example of similar technological design principles. Calatrava is more taken with the skeletons of animals than he is with machines as models for the design of structural frames of buildings. Being in his train station is like being in the rib cage of a giant animal. As parts of animal skeletons join to other parts in a thickening of homogenous material (think of an elbow or knee), so the structural elements of the train station flow into one another. This structural design is based on a biological rather than a mechanical model but the results are much the same. The elements of the building that are responsible for redirecting natural force become the whole of the form of the design.

29

30

Casa Barragán

32 Casa Barragan living room window
33 Casa Barragan plan
34 Casa Barragan roof top axnometric
35 Casa Barragan main dining room window

32

It would not be difficult to conclude that the contemporary architectural use of technology was based solely on advances in engineering. To do so, however, would be to ignore architecture's perennial technical problems. Chief among these is the use of natural light. Sunlight has posed a technical problem for architecture since the first weather enclosure separated people from their surroundings. People who constructed these shelters quickly learned to reconnect the inside of dwellings with their context by cutting holes in this envelope. The vehicle for performing this task was sunlight. It captured the form of all surfaces that reflected it and brought these images within dwellings through windows. The problem of how buildings shape this light and the images that it carries is as old a problem in architecture as gravity and climate. It is a technical problem in architectural design today because natural light is such a significant part of the meaning of buildings. Electric lights have not supplanted natural light in this regard because they remain tiny artificial sources of illumination within the larger construct of natural light that is so central to our conceptions of time and place.

A fine example of the use of natural light might be found in Luis Barragán's residence in Mexico City. In this 1948 building, Barragán restates the central place of the meaning of sunlight in architecture. Every light opening in this house is particular to a space. No two windows are alike. Perhaps this is because Barragán subscribed to a unique design method. He is said to have constructed large models of his buildings, placed them on a table with a whole cut out of it, and then placed his head within this model through the hole. In other design work, human perception is registered as an imagined presence within a plan or model of a building. Barragán's presence was literal and gave rise to visceral senses of being within a space. In this design strategy, the order of windows in building façades gave way to unique qualities in each room lit by windows. Every window was different in size, location, and shutter treatment because the sensibility of every room called for different kinds of daylight. The entry hall is lit from above by an invisible source of light that bathes the walls of the stair. The living room is lit by an over-scaled square window that has its own room. This window connects the living area of the house with the garden beyond with an 8-foot-wide space created to give this window a special place of its own in the design. The rear window of the living space faces the street and is elevated and translucent to obscure images that might have flowed through it. The dining room window has a sill height at hip level yielding a horizontal view of the garden while holding occupants firmly within the room. The tiny dining room for one or two people next to the larger dining room also has a horizontal opening to the garden but one whose sill height is such that only the sky can be seen through it. Each bedroom has wall or corner windows with multiple shutters so light qualities can be adjusted. The original design of the window in the master bedroom was an oversized floor-to-ceiling opening recalling the living room window but on the second floor. And, finally, there is the completely walled roof garden, which only sees the sky.

33

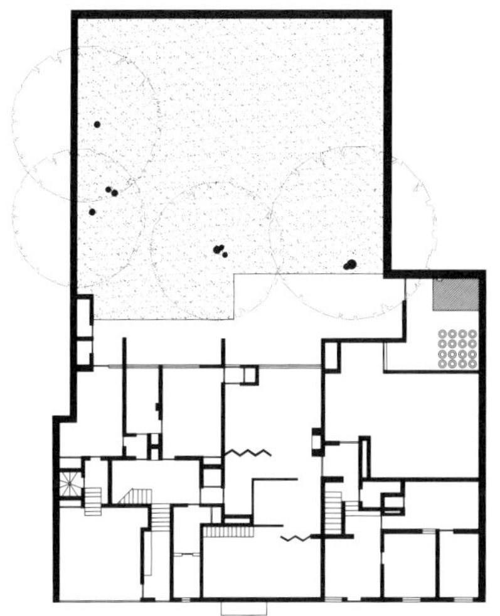

34

35

Of course, simply enumerating these different window conditions communicates little of their effect. Natural light in buildings is not a matter of calculation or efficiency or even of spatial conditions captured in dramatic photographs. It is both the subtlest and the most moving characteristic of architectural technology. People are intuitively aware of its presence or lack thereof. Natural light in buildings is a condition that must be felt directly by occupants of buildings. It cannot be understood at an abstract distance because its impact on our senses cannot be captured by symbols. Perhaps that is why so little is written about this central quality of architectural presence.

36

Casa Barragán is not a dictionary of the use of natural light in architecture. It is an accretion of individual spaces each lit in ways that give them a particular meaning. How could an architectural technology be more different from issues that were propelled by the industrial revolution? The immeasurable capacity of natural light to locate people in their surroundings underlies much significant modern architecture. This capacity ranges from the exuberance of a brightly lit landscape to the subtle gradation of light from a small opening along a wall. Casa Barragán sought to discover the meaning of this light for one individual. But, as is so often the case in architecture, what was profound to one of us strikes a similar chord in others. Long after the particulars of Luis Barragán's personal habits and preferences have disappeared, an unmistakable residue of care for the design of natural light remains in this work. Most of us seek places that are meaningfully lit. Perhaps that is why the repetitive nature of curtain-wall, enclosed office buildings is so alienating. The windows fitted to individual rooms of Casa Barragán remind us that we remain individual personalities in the face of the banal repetitiveness fostered by the industrial revolution. We are as moved by the subtlety of well-shaped natural light in buildings as were medieval people by the light of Gothic cathedrals.

38

Closing thoughts

Technology presents a more complex set of issues for architecture than it does for engineering. The place of people in the natural world of empirical force is not always represented adequately by the tenets of technological efficiency. Buildings respond to natural force in ways that both have and have not changed with the development of a technological society. Structures are profoundly different today than they were 150 years ago because of technological inventions. The steel frame, electric light, and mechanical air conditioning forever changed the form, design, and construction of buildings. New modes of transportation propelled the development of cities that concentrated populations at unparalleled levels. But architecture's use of natural light stands as a reminder that although machines have changed our lives, we remain much the same organisms that we have always been. Casa Barragán represents an architecture of technological resistance that is also part of architecture's search for the role of the natural forces of climate, gravity, and sunlight in buildings. Technologies that profoundly house us in climate, gravity, and sunlight apparently cannot be reduced to technological progress.

This description of the use of technology in a building is surely different from what might be put forward by other disciplines. While it is true that Gothic cathedrals of the Middle Ages were triumphs of engineering, it is equally true that these triumphs of material form over natural force are manifestations of architectural ideas that are not empirical. Soaring light bounded by an elegantly articulate identification of spatial order in the section of a column are not empirical ideas.

The rigor and elegance, both empirical and symbolic, of the Gothic cathedral's stone frame was challenged by the industrial revolution. The tenets of the industrial revolution stress a kind of technological elegance but not one that might make faith clearer to the imagination. The values of industrialization are those of standardization and economy. In this doctrine, much is made available to many because material goods are manufactured in few forms, allowing goods to be made rapidly and cheaply by machines. Building technologies took on this mantle rapidly in the 19th century. The Crystal Palace is a wonderful example of this technological logic. Its 33,000,000 cubic feet of volume is supported by 3,300 columns of only 17 slightly different shapes.

Both the Eames House and Casa Barragán challenge normal conceptions of industrial societies. The Eames House seeks original design outcomes within the constraints of standardization imposed by industrial production. Instead of allowing design to be driven by the banalities of standardized kits of building parts, this tiny building explores the creative potential of industrialization. The Barragán House also rejects much of the industrialization agenda but in a different way. Instead of economy of means, it uses natural light to seek age-old meanings of architectural technology.

Though historic solutions to the problems of how to separate climates, hold buildings aloft, and allow the passage of sunlight have been supplanted by modern technological means, the roots of these problems remain unchanged in human consciousness. The role of architectural technology in linking human consciousness to that of our natural context presents a perennial problem for architects. A profound understanding of this problem will not be found in ever more efficient technology. It will always be sought in speculations like those of the Gothic cathedral, Eames House, and Casa Barragán that ask what this age-old connection might mean to us.

As a culture we have made enormous technological strides over the last 200 years. Many of the technologies that have emerged from this fertile period of invention make our lives convenient, comfortable, and rich. Technological progress comes at a price, however, to the constructed environment. Our level of material production challenges the ability of the earth's resources to sustain us. The dictates of mass production endanger our ability to create rich, individual thought. Our lives and our buildings are in danger of a tyranny of standardization that often attends machine production. Architecture has been aware of all of these problems. It is just as capable of applauding the resourcefulness of the Crystal Palace as it is the romantic image of the machine in the façade of Centre Pompidou. It seeks creative use of the new possibilities of industrialism in the Eames House as it seeks the transcendent nature of architectural technology in Casa Barragán. The machines of technology are an inseparable part of modern lives. Their role in those lives is as complex as the issues pointed to in these four buildings.

40

KATSURA IMPERIAL VILLA

AND THE IDEALIZED LANDSCAPE

Transforming nature to become what we think it ought to be

Issue

We inhabit two kinds of landscapes. The first is the landscape that has not been modified by people. Mountains, seashore, islands, and primal forests are all environments that are solely the product of natural forces. Mountains well up as tectonic plates collide or because of pressures within the earth's mantle. The seashore is where oceans reorder the land by rhythmic waves set into motion by the pull of the moon's gravity. Islands are small pieces of land whose substrate has been able to withstand the erosive power of the water that surrounds them. Forests grow where conditions of water, soil, and sunlight promote them. Plant species replace one another over extended periods of time until the final form of a climax forest is reached. There is a precise balance in each of these examples between natural material and natural force. The shapes that we see in the natural landscape that do not reflect human intervention are the result of this balance. This landscape, with all its varied characteristics, is the product of force and material interacting within a complex matrix of relationships in search of equilibrium. As the terrain, atmosphere, and hydrology of the earth continue to mature, this balance is always sought in new landscape forms and organizations of the life forms it supports.

But the landscape that people more commonly prefer is the natural world that has been reorganized for human habitation. This landscape remains largely the product of natural process but is modified to reflect human concerns. Noted writer J. B. Jackson commented that the natural landscape unaltered by people is often threatening. In an unaltered natural environment, people feel to be at the mercy of their natural surroundings rather than comfortable within them. A humanly modified natural context creates a more congenial sense of human location. This is no longer a primitive

01 Katsura Imperial Villa

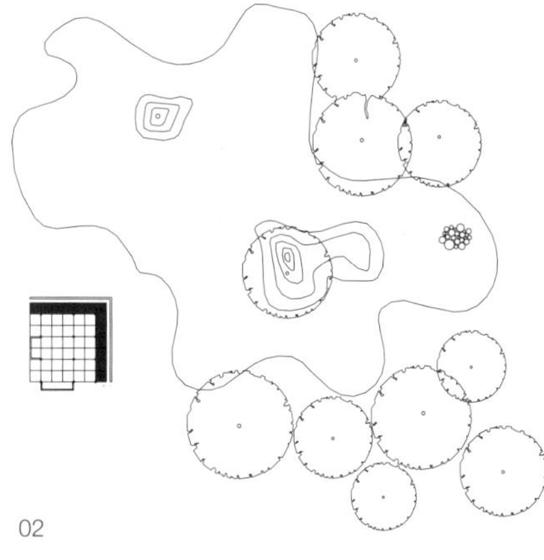

02

landscape that records only a balance between natural force and natural material but one that has been reshaped to reflect human needs and desires. These needs and desires may be as prosaic as a farm field or as abstract as an image of heaven. Between these two poles lie unlimited numbers of ideas about what nature might mean.

There are no purely utilitarian or purely symbolic modifications of our natural context in this regard. Each act of human modification of the natural landscape inherently carries both values. A farm field is biological sustenance but also gives birth to an abstract idea of human control over natural process. A pleasure garden is an abstract concept of beauty that must be watered and weeded to survive. In all of these cases, the human landscape reshapes the natural landscape to become more like what people think nature ought to be. The idealized landscape records these ideas.

What differentiates the idealized landscape from other human constructions is that it is a rearrangement of terrain, water, and plants that retains its predominantly natural form and character. Plants are nurtured and pruned in new locations. Terrain may be changed topographically but is never divorced from the surface of the earth. Water may be rerouted but retains all the characteristics of the original liquid. The underlying idea of each of these manipulations is an interpretation of the natural landscape as people imagine it to exist. Some characteristics of the natural landscape are brought forward in this interpretation while others are suppressed. Interpretations range from literal to metaphorical. But the natural landscape of air, sunlight, water, earth, plants, and animals always lies at the heart of these ideas. The idealized landscape is an intersection of nature's processes and the human imagination. It creates places that people are able to inhabit both mentally and physically from the materials of the natural landscape.

03

Values attached to the idealized landscape

04

As the context of our existence, the landscape has always been a rich source of stories that enunciate the value of nature to people. People contend, for instance, that the natural landscape preceded our existence as a species and that it will continue to exist after our demise. This is an interesting proposition given our inability to know either the world before or after our own existence. This contention demonstrates our belief in the natural world as both our temporal and physical context. In this story, nature is given a place of honor denied our species. We are temporary; nature endures. We are a part; nature is the whole.

Nature is seen to be a set of "difficulties and possibilities" as eloquently stated by José Ortega y Gasset in the early 20th century. All the resources used to construct buildings originate in the natural world. Nature is responsible for the beauty of a sunset or the smell of a lovely spring shower. But nature is also the gravity that attempts to destroy habitable space and the climatic conditions that are uncomfortable or dangerous to human beings. It is storms that threaten life. It is why things wear out. All things on the earth are nurtured by and destroyed by the forces of nature which mould the ever-changing landscape

Nature is the place where people witness a continuum of birth and death that mirrors their own origin and destination. Plants and animals are born, mature, and die. A single leaf on a tree branch contains the full story of all life within nature. Nature gives birth to the leaf each spring and develops a beautiful structure of veins and tissue that absorbs sunlight and powers photosynthesis. As winter approaches, fall leaves turn color, wither, and die. A few drab, grey leaves will cling to branches until the spring as a reminder that birth and death in nature are cyclic. People take pleasure in watching this cycle recur, marking the duration of their own existence.

Our stories about the natural landscape portray the context of human constructions as a coherent and continuous context, as a source of sustenance and of problems, as the cycle of birth and death in our everyday world, and as myriad other values. These are not values that might be attached to other human experiences. They are the unique province of nature as manifested in the landscape that surrounds us.

A good deal of American literature of the 19th century is based on a specific cultural perspective of the natural world. *Moby Dick, Huckleberry Finn,* and *Walden Pond* all take up the issue of the meaning of our natural surroundings. In each case, the natural world is pitted against a maturing industrialization. *A River Runs through It* is a contemporary movie that takes up this recurrent theme in American thought. In this film, a father and two sons value fly fishing next to godliness. The father, a Methodist minister in Montana, teaches his two sons to fly fish each Sunday after the church service. When they grow up, one of the sons remains at home honing his fishing skills while the other goes east to college. The fishing skills of the son who becomes educated (culture) deteriorate while the son who stays in the west develops his own, beautiful casting technique (nature). The son who stays home is killed in a gambling brawl (law of the wild versus rules of humans) just as the West will be acculturated in time.

02 Teahouse in the garden of Katsura
03 Ryonanji Rock Garden
04 Detail of Ryonanji Rock Garden

05

Fly fishing is the central character of this movie. It is a way that people understand the natural landscape by becoming a part of it. The delicate fly rod, waders, and knowledge of waterways signify a direct, intimate, and profound knowledge of the natural landscape that is now denied to most people. That direct human relationship to nature dies with the abstractions of education. To intellectually know about something is not to become part of it but creates, instead, a distance that denies participatory knowledge. The beautiful casting son of *A River Runs through It* must die as knowledge about nature overtakes our culture's direct participation in the natural landscape. This movie returns to the value ascribed to nature in *Walden Pond*. People cannot do without culture, but culture requires a distance from the goodness inherent in a natural life in a natural landscape. This dilemma, one that runs through American values, remains alive in our preference to live in the suburbs rather than the city.

Natural process as counterpoint to human construction

Natural process and form serve as counterpoints to human creative processes. Form shaped through the organic process of nature is different from form shaped by human beings. The human imagination linked to the human hand is capable of reshaping natural resources in ways not possible for nature itself. Buildings are unnatural acts. They defy gravity, isolate climates, and selectively transmit sunlight. Nature does not create villages and cities, farm fields and waste disposal plants, automobiles or computers. People understand these artifacts because they have made them. Nature creates things in a different way. No one is quite sure how natural things come into existence, but it is clear that the hallmarks of this process differ from their human counterpart. Natural creation occurs over extended periods of time. It appears to be able to note the context of its inventions as it creates them. Each new successful invention will become the context of all creations that follow it. All the elements required for this invention appear to be inherent in primal materials and rules. Primal material evolves over time in accordance with rules of behavior that shape a dynamic equilibrium. People ascribe a guiding intelligence to this process because its products seem to manifest an orderly universe. No human creation approaches the elegance of a butterfly wing or the complexity of the human mind.

How could two processes be more different? Nature seems to have a mind of its own as it achieves a dynamic balance of force and material that presents the world with ever-changing forms. The human mind and hand attempt to intervene locally in this process of dynamic change to create moments of understandable stasis. The result is a dialogue of creative possibility. Nature occupies the earth alongside people. Nature is the other, a companion with a different origin, life, and destination. This difference provides a mirror for human thought. Nature offers a counterpoint to human creation and understanding. Each allows the other to be understood more fully in their differences.

06

07

Katsura Imperial Villa

Katsura Imperial Villa is a building, or rather a set of buildings in a garden, that generates a compelling sense of what nature might be from an Asian perspective. This perspective is much different from that held by the West because it is not dominated by the tenets of Christianity. In Christianity, humans were cast from the garden because of self-awareness (culture) and advised to go forward and subdue the other things of the earth. This act has created a lasting fissure in Western thought. We consider nature and culture to be two separate and distinct provinces. Large parts of our Western sense of science and technology may be traced to this division. This division is not as clear in Eastern thought. Humankind was not ejected from nature within these beliefs. Eastern thought tends to see nature not as the other but as a cohabitant of the world. The deep roots of this more unified vision of nature and human culture are found in both the Shinto and Buddhist beliefs that underlie the idealized landscape of Katsura.

Buddhism stresses contemplation as a vehicle to come to know the self and the world around us. Buddha was the awakened one. One is awakened in Buddhism not by taking action in the outside world but rather by attempting to understand that world from inside the human mind. Buddhism contends that everything in the universe is a single force. People see differences in this force because their vision is clouded. This cloud can be lifted only by seeing beyond these images of difference through meditation and contemplation. The enlightened one sees past the veil of appearances.

05 Shinto shrine in Japan
06 Japanese farm house of the 18th century
07 Katsura Imperial Villa

08 Interior of the Villa
09 Shoji screens of the Villa
10 Entry walkway to the Villa
11 Veranda of the Villa

The other major influence on Japanese conceptions of nature is Shintoism, a form of animism. In animism, all things on the earth are considered to contain spirit. People are tied intimately to the natural world through this spirit. The same spirit that inhabits people inhabits the rocks, the soil, the plants, the animals, and the sky. There is no need to reconcile culture with nature in this belief because they have never been separated.

Both of these views stand in stark contrast to dominant European and North American culture. Since the Industrial Revolution of 1750, the West has imagined nature to be either a protagonist or a resource of raw material. We attempt to control and mine nature for the things we need. Katsura will be helpful in establishing an alternate vision of nature and better understanding the roots of our own view.

In Katsura, this vision of nature is manifested in the Japanese tea ceremony. A Buddhist monk, Sen-no-Rikyu, is often credited with changing both the form and the meaning of the tea ceremony in the 16th century. Prior to then, the Japanese tea ceremony was a lavish affair where blindfolded nobles guessed the origin of specific teas much like the wine-tasting parties of today. Sen-no-Rikyu brought a much different form of this ceremony with him from the Chinese mainland. Chinese Buddhist monks sought simplicity. They shared a drink of tea from a common peasant bowl when they

08

completed a meditation. When this form of the tea ceremony was adopted in Japan, it became the heart of a ritual intended to promote insight by focusing complete attention on simple acts. In this ritual, a tea master first prepared charcoal to heat the tea water. This charcoal was formed into a beautiful shape like a flower, washed, and dried. Guests of the ceremony approached a teahouse along a path that helped them leave the problems of their everyday life behind. On this path were places to pause and notice one's surroundings and bowls of water to cleanse hands and feet. Entry into the teahouse was through a door that required entrants to stoop in an act of supplication. Once in the teahouse, participants in this ritual were allowed to speak of nothing else. Their attention was to be focused solely on what was happening each moment. The tea master raked the sand that insulated the heat of the charcoal fire from the structure of the teahouse into a lovely miniature landscape. The beautifully sculpted charcoal and sand landscapes would both be destroyed by the fire that heated the water. Special water chosen from wells with unique characteristics would then be heated, specially chosen fresh tea leaves added, and a tiny cup of steeped tea poured for each participant. Guests would admire the artfulness of the ceremony, the quality of the tea, and the meaning of participating in this ceremony with others. When the ceremony was finished, guests thanked the tea master and quietly departed taking with them the idea that simple things seen in depth might allow the essence of life to be glimpsed.

09

In the tea ceremony, as in the garden of Katsura, each act becomes a work of art. Each form is reduced to a simplicity that might reveal its essence. This model of essence revealed in the unadorned particular is manifested in much Japanese art but may be given its most compelling voice in Ryonanji Rock Garden. This famous garden, composed of only 17 stones placed in a bed of raked gravel, allows those who view it to see anything from 17 literal, if artfully placed rocks, to a vision of the cosmos. Ryonanji couples the material world of nature and the fertile imagination of human beings. Its essential forms promote interpretation. The human mind completes the garden as it does all other manifestations of the idealized landscape. The idealized landscape provides both the context and the subject of this search for what lies beneath the complexity of the material forms that comprise the earth and our lives within this context.

10

Japan suffered 400 years of civil strife from 1200 to 1600 AD. This era ended with the triumph of the warlords over the Emperor. The Emperor and his family were forced to retreat to an isolated residence in Kyoto. As the Emperor's power was stripped by warlords, the royal family became interested in the arts in place of lost political power. The result was royal attention to those things in life that have meaning beyond that of power and wealth.

This search was structured by the tenets of Buddhism. Buddhism came to Japan via China in the 6th, 12th, and 16th centuries. The last of these religious invasions coincided with the royal family's fall from power. The central Buddhist tenets of reduction to simplicity and knowledge through contemplation intersected the royal family's interest in the arts to become the basis for the values manifested in Katsura Imperial Villa.

11

12

12 Rain gutter
13 Tatami mats

This villa, garden, and the teahouses were built by a royal prince and his son as a retreat from the struggles of political life. Soon after 1600, the first owner of Katsura, Prince Toshihito, assembled 14 acres of land where the Imperial Villa now stands. Toshihito built a teahouse in this garden and later the first portion of the Imperial Villa that is called the Old Shoin. Prince Toshihito died in 1620 and work by his son, Prince Noritada, did not resume until 1641. The garden was redesigned from 1641 until 1650, the Middle Shoin added to the Old Shoin, and six teahouses were constructed. Each of these teahouses had a designated role and were named Shokintei, Shokatei, Shoiken, Chikurintei, Manjitei, and Gepparo. All but the Manjitei and Chikurintei exist today. Later, a New Shoin and the Music Room were added to the villa to complete its present day form. The garden is walled and contains a 1.4 acre man-made pond at its center. A path through the garden links the Imperial Villa to the teahouses creating what is called a stroll garden.

The design of Katsura began with the size of a person. The module on which this design was based is that of a tatami mat. A tatami mat is the size of a person lying down, roughly three by six feet. Rooms were formed by adding mats one at a time until an appropriate size was achieved. Rooms may be any number of whole or half mat sizes. Roof members were supported at the corners of these rooms by wood columns of equal size. Walls were made of mud reinforced with straw or delicate rice paper shoji screens that slide apart to allow access to a veranda overlooking the garden or to another room. A tokanoma, or small ceremonial niche, was set aside in important rooms to house a representation of the natural landscape. This representation might be a landscape painting, a simple flower arrangement, or even a single stone. All other rooms served more than one purpose. Utensils necessary to make a room a place to sleep, sit, or eat were kept in storage cabinets. Appropriate furniture was brought from and put back into these cabinets as they were needed.

The materials and forms of Katsura Imperial Villa and the teahouses of the garden were intentionally treated as they might be in a Japanese regional farm house of the 17th century. In this construction, emphasis was placed on maintaining a link between building materials and their source in nature. The wall that surrounds Katsura was made either of cut bamboo lashed together or growing bamboo that is woven together. In both cases, the simplicity of construction and form of the natural materials yield constructions of pristine beauty. The rain gutter of the villa was no different. A small stone trough was embedded in the ground at the edge of the overhanging roof. This lovely trough erodes the earth as a river would but its rectilinear form announces the manmade boundary of the royal dwelling. The tatami mats that form the floor of the structures are woven grasses that retain their natural shape and color. The roof above was built up of successively larger wooden members lashed together and covered with thatch to span progressively larger distances. Special columns were chosen in each structure that retain their form as tree branches. The earth of the garden was molded to make gentle hills and valleys where there were none before. A pond was dredged from the center of the garden that is fed by the waters of the Katsura River that once traversed the site. Trees, shrubs, grasses,

13

14

15

16

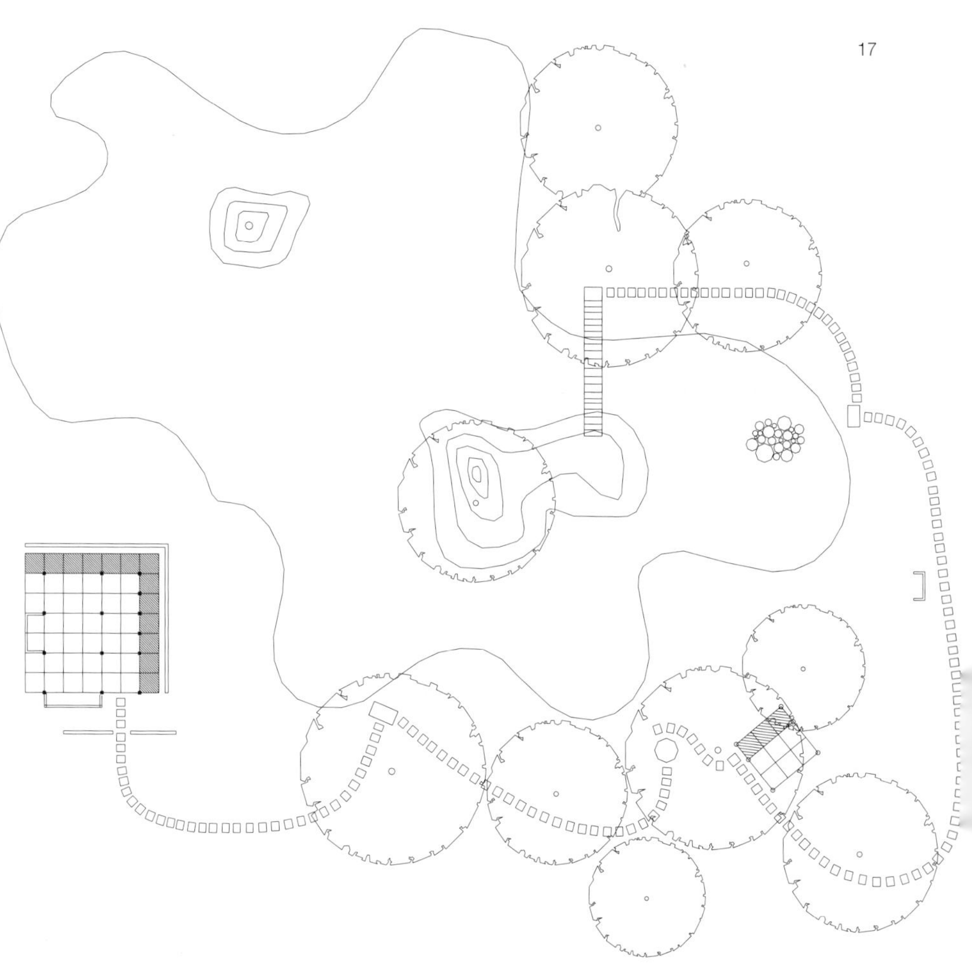

17

and flowers were carefully selected and composed to create scene after scene of natural beauty. The 12,000 stones that make paths through the garden were each individually selected and placed because of particular shapes and colors.

This reorganization of natural material to become buildings or gardens is as artificial as any other human construction. But in the Katsura Imperial Villa, this artifice is easily mistaken for a more perfect vision of how nature ought to look. Both structures and the garden look as if they could have occurred unintentionally. Each could not look less contrived nor could it look less picturesque. Buildings, terrain, water, and plants seem to harmonize here in a way that always recalls the origin of the materials while each element is arranged to create a quiet and seemingly inevitable harmony.

14 Garden path
15 The garden
16 Interior of a teahouse
17 Teahouse in the garden

Katsura as an idealized landscape

18 Buddha as the philosophical underpinning of the Villa
19 Enclosing the garden with a wall
20 A stroll path through the garden

Like all important works of art, Katsura Imperial Villa has given birth to numerous interpretations. Some of these attempt to propel specific ideological agendas such as the writings by early modern architects. Others pay more attention to the role of Katsura in the development of Japanese culture. The following analysis is not different from its predecessors; it also seeks to make a specific point based on the forms of this environment. Simply stated, this point is that the idealized landscape is an intersection of human thought and natural process. Each gives shape to the other. Neither can be ignored. Both are essential to a vision of what people think nature ought to be.

The idealized landscape begins from a point of view that probes the way we think about our natural context. At Katsura, this viewpoint is based on the tenets of Buddhism. Buddhism creates no explicit separation between nature and culture. All that exists is a manifestation of a single force. All is a part of a whole. We are a part of the garden just as it is a part of us. We may understand ourselves by coming to know the garden well.

The wall of the garden creates an island that isolates people from the prosaic concerns of the secular world. This wall isolates Katsura from both the natural landscape and from the city. It is a special place set aside for a special purpose. Its gate admits entrants to another world: a world of contemplation versus a world of either human or natural action.

The stroll garden is a way of placing the human body and thus the human mind within this world of contemplation. There is something about being in a garden that cannot be reproduced in a building. Subtle differences in organic form may be mimicked but cannot be replaced by buildings. The warmth of sunlight cannot be replaced by a fire. The sound and smell of water cannot be reproduced in a basin. The wind rustling the leaves of a tree sounds different outside. Modern people take a special pleasure from natural surroundings. There is a special human feeling that ac-

18

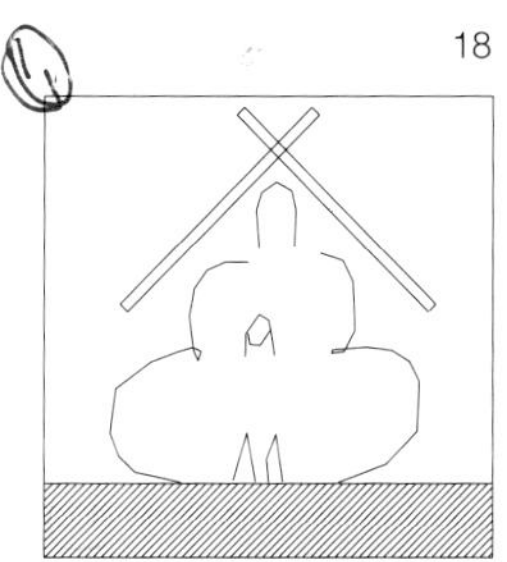

19

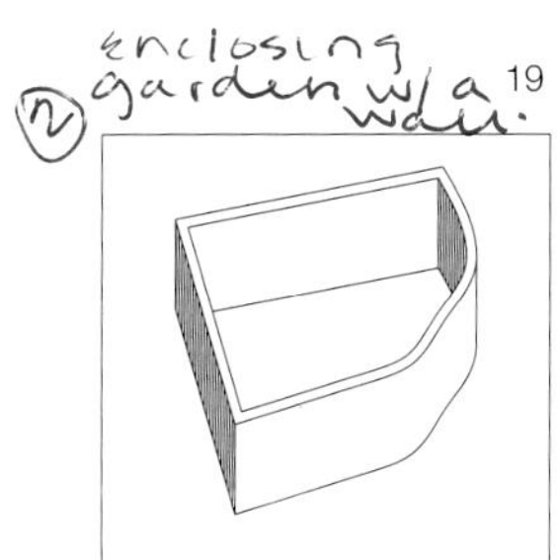

20

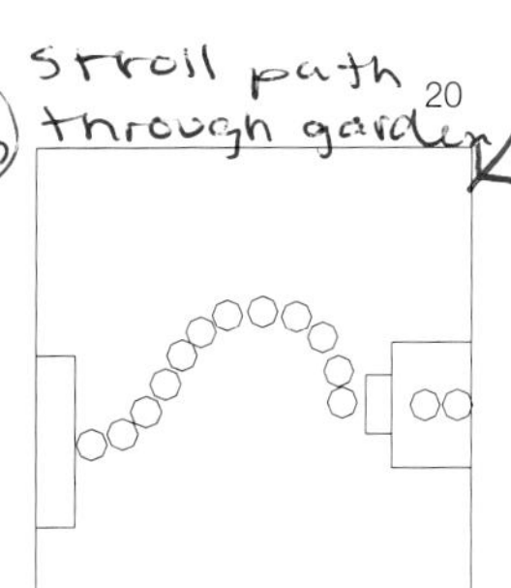

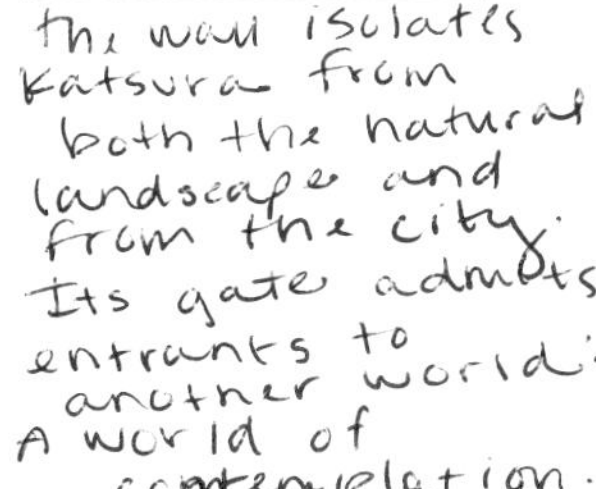

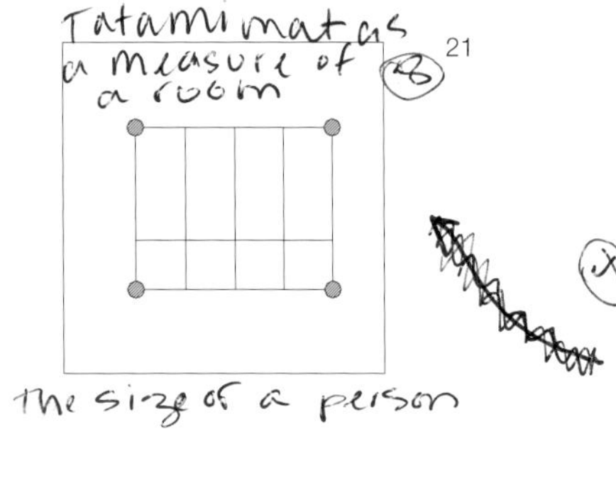

companies being in a beautiful garden that propels a human sense of wellbeing. This sense of wellbeing creates a calm that might promote insight into the significance of our lives and that which surrounds us.

A tatami mat is the size of a reclining person. As the primary planning module of Japanese Shoin-style buildings, it assures that the scale of these buildings arises from the scale of our bodies. This scale might be seen in distinction to more heroic architectural gestures of Western temples. The Parthenon, Pantheon, or cathedral at Chartres represent scales that are intended to make people feel small in relation to a building. The ideas that these larger-than-human scales put forth are those of political, economic, and intellectual power. In Katsura, this scale is reduced to that of our own bodies. Enlightenment is not found in grandeur but in attention to ourselves. Heroic gestures do not serve to understand that which might be glimpsed in a single raindrop.

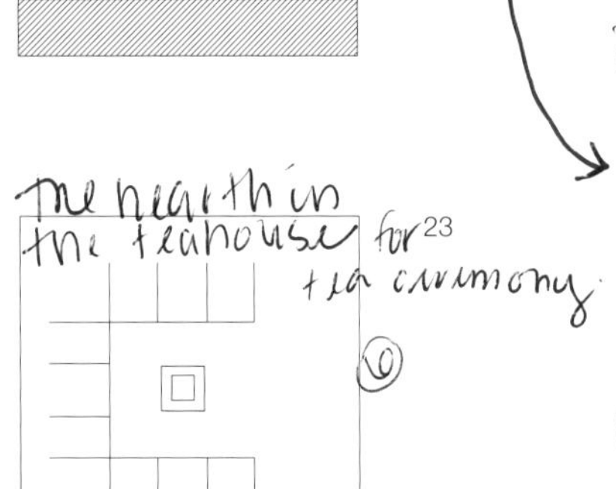

Mental belief requires tangible ceremony to become a part of our everyday lives. The tea ceremony makes the watchfulness and thoughtful contemplation of Buddhism a tangible part of a stroll through Katsura garden. People learn how to see the world around them. Often this sight is trained to see only the surface that surrounds us. To see below the surface requires a different kind of training. The Japanese tea ceremony trains the mind of participants to see all that there might be in a single act.

The hearth for the tea ceremony is supplied by the earth. It is surrounded by a kind of interior veranda of the teahouse in which tatami mats overlook it. The formal hearth for this ceremony is constructed by the tea master while raking the white sand in the base of the hibachi that will be the place of the fire in a miniature landscape. As in life, this landscape will be consumed by the processes of nature. The artfulness of the human hand will succumb to the inevitable death and rebirth of nature.

The path through the garden is a series of events that prepare one for participation in the tea ceremony. It is a path that leaves everyday concerns behind to focus on the immediate beauty and depth provided by the natural world. Each stone of this path is carefully positioned to control the orientation and tempo of those who walk on it. Every pause or change in direction is rewarded with a new vision of the idealized landscape. Within each of these visions lies the whole for those able to see it. It is a path of watchfulness, a path of mental cleansing.

The rooms of Katsura are created by adding tatami mat spaces one to another. This module defines a place in terms of aggregate human bodies and not in terms of a particular use. People rather than function become the center of environments that seek to explore our relationship to the natural world.

The garden is a human rearrangement of natural material that largely retains its natural form. Earth is re-graded, water pooled, crossed, and channeled, and vegetation is planted and pruned. This origin in the organic process of nature serves as counterpoint to the culturally developed tenets of Buddhism. Nature gives birth to and constrains the ideas that form culture in a particular way. The idealism of Buddhism meets the empiricism of nature to create a rich hybrid of thought in Katsura's garden.

21 Tatami mats as the measure of a room
22 The tea ceremony as the center of the garden
23 The hearth in a teahouse for the tea ceremony
24 Pausing along the path to take notice of the moment

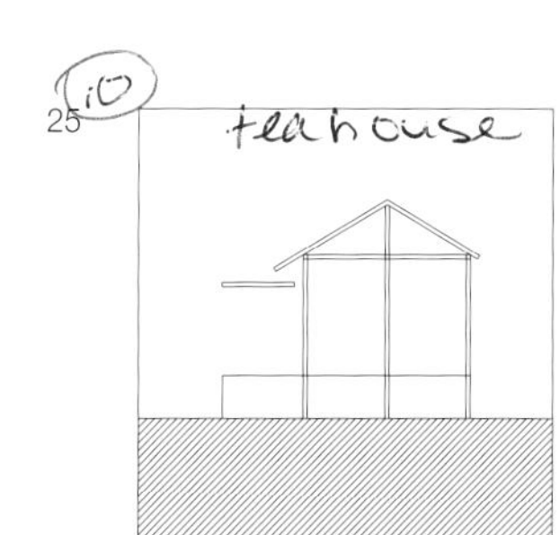

The teahouse is the subject of the garden. It is the place where ceremony prepares the human mind to contemplate our existence. It is the place where narrowed watchfulness might propel a wider insight into the meaning of our lives. The entry, construction, and orientation of the teahouse all are designed to bring a particular kind of meaning to this ritual. How different it would be in a Renaissance villa or a modern house. The teahouse recalls human roots in a simpler time. It enunciates the fundamental-ness of simple virtues.

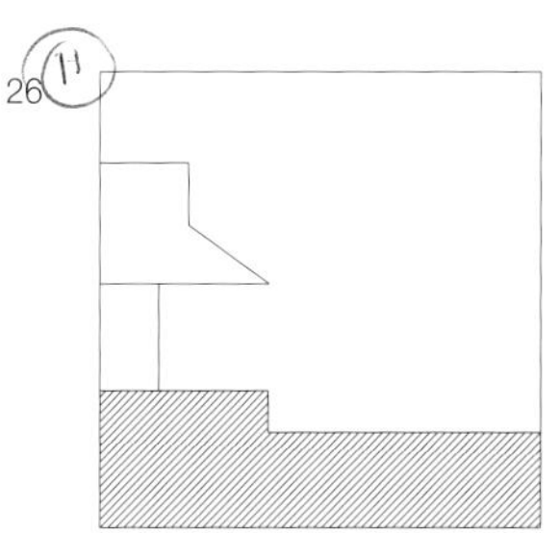

The veranda is a classic place of the in-between. It is between the cultural world of the tatami mat and the natural world of the garden. It is between the shadow at the center of the building and the sunlight and moonlight of the garden at its edge. It is between the physical life of the human body and the mental life of the human mind.

Central to the placement of the rooms at Katsura is their relationship to the garden. The shoji screen wall and the veranda tie each of these rooms intimately to portions of the garden beyond. The edge of these rooms is not a termination but a seam. It melds the artifice of organic processes to the artifice of the human hand.

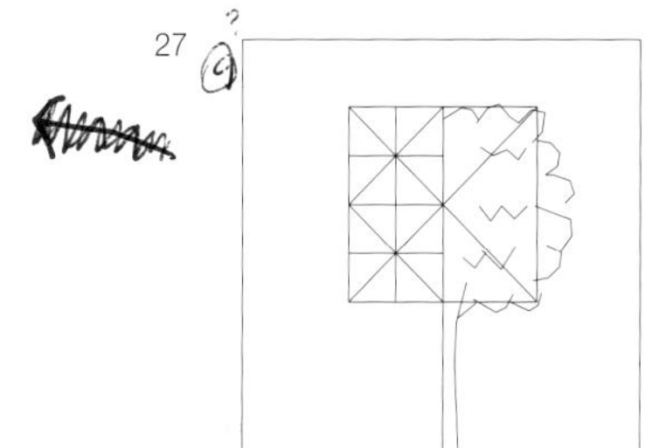

The idealized landscape is a conjunction of natural material that is naturally formed, and human conceptions of what nature is or ought to be. The garden is the search for a definition of perfection of nature. It retains the tangible origins as earth, water, air, and plants but rearranges these elements to become a manifestation of an ideal vision of what nature ought to be. The garden is thus an idea. It is an architectural idea formed with natural materials retaining their natural form. It is the conscious reformulation of that material to express a human value.

This vision emanates from our experiences within a natural world. Human beings have grown up as a species within that world. Our presence within nature has significantly conditioned the way we think. Our attachment to this natural context has been clouded by the invention and multiplication of machines that make the natural world ever more abstract. But our natural origins run deep. Below people's mechanized sophistication lies an abiding need to belong within a nature that is presented to us by Katsura.

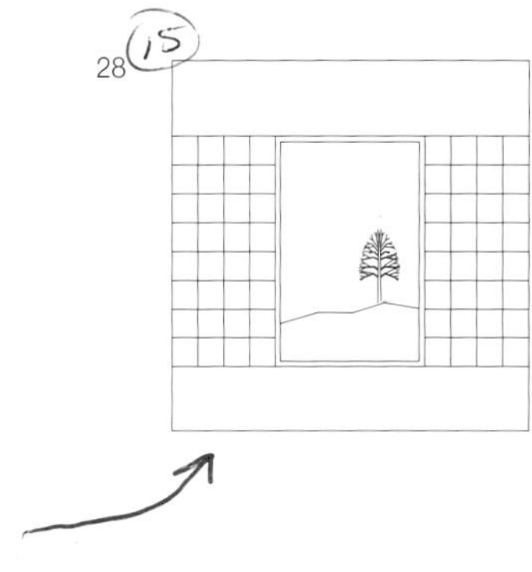

The view of the garden from within shoji is the framed view of an excised portion of the natural world. This opening brings small pieces of land, air, water, and plants within the human domain. The sky, the lush vegetation of Katsura, or an urban street might equally well serve to inform us that our buildings always lie within the broader context of a natural world.

The buildings of Katsura proceed from a dim interior center to a naturally lit edge. There exists a metaphorical correspondence between this order and our own mind. We see our own interiors only dimly in contrast to the world outside of us that is composed of brightly illuminated tangible form. The edge as veranda places inhabitants between the human mind and the tangible qualities of the natural environment that forms our symbolic and biological context.

The natural world begins with natural forms produced through natural processes. People may interpret these natural occurrences in many ways, but they remain the continuous and stable base of our lives and evolution as a species. Our search for an

25 Teahouse as locus of ritual
26 Veranda as the in between
27 Human and natural order in the idealized landscape
28 Framed view of the landscape from within the shoji

29

idealized landscape begins from this essential material that preceded us and that will continue to exist long after we do not.

Nature can be understood in the smallest and most particular of its products. Though we understand little of the underlying structure that produces natural forms, people are surrounded by the products of those processes. Learning to really see these products is a difficult task. Buddhism would suggest that we begin with something small and particular. In the part exists the whole.

The tokanoma is a representation of nature as art at the center of a Shoin structure. It represents the human capacity to think through art. This representation serves as a counterpoint to the actual garden that lies without the shoji screens of the house. The garden is literal artifice made from natural material. A painting of the same or a flower arrangement abstracts the elements of the natural world for human consideration. People manipulate and understand the world through ideas. Ideas are comprised of symbols. Symbols are the ground of mental abstractions that promote an intellectual understanding of nature.

The mind's eye represents the idea that the world is as our thought configures it. There certainly exist tangible natural material and process. But the significance that we ascribe to that material is the product of the ways we have learned to think about it. The garden in architecture is a projection of this mind's eye.

30

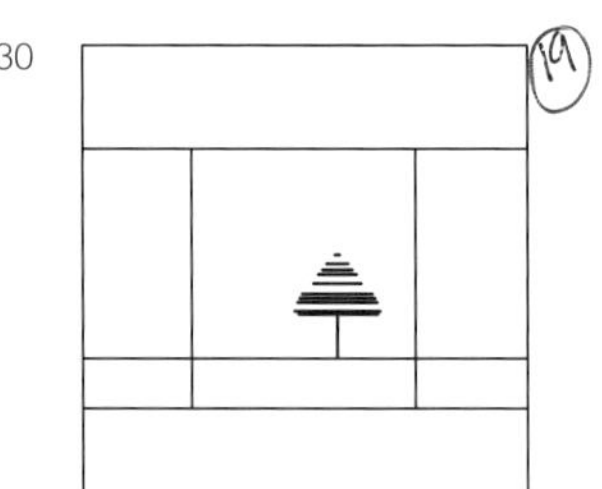

31

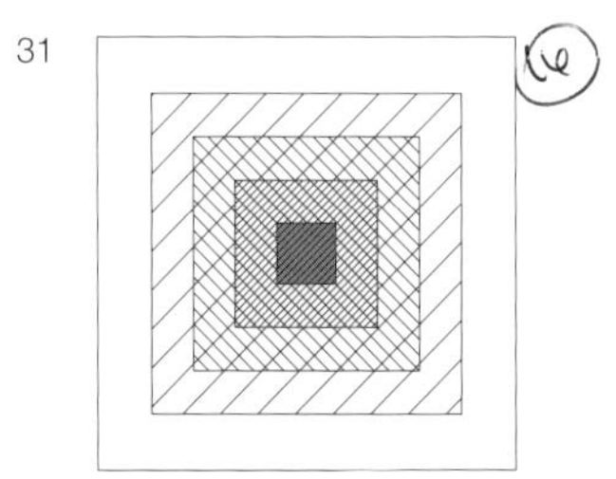

32

33

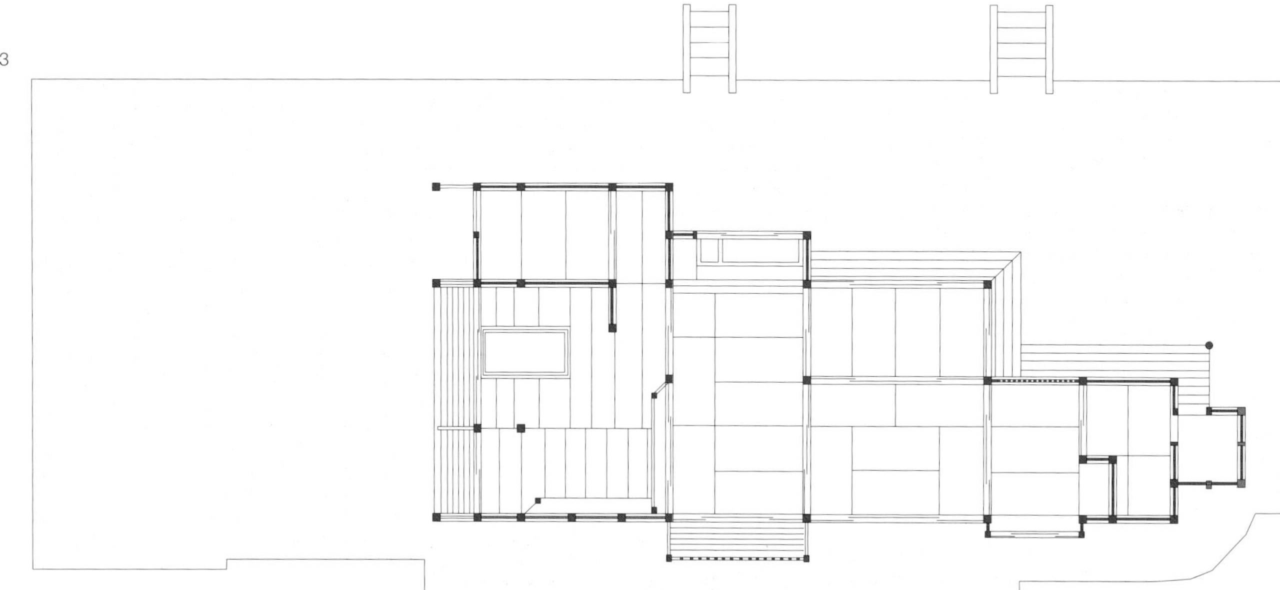

Closing thoughts

34

Katsura points out what often remains unclear to the Western mind as it considers our natural surroundings. Modern science has become so thoroughly enmeshed in our considerations of what nature is that, as a culture, we seem to have some difficulty accepting other points of view. Yet each of us who visits Katsura Imperial Palace is reminded that the garden is a tangible landscape with significant meaning. This is not a nature of quantum mechanics but a landscape of earth, water, air, plants, and sunlight. We continue to attribute specific values to this idealized landscape because we continue to need to understand the human dimensions of nature. There is substantial history of this search in the gardens of both East and West. Chinese poets created famous gardens as did European royalty. The Alhambra, Versailles, Villa Lante, and Castle Howard all remain examples of this search that cuts across cultural boundaries and time. Though these landscapes occur late in architectural history, they were inevitable. It was probably only a matter of time before the natural world, so necessary for our existence, came under the scrutiny of the interpretive mind. Science makes of nature a mechanism. The garden makes of nature a habitation of values.

Two pairs of ideas structure the creation of idealized landscapes. The first of these is mental. It weaves together our systems of cultural beliefs and the mind's eye. People seem to need to understand what lies below the tangible surface of their existence. The search for these intangible answers to the question "Why?" drives a symbolic understanding of the human circumstance. Nature is part of that circumstance. Cultural value as a product of the mind's eye provides the motive power for the rearrangement of the natural landscape to become the idealized landscape. The other ideas that

29 Seeing the world in its smallest part
30 Tokonoma as representation of nature within
31 Center to edge as dark to light
32 The mind's eye
33 Plan of teahouse
34 Taking note of the particular

35 The Alhambra courtyard of the Myrtles
36 The Alhambra as a window to the garden

give birth to the idealized landscape are physical. People have physical bodies that place them in the physical forms of the landscape. The idealized landscape cannot be understood solely as a mental construct. Its mental abstractions find their origin in a human physical presence within a physical context. The particular size of the human body and the human hand are seen against the particular size, shape, and textures of nature, from the smallest leaf to the largest mountain, as the base of ideas that emerge from this relationship.

The garden as an idealized landscape is so interesting because it is such an impure idea. It is neither solely composed of abstractions that allow the development of ideas, nor of the natural ecology of the biosphere; it is a bit of both. Plant tissue is the product of natural process, but the placement of that plant and its care require human action. The form of the plant is the form that natural processes produce, but the form of the garden where it is located is human artifice. This intersection may be stretched in either direction. The idealized landscape might be as dominantly natural as a path in a forest or as dominantly human as a square in a city. But the conception of the impure, neither nature nor culture but the intersection of the two, remains the heart of the idealized landscape.

People's ability to discriminate between what does and does not constitute an idealized landscape is based on a long and special history of human experience within a natural setting. Human beings remain, at some level, wedded to the natural context that has supported them throughout their development as a species. People seem to store this memory to be recalled when appropriate. Perhaps, it is this primal relationship that makes the idealized landscape such a special construction.

The Japanese tea ceremony represents only one of the rituals that allow people to be part of an idealized environment. Today, this ritual is often that of a vacation. People spend leisure time at the shore of an ocean, in the mountains, in a forest, or near a lake in an attempt to reconnect with the natural landscape. Perhaps, these rituals are based on a less profound understanding of our relationship to nature than that of the tea ceremony, but they serve nonetheless to remind us of the pleasure of being in the natural landscape. People continue to develop gardens for their own homes that bring them close to organic processes. Landscape painting and flower arrangements still abound in our residences. People make parks, squares, and streets as gardens that structure our cities. Each of these idealized landscapes gives rise to a ritual of occupation. People behave within each in accordance with the tenets of these rituals.

People's ability to symbolically rather than biologically reconstruct nature is fairly recent. More than 11,000 years elapsed between human intervention in the natural landscape to grow crops and the rearrangement of that landscape to create pleasure gardens. But, in the final analysis, this form of scrutiny was inevitable. The natural landscape, which has always served as our human context, could not avoid the same sort of examination that dominates other human pursuits. The idealized landscape offers glimpses into the possible meanings of the earth, air, sunlight, water, and plants that have always been the home of human beings. Rearranging these commodities to represent human value restates the human need to understand our place on the earth.

35

1

Buddha/Shinto

2

walled world

5

tea ceremony

6

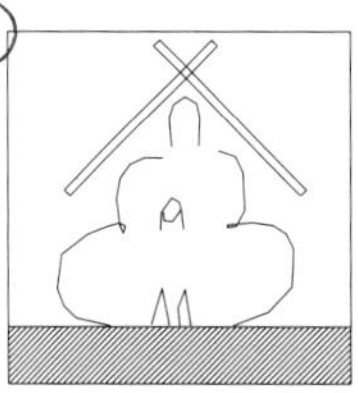

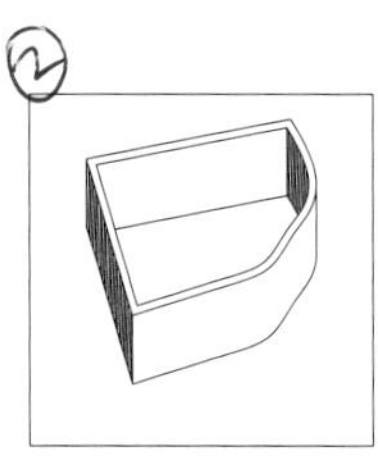

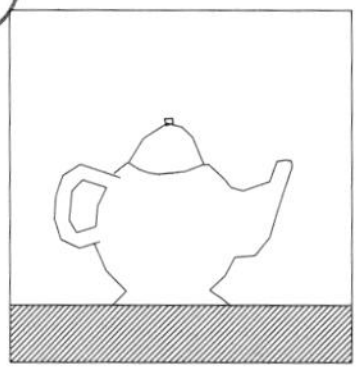

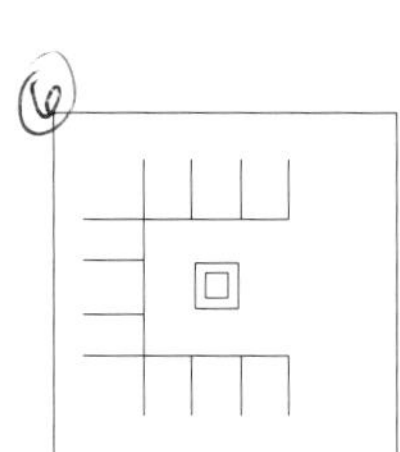

hearth for tea
ceremony

9

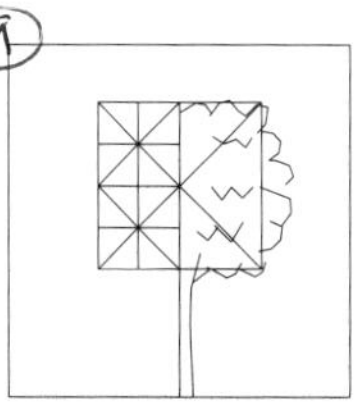

mental & natural
order in the world

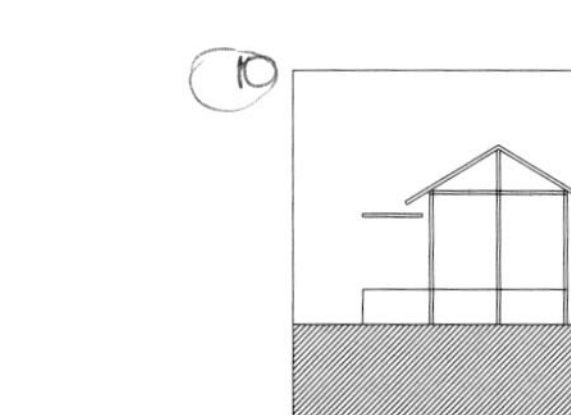

10

tea house

13

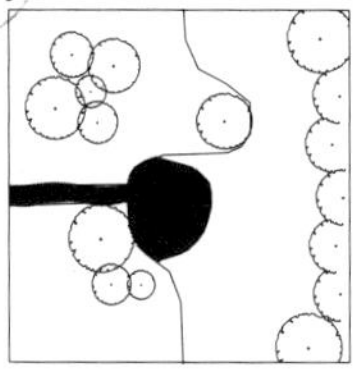

the garden as the
rearrangement of
natural landscapes

14

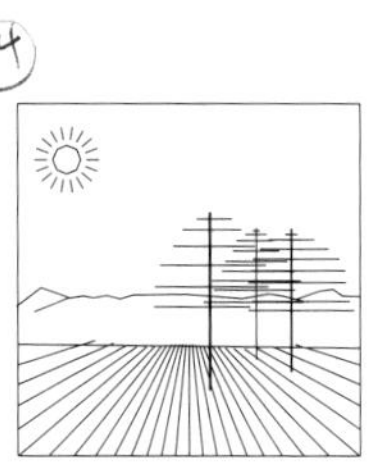

the garden as vision
from within nature

17

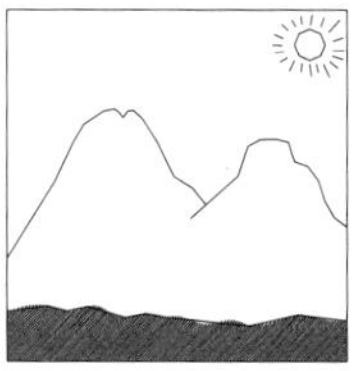

untransformed
nature

18

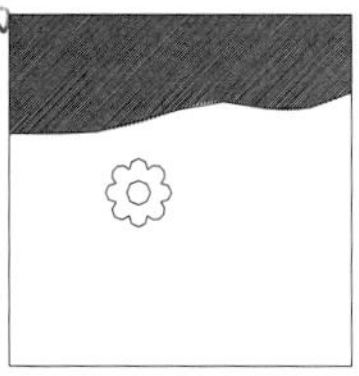

a water lily
in a pond,
a drop of rain

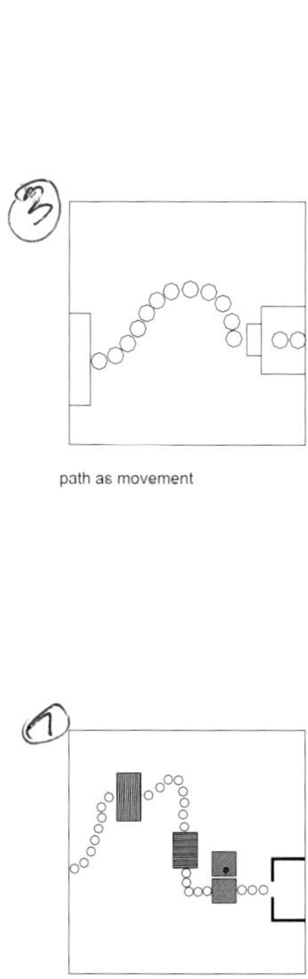

path as movement

tatami and the
human body

path as a sequence
of events

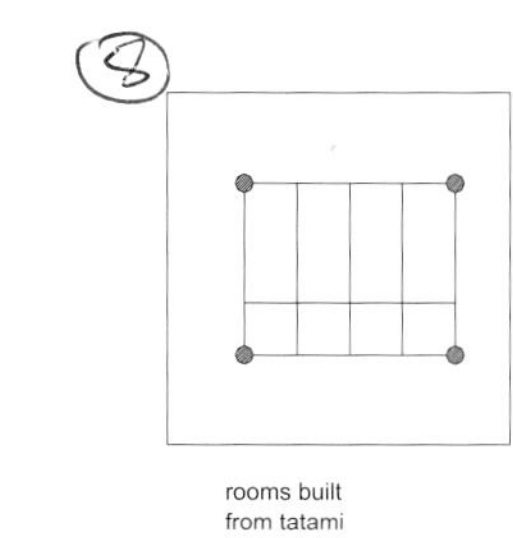

rooms built
from tatami

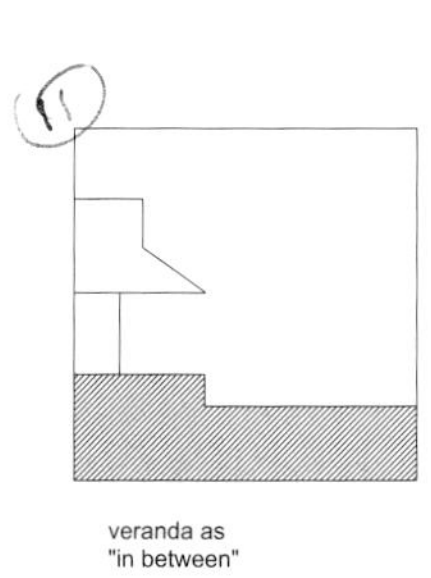

veranda as
"in between"

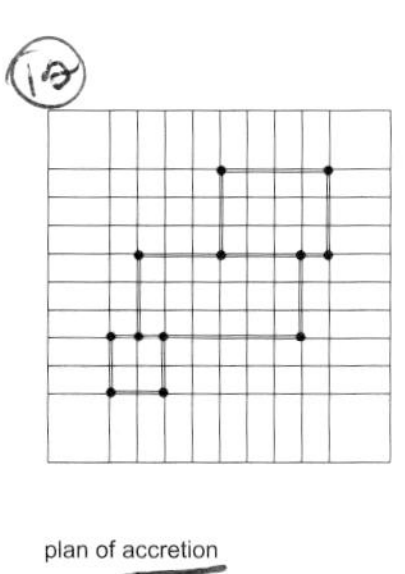

plan of accretion

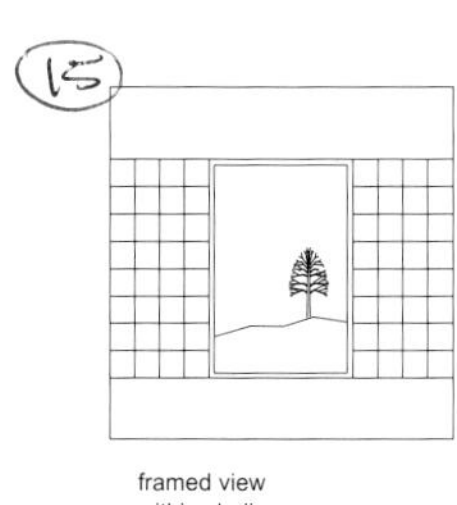

framed view
within shoji

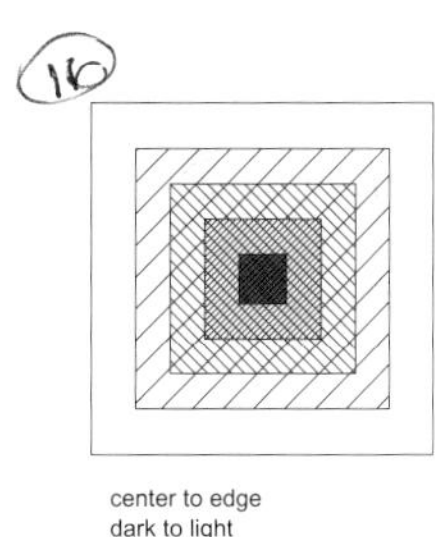

center to edge
dark to light

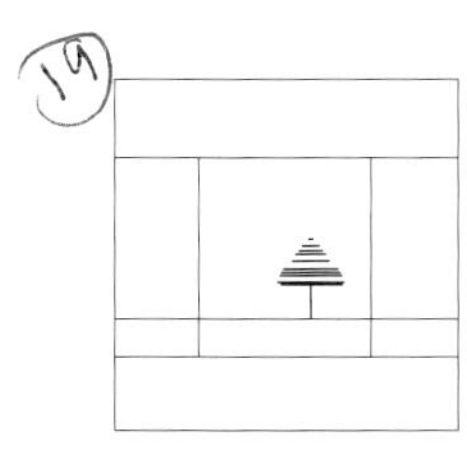

tokonoma
as representation
of nature

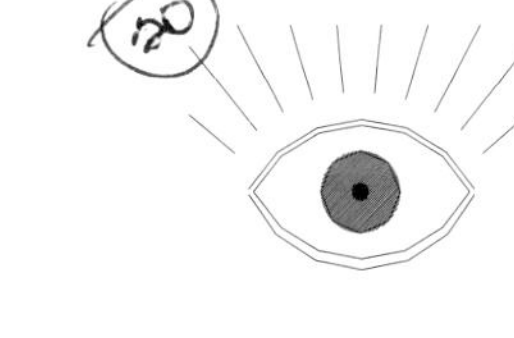

the mind's eye vs
perception

THE IDEALIZED
LANDSCAPE AFTER 1850
Seeing nature as mechanical process or as poetic image

Background

The modern world has divided in two our understanding of both natural and idealized landscapes. One of the ways contemporary people attempt to understand their natural surroundings is as poetic image that retains a transcendent core. The structure of our bodies and minds on which we base our understanding of our natural context has changed little over the 3 million years of our development as a species. We bring the same basic equipment to the task of understanding our natural surroundings as did our predecessors. The way we gather information with our senses and process it through a filter of human feeling probably remains much like that of people who came before us. The landscape continues to be as emotionally moving as it apparently always has been, albeit with different cultural interpretations. The culture of any particular place and time reconstructs the landscape to manifest different values, but the emotional root of thought that propels these interpretations remains unchanged.

01

People sense and interpret these values in their everyday contact with a natural context. The radiance of the sunrise, warmth of the day, smell of the rain, tenderness of a rose petal, power of rhythmic tides, and quiet of the forest probably move us much as they moved our forebears. People continue to construct a world of interpreted value from these common experiences that identifies what they think nature is.

What has changed since 1600 is the human perception of our natural circumstance due to science and technology. Modern science purports to lay bare the mechanical substructure of nature as technology harnesses the energies of the natural world for human convenience. Both have transformed human thought about the landscape. Science outlines the mechanical processes that formed the earth and gave rise

01 Central Park

to life. Quantum physics portrays the forms of the universe to be the result of infinitesimal particles. Biology traces the development of our planetary life forms from the first single-celled organism to human beings. Genetics has unlocked the code that provides directions for specific organisms and the mechanism for new species. All matter and energy are entwined in a dynamic equilibrium that serves as a guide for the development of all physical things in the universe. Quantum physics, biology, and genetics have created a penetrating and powerful lens into the underlying processes of the physical universe. People have never before achieved the empirical insight offered by this vision of nature.

Technology has come to manipulate these forces at a level without historic precedent. Fire began a parade of human inventions that altered natural circumstance to fit human need. These inventions accumulated slowly until 1750 when the industrial revolution initiated a rapid stream of new ways to manipulate our physical surroundings. Steam engines led to locomotives and internal combustion engines to automobiles. Water, then steam, then coal, then petroleum, then electricity powered new productive capacities. The size of the globe was reduced through ever-faster travel and communication. The natural environment remained the source of material and energy for these transformations that were asked to serve ever greater numbers of people. The result has been both a blessing and a cause of concern. If the natural environment that fuels these technologies is considered to have finite capacities, then the amount of energy and material it can be asked to produce is limited. The waste products of these technologies similarly challenge the capacity of the earth to process them in a manner that retains the conditions on earth necessary for the survival of our species.

Modern science, technology, production, consumption, and waste products are all tied together in a vision of the natural environment as ecology. Ecology stresses an understanding of nature as process. The natural landscape in this vision is like a very complex, highly interrelated machine. Each part of nature has developed over extended periods of time to fit with all the other parts. As each assumes a proper place within the whole, equilibrium is established that governs the capacity of the natural context to support any and all of its parts. This process is wonderfully complex and only partially understood. The problem with people is that they have the ability to willfully modify this. As they transform the natural environment to meet their own needs, these transformations may violate the equilibrium created by all other natural things. Nature does not look upon human beings as anything special. If our species violates the rule of nature in ways that upset the balance, nature may do away with us. The human capacity to self-consciously modify our natural surroundings may prove to be our undoing as a species.

These two visions of the natural landscape are not mutually exclusive, but they are very different. The first as poetic image enunciates a tactile understanding of our natural circumstance that gives birth to ideas of its cultural value. The second provides a more abstract and mechanical vision that stresses nature as a quantifiable process with systemic limits. Both provide a powerful base for developing a modern concept of idealized landscapes.

02

Pastoralism as a poetic image of the landscape

The idea that the landscape gives rise to cultural values is beautifully discribed by Leo Marx in his seminal work, *The Machine in the Garden.* Marx is interested in a literary definition of a symbolic relationship of people to their natural surroundings. He traces the history of a particular vision of this relationship from the Roman poet Virgil to our present day. Virgil characterizes the pastoral landscape in a conversation between two sheepherders. The first tended his flock peacefully in a field that was neither the city nor the wilderness. The second had lost his field and was in search of new pasture. As the two talk, it becomes clear that a satisfying human location within a natural context is dependant upon a permanent location that is neither the city nor the wilderness but exists between the two as a middle kingdom. A sheep pasture is not divorced from its natural setting but also does not represent a primitive life that is dependent on the vagaries of an unmodified nature. Herding promotes a participatory sense of the landscape rather than the more distant, intellectual, and abstract vision of nature created by the cultural city. Pastoralism represents a vision of a satisfying relationship of people to nature as lying midway between the poles of the artificial culture of the city and the dangers of the wilderness. It seeks an appropriate balance between cultural needs and the ecological capacities of the earth to support our existence. To find that balance is to be located within our natural circumstance in a manner that breeds human contentment. When this balance is reached, people find their biological and symbolic home in nature. They need no longer roam in search of a satisfying life. They find that satisfaction by reaching an accommodation with the natural landscape.

Pastoralism is a perennial theme in Western literature. Few eras of Western thought have failed to take up the issue of a satisfying way for people to belong in nature. Few have found a more consistently compelling answer to this question than that put forth by Virgil's sheepherder. The pastoral ideal seeks a human place in the natural landscape that is at peace with both human desires and the natural landscape. Fly fishing in the movie discussed in the last chapter, *A River Runs through It,* is a recent and compelling pastoral vision of the landscape.

02 Concert in Central Park

03 Machu Picchu
04 Temple in Machu Picchu
05 Opening to the landscape, Machu Picchu

This fascination with the less artificial relationship of the sheepherder to the natural landscape has shaped a good deal of the way in which Americans view the idealized landscape. Pastoralism looks to the simpler life of an agrarian era as a solution to the stresses of an industrial culture. In this vision of civilization is a sense of the felicity of the unspoiled landscape. It argues that art and industry are essentially artificial and that the simplicity of nature is preferred over the sophistication of the city and the culture that thrives there. In the United States, we have set aside large tracts of land as national and state parks to honor this ethic. Major development is prohibited in these refuges that hope to preserve samples of a natural landscape in the face of continuing industrial development and urbanization. City parks and boulevards do the same, albeit on more modest terms. The yards of our houses restate this ethic as do the cut flowers that we arrange in vases. All represent a kind of pastoralism: the emotive power of the landscape, nostalgia for the simple life as a sheepherder.

03

Machu Picchu

04

Machu Picchu is the ruin of a 15th-century Incan religious city constructed in the mountains of Peru. Unlike most Incan cities and temples, it was not destroyed by the Spanish conquistadores because a cunning Incan prince told them that the native people of Machu Picchu were dying of the plague. The Spanish invaders skipped plundering and destroying Machu Picchu in search of safer treasure. Today the ruin of this religious center for 500 people remains perched atop a 9,000-foot peak. It is surrounded by similar mountains creating a dramatic natural setting for this once-important Incan center.

The city was abandoned when the Incan empire fell to European invaders in the 16th century and was rediscovered by archeologists in the early 20th century. Today over a million people visit the ruin of this religious construction each year because of its sublimely beautiful natural setting. To heighten their experience of this ruin, many visitors walk for days along the old Inca Road that originally provided access to this site.

The importance of this site to an understanding of the modern idealized landscape is twofold. First, it exemplifies people's continuing search within the natural landscape for places of particular power as sites for significant rituals. People often reserve special natural settings for the ideas that mean the most to them. Machu Picchu was that for the Incas. Waterfalls, mountains, lakes, and forests provide much the same for the modern secular mind. People often select a particular place within the natural landscape that reaches within the human psyche to propel an idea of awe or

05

06

wellbeing. Such places have been venerated in literature and handed down through generations in stories about such places. In *Landscape and Memory,* Simon Schama claims that specific cultures have root definitions of this landscape that are integral to their cultural identity. Each of the definitions of a particular cultural landscape that shapes a peoples' corporate memory is rooted in particular characteristics of the physical landscape in which their societies developed. Settings like Machu Picchu seem to reverberate with all people. There is something compelling to all of us in natural settings that exhibit unusual characteristics. People seem to attach particular meanings to these natural structures. As they do, parts of the natural landscape become idealized.

The second is that Machu Picchu has become a destination for vacations rather than a setting for religious observances. Natural settings like Machu Picchu are now consumed as experiences by the modern traveler. We acquire these experiences as we acquire other goods. The natural landscape of the earth is fast disappearing under the pressures of population growth and industrialization. Few patches of the natural landscape capable of inspiring awe or feelings of wellbeing have avoided modern development. They are often set aside in remembrance of a landscape that was once more prevalent in our lives. We visit these landscapes as places in an attempt to reconnect with this past. The landscape of Machu Picchu represented a profound cosmic place to the Incas. Modern visitors to this site are awed by its natural beauty and entranced by ruins that testify to past occupation but are unable to comprehend this site in any other than the terms that tourism allows. In this sense, our era is a voyeur of once-significant idealized landscapes.

06 Dwelling, Machu Picchu
07 Entry walk to Woodland Cemetery
08 Crematorium
09 Walkway, cross, lawn, and woods

Woodland Cemetery

Woodland Cemetery was designed in the early 20th century by Erik Gunnar Asplund and Sigurd Lewerentz as a burial place that challenged the European conception of a cemetery as a city of the dead. Traditional American and European cemeteries line graves up along paths as houses might be arranged along streets in cities. This order of the dead is in stark contrast to the cemeteries of Buddhist monks in Japan. In these cemeteries, graves are scattered among trees in beautiful cedar forests. In these Japanese forest-cemeteries lies a much different sense of our place in the natural world. Instead of returning us in death to the civilized order of the city, these graves seem to return us to a more primitive sense of our origin. The forest is a place of organic process. It symbolizes nature's transcendent cyclic order of birth and death in contradistinction to artificially imposed cultural order. Organisms arise from the nutrients of the natural world, live briefly, and return to that world to become nutrients for new life. There is a sense of satisfaction in this cycle of life that transcends the limits of particular societies. It reminds people that we are part of a process that is larger than human histories.

07

08

Woodland Cemetery brings this Eastern sense of burial to 20th-century Western Europe. The cemetery is entered through an opening in a wall. A long, straight stone walkway brings visitors by a crematorium on one side and a grassy knoll on the other. Two-thirds of the way down this path a large, wooden cross looms against the grassy

09

10

knoll. The effect of this symbol of Christian belief against the lawn of the cemetery is dramatic. The cross seems to stand out against its landscape background in a way that would not be possible in a different context. The idealized landscape of the grassy lawn with trees in the distance is a reminder not of a church but of the Garden of Eden. It was this idealized mythological landscape that served as the original home of an unselfconscious people in Christian theology. The cross against the lawn of Woodland Cemetery reminds people of this origin.

The portico of the chapel that follows is a classical construction. The landscape is viewed from here as a framed, picturesque lawn brought within a constructed domain. The portico acts as all porches do: it places people between a constructed environment and an idealized landscape. In Woodland Cemetery, this portico is clearly a cultural rather than a natural construction.

The small chapel that follows its larger counterpart is nestled in the woods. The forest becomes more dominant in this setting as the cultural meaning of the building begins to recede in prominence. This second, small chapel is part classical and part vernacular design, but its relationship to the forest that surrounds it is less one of overlook and appropriation than it is one of nestling in a wood. The natural landscape is not a distant vision here but an immediate tactile presence. The small dome of this structure hollows out a tiny space from this natural context, but it is the landscape that has become dominant.

11

10 Portico of large chapel
11 Entry to small chapel
12 Front façade of small chapel
13 Looking out from portico of small chapel

12 

 13

This second chapel is followed by the forest itself with the headstones of graves scattered in the openings between trees. Here the space of human occupation is what the natural landscape allows as the forest becomes the primary structure of this environment. Headstones appear small in comparison to the towering tree trunks that provide their context. Headstones of graves mark cultural constructions as small, limited, and temporary in relation to the ongoing process of the natural landscape in this cemetery.

Perhaps this analysis of the progression from environments where human constructions are dominant to one where the organic structures of nature prevail over-intellectualizes the experience of Woodland Cemetery. Perhaps this analysis cannot access the emotions that attend such human experiences. While it is true that symbolic representations do not convey the actual richness of the territory that they purport to represent, it is also true that people continue to create such maps in an attempt to understand their own location within this territory. As a species, we are driven to not only experience our surroundings but to attempt to understand why they are meaningful to us. The organization of Woodland Cemetery from the stone wall that separates it from the city, to the forest that provides the final resting place of human remains, is able to support such an analysis because it is a compelling idealized landscape. This landscape makes the final act of life, our death, a palpable story. Death is a constituent part of every life. Burial mounds may have been the first architectural constructions of symbolic rather than of utilitarian significance. Woodland Cemetery continues this tradition. Its ideas resonate with 21st-century minds as the first burial mounds did with our forebears. The natural environment has always been our home. A return to that home seems to many to represent a satisfying conclusion to our lives.

14

The Kings Road house

The Kings Road house was designed and built in 1923 by Rudolf Schindler as a residence for two couples. Schindler and his wife occupied this house with a couple who were friends and business partners. Schindler migrated from Vienna to Chicago in the early 20th century to work with Frank Lloyd Wright. Later, he moved to California to begin his own practice. His architectural interests were guided by a faith that the outdoors provided a healthy context for our lives. His contention was that houses should reflect this link of human wellbeing to direct contact with natural surroundings.

The Kings Road house is designed to manifest this philosophy. It is not a conventional house but rather a set of rooms, one for each occupant. Each of these rooms was a complete place to live in and reflected the individual interests and propensities of its occupants. Common rituals like cooking and eating were conducted in the house's shared space. Each room had a fireplace, a corner sitting area, and a work space that was connected to an adjacent garden area with the Schindler Frame. The Schindler Frame recognized two critical elevations of a room. The first is that of the ceiling. The second is door height. The second of these frames creates both the intimacy of the

14 Kings Road House
15 Schindler's room
16 Sleeping loft on roof
17 Plan of the Kings Road House

corner sitting areas of living rooms and passage from the interior of the room to the garden beyond. The back side of each of these rooms, the side that does not face the garden, is constructed of tilt-up concrete panels. These panels were formed on the ground and then rotated into place once the concrete had cured. The residue of this process is found in the glazed slits between each of these panels that represent a formal memory of board forms for panels that lay side-by-side on the ground. These concrete backs of rooms are as opaque to the outside world as their open Schindler Frame fronts are transparent to the garden. The room floor at the same level as the garden outside reinforces the strength of the partnership of room and garden stated by the Schindler Frame.

15

The enclosed room represents only half the space of each Kings Road living room. The shared garden contained by the rooms of the house completes each of these spaces. Together, this configuration creates two shared courtyards. As in other houses of this typology, outdoor space is captured at the heart rather than at the edge of a domain. Its position at the center of the domain gives this outdoor space a special position in the Kings Road house. The garden is no longer a vehicle to separate residences one from the other, as in conventional houses, but has become the symbolic as well as physical center of the house. This linkage between landscape and dwelling is extended by sleeping spaces located on the roof of the house in a minimal shelter. Attaching our lives to the night sky is as important in this house as attaching our lives to the daylit landscape of terrain, plants, and animals.

16

The Kings Road house represents a long-standing American interest in pairing our homes with an idealized landscape. We are not a very urban people. Our mythology centers more often on the goodness of the natural landscape than it does on the cultural value of cities. Our urge to live in suburbs manifests this value. The Schindler

17

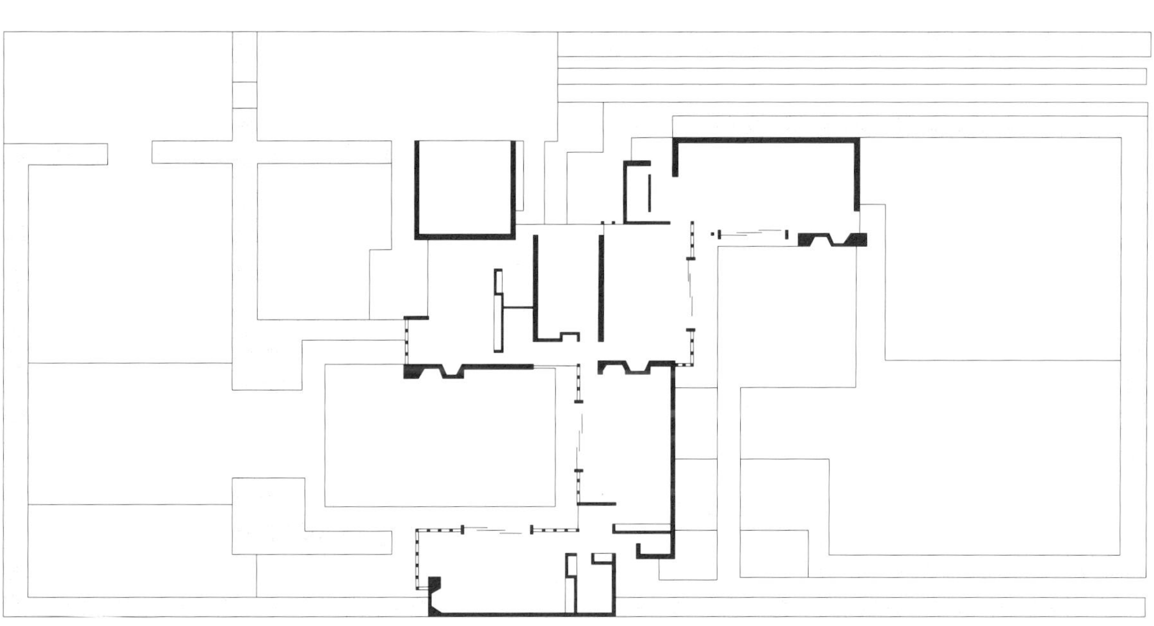

18

18 Tilt up concrete panels
19 Garden
20 Interior skylight and Schindler Frame

House exemplifies this ethic through the power of the formal mechanisms it employs to incorporate the idealized landscape within the structure of the house. Poured concrete walls enclose space from its urban surround. Fireplaces center these rooms with a return to the values attached to this atavistic technology. The space within each room is wedded to the garden space that it faces, because the Schindler Frame, partnered with a continuous floor level, suggests unimpeded passage from one to the other. To sleep on the roof is to be directly connected to the night sky, moon, and stars.

Many contemporary residential designs point in a direction that is similar to that identified in the Schindler house. Few are able to unite the idealized landscape with a residence in as pure, thoughtful, and carefully developed a way as is accomplished in this design. Conventional houses represent compromises with social values that Schindler chose not to observe. A family unit as a group of individual rooms centered by gardens does little to engage even the most independent of contemporary family lifestyles. This intentional disregard of social convention focuses the ideas promoted in this design on its connection to the idealized landscape. In this house, we are part of the natural landscape before we are a part of a social group. Our rooted wellbeing as animals depends upon recognizing our origin and personal need to recall our place within nature. The garden is our population's modern vision of a more primal state. It should center our homes as an intuitive sense of the value of the natural landscape has always centered our existence.

19

Central Park

Portuguese architect Gonçalo Byrne contends that the life of cities is to be found in their voids. This sense of the importance of the public life of cities is not conveyed in buildings, that dominantly represent private use, but in the spaces between buildings that represent the common ground of a people.

Central Park in New York is the most significant urban idealized landscape in the United States. Designer Fredrick Law Olmstead was America's most prominent 19th-century landscape architect. New York City is the symbol of American urban vitality as well as the largest city in the country. To set aside the entire midsection of Manhattan in 1860 as the center of an emerging country's largest metropolis was an act of modern city planning hubris.

Central Park spans four Manhattan avenues and is 55 blocks long. Its 840 acres is more than double the size of Hyde Park in London (360 acres) or Grant Park in Chicago (303 acres), though it is a bit smaller than the 1,107-acre Golden Gate Park in San Francisco. Olmstead toured English Parks before designing Central Park, and its design reflects this influence. As in early English parks, Central Park was intended to raise moral standards of an urban populace. The working poor of the city were thought to be untrained in conduct that to upper classes represented civilized behavior. The values that these masses pretended to were not the more gentile attitudes about nature that a newly developed American mercantile class borrowed from their aristocratic predecessors. English romantic poets and American essayists echoed the common 19th-century theme that the city was a place of moral degradation while the natural landscape had the power to rekindle healthier ethical structures of an earlier agrarian age.

There is something for everyone in Central Park. There is a zoo and a major art museum, the Metropolitan. There are walking paths of every description and bridle paths for horses. There are places to play all sorts of games and places to sit and talk or to just watch people pass by. There are meadows, forests, and lakes. A large reservoir helps provide the water while urban roads that connect the city on either side of the park are depressed.

21

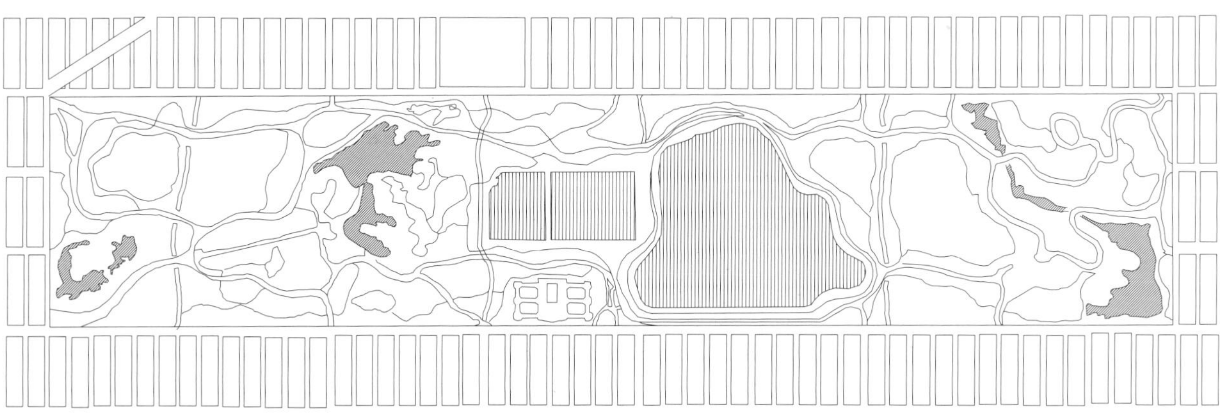

22

Central Park is the English romantic vision of the idealized landscape brought to the heart of a city. As befits the conception of the industrial city in an emerging democracy, the objective of this park was to fulfill the recreational needs of the common person. All who lived in Manhattan and provided the labor for this quickly growing manufacturing center had access to this enormous public recreational area. The squalor of tenement living conditions in New York (outhouses for multiunit housing for workers extended well into the 20th century) was in small measure ameliorated by this green open space. Central Park provided relief from summer heat, relief from oppressive living conditions, and relief from being poor. It has become the symbol not only of the egalitarian vision that propels American cities but of the importance Americans place on the idealized landscape as balance to the stress of urban culture.

But this vision of goodness is not without its problems. In Nathaniel Hawthorne's *Sleepy Hollow,* Marx outlines the problem of this view. As a poet sits overlooking a quiet, pastoral valley listening to the beautiful songs of birds and examining the activity of ants, his reverie is interrupted by the shriek of a locomotive whistle in the distance. The machine bursts into the natural landscape. Tension replaces repose and

21 Plan of Central Park
22 Central Park

23

24

tranquility. The pastoral landscape is forced to accept the invasion of machines because they are the foundation of our culture. The landscape will never again be the same after this invasion. People can look for isolated places where they can enjoy the gifts of the idealized landscape but that landscape will become the exception rather than the rule. The history of Western culture is the history of its technological development. These technologies do not sit comfortably beside the idealized landscape because they view nature to be a resource for production rather than as transcendent poetic value. History has given up the idealized landscape for technological progress. The landscapes that we produce now hearken back to a time of simpler pleasures.

25

26

Ecological visions of the idealized landscape

To ecologists, nature is not simply a passive receptacle for poetic development. It has its own way of doing things and its own rules. To break those rules is to risk nature's wrath. Ian McHarg gives voice to this understanding of the landscape in *Sea and Survival.* This story is a short morality play dressed in professional clothing. Its main actors are an intelligent nature that produces sand dunes as an effective way to combat the power of ocean waves that erode the seashore and human beings who are ignorant of the elegance of these natural systems. The land of the seashore is protected from ocean storms by a series of three ranks of sand dunes. The first is held in place by vegetation that is very sensitive to human development. The second set of dunes is a bit hardier and the third is hardier still. Together, they form a complex defense against ocean waves that gives as these waves crash into them rather than attempting to maintain a rigid boundary in the face of the power of this water. The Dutch learned this lesson when they first attempted to hold back the sea. Their first dikes were rigid and soon broke under the relentless attack of waves. Their second attempt was patterned on sand dunes. They were constructed of material that deformed but did not break as waves crashed against it. When people build vacation homes on the ocean, they choose primary sand dunes as building sites because this land directly overlooks the ocean. Unfortunately, they are building structures on terrain that is very sensitive to development. The houses kill the vegetation that once grew on primary dunes and with it the root structure that once held the dunes together. All is well until a hurricane drives the ocean into the land with a force that the weakened dune is no longer able to withstand. As the primary dune erodes, the foundations of the vacation houses go with it. The natural system of dunes as flexible barriers to waves, undermined by the ignorant actions of human development, allows nature to wipe the human slate clean. Such will be our fate on a much larger scale, warns this tale, if we do not observe the process and limits of the natural world when we build within it.

23 Central Park
24 Nature in the city
25 Lake in Central Park
26 Ouroboros

27

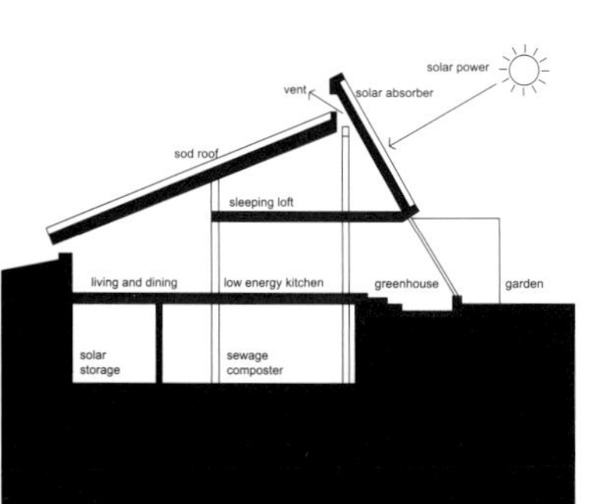

28

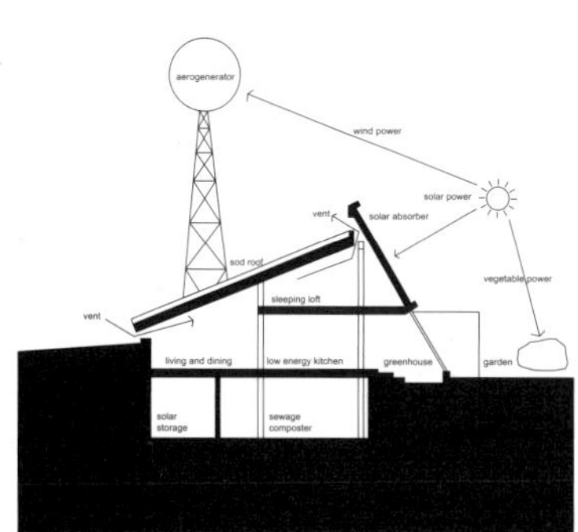

29

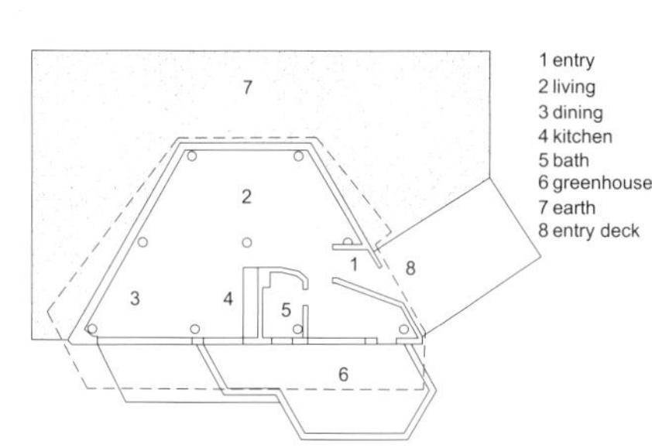

This play does not see the tension between the technologies of civilization and the requirements of nature to be incompatible. Rather, it sees the need to develop human technologies within the intelligence of existing natural systems. What matters most is natural process. That process is seen as complex, intertwined, and the base of human sustenance. To damage it is to damage nature's ability to provide for us. When houses are built on the vulnerable portions of sand dunes, people suffer just retribution for their ignorance of the elegance of the natural processes that have sustained the earth for billions of years.

A politically engineered oil shortage in the early 1970s presented this idea of resource limits dramatically to the industrialized world. As the Middle East withheld a portion of its large petroleum output, countries that depended on this oil staggered under the shortages. Long lines of private automobiles formed at gas stations, the cost of flying went up, and energy for industrial production and to heat buildings became expensive. This tremor in the central energy supply of industrial countries shook their confidence. Conservation of energy supplies became a political issue overnight.

A broad ecological commentary emerged in this era. Garrett Hardin's *The Tragedy of the Commons* repeated McHarg's message in broader and more critical terms. In this tale, farmers maintain only the number of cattle in their herds that can graze a common pasture without damaging its capacity to renew itself. Then a farmer with more daughters than sons decides to increase his herd size to prepare for his daughters' dowries. The action of this single farmer has no impact on the viability of the common pasture, but it gives birth to an attitude among other farmers that larger herds would be individually beneficial. All the farmers using the pasture decide to increase the size of their herds because their neighbor did. The result is too many cattle grazing on the pasture. The land is no longer able to regenerate itself. The grasses die off and with them goes the food for the cattle. The cattle die of starvation leaving their human masters in an equally precarious position. The action of an individual, not harmful to the environment in itself, has led to a breakdown of cultural controls. The result is the same retribution that the sea took on the vacation houses that weaken the dunes.

30

Barry Commoner summarized many of these contentions in *Closing Circle* with these four rules of human conduct to preserve the capacity of natural systems to maintain human beings: "everything is connected to everything else; everything must go somewhere; there is no free lunch; and nature knows best."

These elegant little sentences written in everyday language outlined a new societal attitude toward the natural environment. The era of exploiting this environment independent of consequences came to an end with these statements. The first recognizes nature as an intricate system of interdependencies that have developed over the 3 billion years of life on the planet. Commoner compares human intervention in these systems to a blind man plunging a screwdriver into the mechanism of a fine watch in hopes of fixing it. The 6 billion plus people of the earth who now consume resources all produce waste products that must be processed by the biosphere. Ozone holes in our atmosphere that admit radiation and endanger reproduction are apt testimony that these systems have limits that human development can violate. Societies have treated the natural environment as a limitless system for thousands of years because their numbers and demands on this environment were trivial. Industrialization and population growth altered this relationship dramatically. We can no longer treat the environment as a "free lunch" because each human action in our contemporary ecological situation has a consequence much as in Hardin's cattle on common grassland. And finally, natural systems have developed over extended periods of time independent of human intervention. We are the animal with both the desire and the capacity to alter these systems in major ways. In these capacities lies both what makes us most human and what threatens the capacity of the natural environment to support us. Nature has developed her systems over the history of the universe. Human beings are but the most recent of nature's experiments. Should we violate the intelligence that nature has developed over her history, our fate might well be that of *The Sea and Survival* or *The Tragedy of the Commons.*

There is good reason for architecture to take note of this process-oriented vision of the idealized landscape. Buildings in the U.S. account for over 30% of our total energy use and transportation for another 25%. Both are dependent on the way we construct our environment. Nearly 60% of our energy use is consumed by the technologies of the constructed environment. The question is whether or not the earth can sustain this level of use or, as in the weakened sand dune, we will be swept away by the natural systems that our level and kind of constructions violate.

27 Section with solar collectors
28 Section of energy production and distribution
29 Ouroboros plan
30 Ouroboros, north façade

31

Ouroboros

Ouroboros was a university research project of the mid 1960s. It was small house in the woods that was designed and constructed to explore an ethic of cooperation rather than confrontation of buildings with the natural environment. Its technical systems were intended to make this house self-sufficient. Solar panels provided heat and hot water; a windmill generated a small amount of electricity; the house had its own water well; and toilets were aerobic, a waste-disposal system that required only bacteria to naturally turn solid waste products into rich black soil. This research house was named after a mythical serpent that consumed itself by eating its own tail, unaware that its own life was at stake. Its goal was to create a building that prospered within natural systems and their limits by using only renewable energies rather than petroleum. It is estimated that in 120 years the industrial world will consume roughly 80% of petroleum stores that required 600 million years to form. Some estimates indicate that world petroleum production is scheduled to peak between 2010 and 2020. Either the industrial world discovers another source of energy and better mitigation strategies for the pollution that consumption of this amount of petroleum entails, or our species is in for a rude awakening.

The renewable energy systems of Ouroboros outline a construction strategy that is intended to cope with these environmental problems through the use of renewable energy systems. Every day the sun brings the earth enormous amounts of energy. All other living things on the earth have learned to operate within the limits imposed by this daily solar ration of energy. It may be stored in crops for later use, but the annual energy balance of living things other than human beings is zero. An ecological idealized landscape requires the same balance for human construction.

A great deal of progress has been made in this area in architecture since the 1960s. Many states in the U.S. have instituted energy codes to reduce excess energy use in buildings. Some European countries have instituted more aggressive conservation policies for buildings. Programs to reduce the energy use in both public and private buildings are common. New technological approaches to these problems appear annually. But the vast majority of construction in industrial countries continues to take place as if the supportive natural systems are limitless. An environmental ethic in architecture exists but is not powerful enough to cope with economic forces and cultural attitudes to make differences on the scale necessary to assure that individual buildings do not become a tragedy of our common natural environment.

32

Closing thoughts

The first of our visions of the idealized landscape as poetic image is a heritage of an extended past. People have always recognized a grandeur and elegance in the natural landscape that falls beyond human creative capacities. There is both a joy and a fear inherent in this recognition. Only a self-conscious organism like humans is capable of recognizing and valuing nature's creations in other than survival terms because our cerebral cortex allows us to symbolically represent the world around us. Symbols allow literal experience to be understood as abstraction. Abstractions give birth to a world of ideas as a partner to an empirical natural context. Machu Picchu, Woodland Cemetery, Central Park, and Kings Road house all give voice to architecture's ability to treat the natural landscape as symbolic ideas. Each of these treatments gives birth to a different kind of architectural idea about the poetic value of the landscape in our lives. This tradition is carried on in our daily lives as we tend our lawns, meet in public squares and parks, or travel to natural sites for vacations.

The second contemporary view of the idealized landscape as ecological system is based on how people have come to scientifically understand the natural landscape. It is a mechanical vision of this landscape that predicts empirical consequences of our development of buildings. No one knows if these predictions are accurate; but if they are, the consequences of ignoring them are dramatic. Our species cannot afford to ignore the early warning signs in waterways, air, and atmosphere that something has gone awry. If ecological predictions of the consequences of current resource consumption and waste production are right even in part, our progeny will face the dire consequences of our own environmental hubris.

What these two very different architectural visions of an idealized landscape have in common is an assumption that the natural landscape is an integral component of the design of buildings. Whether this intimate relationship is expressed as poetic vision or as resource-conscious development is less important than is the recognition that the natural landscape is and has always been the context for buildings. The ways people choose to manipulate that context are little different from the ways they choose to build buildings. In this sense, context is not background but active ingredient in design thought. To make a building is to make a site for that building. To make a site is to remake the natural landscape. To remake the natural landscape is to give birth to a symbolic landscape that manifests human ideals.

31 Ouroboros in the winter
32 Ouroboros entry

THE DIFFERENCES
THAT ARCHITECTURE MAKES

Twenty buildings, five symbols and an infinite array of habitational ideas

These 20 buildings begin to outline the breadth, depth, and richness of the ideas that architecture might be interpreted to suggest about people, their values, and their context. This attenuated library of architectural thought is the dual outcome of both the human propensity to construct and inhabit places of significance and an equally natural and compelling desire to understand the significance of what we construct. This cycle of creation and interpretation permeates all architectural production. There exist few boundaries in this speculation because the central problems of habitation appear to exist for all people in all eras and cultures. In this sense, Dogon domains are not distant African artifacts that make little difference to us but rather a mirror for our own cultural constructions. Do we invest our buildings with as rich a set of symbolic values as do the Dogon? The Parthenon is not simply an intellectual idea excavated from Classical Greece but a structure that deserves continued architectural admiration because it poses perennial questions about the problem of architectural order. The cathedral at Chartres continues to ask if the industrial technologies of today's buildings are meaningful enough to fulfill all our needs to understand the natural forces that they redirect. Finally, Katsura Imperial Villa remains not only a beautiful garden but also a vehicle to question Western versus Eastern views of reality. This is neither a limited nor an irrelevant set of issues for contemporary people. Canonic architectural environments remind us that thoughtful people have always struggled with the meaning of the places they have constructed to inhabit.

01 Dogon village

Certainly, some of the conditions that create these meanings have changed over time. The 20th century, in fact, may have constituted a break with the past of such a

02

degree and profundity as to be declared a new age. But history was not swept aside by these changes; new architectural concerns were simply added to an older base of thought. A Dogon village, the Parthenon, the cathedral at Chartres, and Katsura Imperial Villa remain vivid and meaningful standards of architectural thought because each eloquently says something about our need to belong with one another in nature in the places that we construct. It is the quality of constructed architectural ideas that preserves them in architectural thought. This quality is neither diminished nor rendered obsolete by time. If anything, the power of these and like buildings needs to grow in architectural thought today as technology makes it progressively more difficult to differentiate between what is possible to construct versus what is insightful about constructions.

Post-1850 buildings do not take second place to these historic exemplars as modes of architectural thought. These attempts to understand and make pronouncements about the architectural issues and values of a modern era are as interesting as the canonic designs they follow. Contemporary architecture continues to attempt to understand how domains reflect our values. Villa Mairea rightfully asks if we might disregard our cultural histories with impunity. Sea Ranch convincingly reminds us that as the conditions around us change, our bodies and associations with how we are tangibly located in buildings do not. Our battle to retain individual personalities in the midst of the bureaucracies of the modern world is placed provocatively before us by Central Beheer. What does or should center our communities is questioned by Southdale Shopping Center. Issues of order, technology, and the idealized environ-

02 The Parthenon
03 Chartres Cathedral
04 Katsura Imperial Villa

ment are no different. Each of the contemporary buildings in these categories restates the need of buildings to allow meaning to emerge from pattern, to create symbolic forms that redirect natural forces, and to rearrange the natural landscape to become what we think that nature ought to be.

03

These contemporary buildings and the questions they ask are not solely about rarified buildings that command critical attention. They are ideas that affect each of us every day in the places we live, work, and recreate. Great buildings provide clues to what we value in our everyday lives. Few of us would want to live in Villa Savoye or the German Pavilion in Barcelona, but the intellectual craft of these buildings reverberates in the best of current design. Conversely, clues for great architecture also exist in the buildings we inhabit every day. What better way to try and understand what matters to people than to look in the places they mold to reflect personal and corporate values?

The best of our everyday environments are not imitations or even reinterpretations of the canonic environments whose architectural values they echo. They ask, rather, the same questions as do their more illustrious predecessors. Our domains ask how buildings might represent not our most shallow but our most profound concerns. Contemporary examples of architectural order ask what kinds of meaning we might expect to emerge from the complex patterns that typify the modern experience. Technology asks if we should continue to push back the boundaries of the possible with modern construction techniques or perhaps look to ecological economy as a better guide for designing contemporary buildings. Modern landscapes ask if we are just as given to being in nature as we have always been, or if this desire to be in idealized on landscape is nostalgia for a disappearing cultural era.

These and similar questions are not always thought to be of parallel importance to architecture. Different forms of analysis have different architectural objectives. Each takes up different kinds of architectural issues in hopes of revealing something special about the places people create to inhabit. These viewpoints are part of a kaleidoscope of issues and ideas that represent the complex form of thought called architecture. They arise because so many facets of the constructed environment are important to us in so many ways.

04

Comparative understanding

One of the ways people grasp meaning in architecture is through difference. If they can identify differences between two environments then what each represents becomes clearer. The comparisons that can be made between and among buildings of this study are infinite. All good design in architecture promotes comparison with other good buildings as a means to ascertain their value.

05

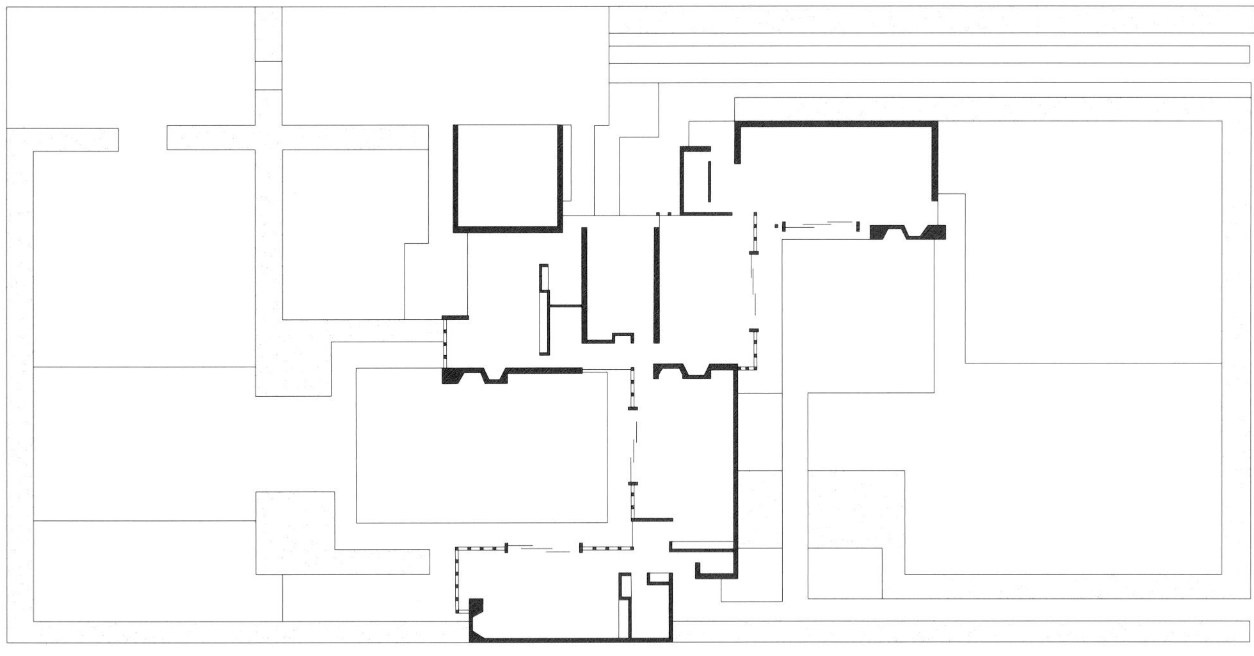

06

Idealized landscapes, Villa Savoye, and the Kings Road house

Villa Savoye and the Kings Road house were constructed within 10 years of one another. Both were by architects educated in Europe. Both treat the meaning of the idealized landscape in a house but to much different ends. In Villa Savoye, the landscape is represented by a series of intellectual abstractions. The earth flows up a ramp first to a living floor and then to a roof garden above as an unbroken surface. The new ground as garden of the house's living floor is bounded by a wall with a continuous horizontal slit window that represents the natural horizon. In Villa Savoye, a new abstract earth is bounded by a new abstract horizon to become an intellectualized idealized landscape in the courtyards they create. The garden of the Kings Road house is a palpable and intimate partner of each room that it adjoins. Gardens are tilled from the earth and contain arranged plants. The connection between the interior of rooms and gardens is direct as architecturally spelled out by the Schindler Frame and continuity of floor and earth.

Nature in Villa Savoye is a matter of cerebral symbols; in the Kings Road House, it is of sensual experience. Both ways of understanding nature are common to all of us. Although quite different visions of the same phenomena, our modern minds have little trouble understanding nature as physics calculations or nature as a walk in the forest. Is the center of a contemporary architectural understanding of nature to be found in the cerebral abstractions of Villa Savoye or in the sensually driven emotions of the Kings Road house?

05 Main courtyard of Villa Savoye
06 Plan of the Kings Road House

07

Domain, Dogon, and Central Beheer

It may be unfair to consider domain in architecture by comparing buildings of different eras and cultures, but it also may also prove instructive. The myth of origin is the cultural foundation of the Dogon that gives form to their compounds. This rich and poetic myth is manifested in the construction of Dogon domains to constantly remind people of its significance in their lives. It is a myth that defines all history, all knowledge, and ways to understand and value human experience. By contrast, the domain of Central Beheer is formal, scientific, and methodical. Column placement creates streets, streets create corners of territory, and corners of territory might be furnished to reflect the values of individuals who occupy them.

In Central Beheer, geometry replaces Dogon myth as the substructure of domain. Perhaps this comparison encapsulates the modern problem of finding a sense of authenticity in our designed environments. The modern world emphasizes the rights of the individual over those of the group and the place of scientific reason over more poetic and emotionally satisfying myths of creation. Have we become prisoners of our own intellectual progress? Modern people seek a satisfying sense of domain in their cities but are frequently reduced to the calculated logic of streets and individual territories to hold them together. We are alone in our cities because we intend to be. Our sense of community is premised less on common values than on self-interest. The rigorous formal logic of the domains of Central Beheer in comparison with the poetically rich domains of the Dogon could not make this clearer.

08

Technology, Katsura, Centre Pompidou, and Phillips Exeter Library

The structural frame of a Katsura teahouse, the unapologetically mechanical frame of Centre Pompidou, and the exterior walls of Phillips Exeter Library seem to have little in common. One is wood lashed together with rope; the second is stainless steel tubes connected by iron joints; and the third is brick. What might such different materials applied to such different ends have in common?

The lashed wooden supports of a Japanese teahouse roof display the elegant order of gravity as progressively larger-diameter elements span larger distances to transfer progressively greater loads to supporting members. The lashed joints of this structure record this transfer of weight from smaller to larger member until the whole space is spanned. In many ways, this joint differs little from the scaffolding that supports Centre Pompidou. Here rope has been transformed into cast iron and wooden spanning members into stainless steel tubes, but there is a common elegance with which each system traces the way it brings gravitational forces to the earth. The brick exterior of Phillips Exeter Library records the same elegant transfer of loads in the spring line of the brick arch that spans progressively wider openings as the wall rises and creates columns of diminishing width as they carry progressively lighter loads.

The commonality in these three structural systems lies not in their construction material but in their attention to joints. Joints are where architecture records a shift from one thing to another. A joint that redirects gravity is always asked to respond to the kinds of loads it transfers and the way it does so. A Katsura teahouse roof, the frame of Pompidou, and Phillips Exeter's exterior brick wall all accomplish this transfer with an ingenuity that becomes beautiful in its thoughtfulness. It is this understanding of the obligation of a structural joint that these three buildings hold in common.

09

10

11

07 Dogon granary door
08 Corner offices of Central Beheer
09 Underside of teahouse roof
10 Centre Pompidou, structural detail
11 Wall of Exeter Library

The order of natural light in Casa Barragán and the Robie House

Casa Barragán and the Robie House both use natural light to create order. At first glance, these two uses of sunlight appear to have much in common. Both create openings specific to particular rooms. Natural light in both houses is central to the character of rooms. Both create memorable luminescent spaces. But beneath these similarities lie major differences in the goals of their respective use of light. In the Robie House, this light is central to the geometric order of the house. Just as the ceiling is raised along the axis of the living and dining rooms, so the rhythmic openings of French doors along one side create cross axes of light. The windows and glazed doors at the ends of these rooms extend the lineal axes of this raised ceiling. The higher windows on the side of the room opposite the French doors suggest that the larger French door openings constitute the front of these rooms. The use of light in the Robie house is formal. It extends and clarifies other formal compositions of this house that give it order.

The use of sunlight in Casa Barragán is much different. No two windows are the same. They never reinforce a larger spatial logic. Each window is what it is because it shapes the way an occupant feels. The living room window is larger than it should be to give a feeling of expansiveness that exists nowhere else in the house. The dining room window holds occupants within the room at hip level while bringing a portion of the garden inside. The individual dining room is lit by a eye-level window that contains occupants securely in this space with an opaque wall and at the same time

12

allows the sky instead of the garden to enter. Every window of this house locates an individual imagination in a special way. Their light is about ideas that people attach to particular openings in relation to particular spaces. The order of the rooms created by this light is serial. The light of the preceding room defines the light of the present room just as that present experience will help define the meaning of light in the next space. Order here is not formal but is housed in a human consciousness that remembers, compares, and projects.

This list of comparisons is endless. It continues in refreshing new insights gained from likely comparisons and in surprising junctures forged by making less likely comparisons of buildings. It is the mode of thought that critics employ to decipher messages interpreted from great buildings and the method most of use to discriminate among our everyday environmental experiences.

12 Casa Barragán living room window
13 Robie House living room

People as the subject of architecture

These comparisons would be empty if people did not stand at the heart of them. Architecture seeks to understand who we are and how we are emotionally, intellectually, and spiritually located in the world. It is about us. No floor, no matter how elegant a construction, calls out to be interpreted. No frame suggests its own meaning. No opening becomes significant in architecture without us. Each of these constructions becomes meaningful only in relation to the thoughts, needs, and desires of people who live in and think about them. Architecture could not be differentiated from a fine painting, an elegant camera, or the Golden Gate Bridge if it were to lose habitation as its central issue. Our habitational values only become real when they are presented to us in things that we create. The objective form of buildings is wedded to the subjective search for human meaning through interpretation of the human significance of these forms.

Our ability to belong in nature with each other constitutes a specific view of this problem of habitation. It suggests that architecture is first a social art. This does not mean that architecture is a subcategory of sociology or anthropology but rather that finding our physical and symbolic place in the world is a central condition of human identity. We do not choose to live alone. We group in families, tribes, and nations in an attempt to forge a common understanding of ourselves, our species, and our surroundings. We group to find satisfaction in our own being. Expressions of this search extend in an unbroken line from the original pit house of our ancestors to the suburban shopping center. Architecture both today and in ancient times struggles with the same issue of symbolically satisfying location.

Similarly, we need to belong in nature. Nature has been objectified by modern science but that is not how we as individual human beings inhabit it. We are not likely to sit with a loved one watching a beautiful sunset and comment that we are seeing 4-7 micron wavelength light that is 8 minutes old. These are ways that we understand nature as quantifiable abstractions, not as human events. Marveling at sunsets and a host of other familiar responses to our natural context are the ways we are in nature as sensing, feeling, and interpreting animals. We organize the events of nature in our minds much as we organize our social and cultural values. As we form mental constructs that allow us to belong with one another in buildings, so our buildings form a web of ideas that make nature a place in which we might belong.

These subjective virtues of architecture are present in all the buildings. Each expresses a different idea about belonging in nature with each other as its tangible forms promote different interpretations about how and why this act of belonging might take place. In this regard, there is little difference between the construction of a Dogon granary and the Parthenon, between the courtyards of Villa Savoye and the garden of the Kings Road house, between the walls of Phillips Exeter Library and the frame of Centre Pompidou. All render a subjective vision of how architectural form explains the human significance of culture and nature.

14 The Zócalo in Oaxaca, Mexico

More than compositional image

15

16

What is clear from this interpretation of architecture's purpose is that building design is much more than a matter of compositional skill. Buildings are often presented in media as staged photographs that dramatize the visual forms of buildings to the exclusion of all else. There are no domains in these photographs because they rarely show people in them. There are no issues of order because a photograph is necessarily a small fragment of the building. Technology is reduced to another visual object. The idealized landscape is similarly reduced to pretty images of plants and terrain. A reasonable person paging through most architectural publications would justifiably conclude that architectural design is primarily concerned with the artful composition of form.

Beneath the image of a well-designed building, however, lies so much more. People do not think that the Sea Ranch condominiums are intrinsically beautiful. Beauty emanates from the care this building takes with the site it occupies and the well-wrought places it creates for people to occupy. The idea of order put forth in the forms of the Phillips Exeter Library is certainly more meaningful than pretty. The image of Centre Pompidou may be disconcerting, but the beauty of its sand-cast joints, articulate structure, and powerful elucidation of exposed mechanical systems allows this design to be considered in the same aesthetic terms as an elegant suspension bridge or a 12-meter yacht. Translating Woodland Cemetery into a simple visual image of a well-kept forest would demean the sense of our own death. Beauty emerges from the ideas of place, meaning, building craft, and ritual put forth by these buildings. This beauty is not independent of the insightfulness with which these structures take up issues of domain, order, technology, and the idealized landscape. Beauty in architecture emerges from insightful interpretations of these issues proposed in well-wrought form.

Our contemporary dependence on image in architecture parallels that of the rest of our culture. Television and advertising have made us aware of rapid-fire images as the content of messages. But few of us would be content to live in a television sitcom or see the values of our own lives as an advertisement. We expect more of our constructed environment. We expect it to represent and respond to us in ways that extend well below the surface of images. We expect it to contain us with our values, to present patterns that we find meaningful, to create symbolic form that redirects natural force, and to present the natural landscape of our imagination. These are the underlying benefits of great architectural design.

Architecture is, by nature, a positive pursuit

In the final analysis, architectural ideas stand out against much contemporary thought because they intrinsically promote a positive vision of the human condition. Much of contemporary philosophy, literature, art, and media have focused on the intractable problems faced by modern people. They often paint pictures of displacement, confusion, and anxiety. There is good reason to assume this intellectual stance. The Industrial Revolution and its accompanying changes profoundly affected the way people view their own lives and place in society. But there is another vision of the human condition not enunciated by the despair and alienation so common in modern thought. People continue to be born, love one another, form families, build houses, and be members of a community. They appear to be as enamored of their ability to create things as they have always been. Each of us continues to search for significance in our own lives much as people have always done. In these transcendent conditions of humanity lies a rich base for the buildings we construct to represent our values. While some of these buildings represent these aspirations in more superficial terms than others, the people of the world seem to be compelled to continue to create domains that are truly significant to them. Good architecture is an intimate reflection of what people value most — architecture is, by nature, a positive pursuit. The resources and energy required to create buildings assures that we take them more seriously than more temporary ventures. The best of our buildings represents what we hold most dear.

18

17

15 Sea Ranch bed atop interior tower
16 Study carrel of Exeter Library
17 Centre Pompidou front façade
18 Woodland Cemetery gravesites

Domain, Order, Technology, and the Idealized Landscape

	domain	order	technology	idealized nature
dogon domain				
pantheon order				
chartres technology				
katsura idealized nature				
order in the landscape order in the landscape				

INDEX
OF IMAGES

Chapter 1

Chapter 2

Chapter 3

Chapter 4

Chapter 5

01 Lance LaVine (p. 89)
02 Simon Beeson (p. 91)
03 Benjamin Ibarra (p. 91)
04 Simon Beeson (p. 91)
05 LaVine/Ibarra (p. 92)
06 Simon Beeson (p. 92)
07 LaVine/Ibarra (p. 93)
08 Simon Beeson (p. 93)
09 Simon Beeson (p. 94)
10 LaVine/Ibarra (p. 94)
11 John Thorpe (p. 95)
12 LaVine/Ibarra (p. 95)
13 John Thorpe (p. 96)
14 Lance LaVine (p. 97)
15 Benjamin Ibarra (p. 98)
16 LaVine/Ibarra (p. 98)
17 LaVine/Ibarra (p. 99)
18 Andrzej Piotrowski (p. 99)
19 Lance LaVine (p. 100)
20 Andrzej Piotrowski (p. 100)
21 Lance LaVine (p. 101)
22 LaVine/Ibarra (p. 102)
23 Lance LaVine (p. 102)
24 Lance LaVine (p. 103)
25 LaVine/Ibarra (p. 103)
26 Benjamin Ibarra (p. 104)
27 Andrzej Piotrowski (p. 105)
28 LaVine/Ibarra (p. 106)
29 Lance LaVine (p. 106)
30 Lance LaVine (p. 107)
31 Benjamin Ibarra (p. 107)
32 Lance LaVine (p. 108)
33 LaVine/Ibarra (p. 108)
34 Lance LaVine (p. 109)
35 Lance LaVine (p. 109)
36 Lance LaVine (p. 109)
37 Lance LaVine (p. 110)
38 LaVine/Ibarra (p. 110)
39 Lance LaVine (p. 111)
40 Lance LaVine (p. 111)
41 Lavine/Ibarra (p. 112)
42 Lance LaVine (p. 113)
43 Benjamin Ibarra (p. 113)
44 Lance LaVine (p. 114)
45 LaVine Ibarra (p. 114)
46 Simon Beeson (p. 114)
47 Lance LaVine (p. 115)
48 Lance LaVine (p. 116)
49 Simon Beeson (p. 117)
50 Lance LaVine (p. 117)
51 Simon Beeeson (p. 118)
52 Lance LaVine (p. 118)
53 LaVine/Ibarra (p. 119)
54 Lance LaVine (p. 119)

Chapter 6

01 Andrzej Piotrowski (p. 121)
02 LaVine/Ibarra (p. 122)
03 Lavine/Ibarra (p. 123)
04 Lavine/Ibarra (p. 124)
05 Simon Beeson (p. 127)
06 Lavine/Ibarra (p. 129)
07 Andrzej Piotrowski (p. 130)
08 Andrzej Piotrowski (p. 131)
09 LaVine/Ibarra (p. 131)
10 Andrzej Piotrowski (p. 132)
11 LaVine/Ibarra (p. 134)
12 Simon Beeson (p. 135)
13 Benjamin Ibarra (p. 136)
14 LaVine/Ibarra (p. 136)
15 Simon Beeson (p. 137)
16 LaVine/Ibarra (p. 138)
17 Andrzej Piotrowski (p. 138)

Chapter 7

01 Simon Beeson (p. 143)
02 Corbis (p. 147)
03 Corbis (p. 149)
04 Corbis (p. 149)
05 Corbis (p. 150)
06 Benjamin Ibarra (p. 150)
07 Corbis (p. 151)
08 Corbis (p. 151)
09 Corbis (p. 151)
10 Corbis (p. 152)
11 Corbis (p. 152)
12 Corbis (p. 153)
13 Eric Olson (p. 153)
14 Corbis (p. 154)
15 Simon Beeson (p. 155)
16 Simon Beeson (p. 155)
17 Benjamin Ibarra (p. 155)
18 Lance LaVine (p. 156)
19 Simon Beeson (p. 157)
20 Simon Beeson (p. 157)
21 Lance LaVine (p. 158)
22 Lance LaVine (p. 159)
23 Lance LaVine (p. 159)
24 Lance LaVine (p. 160)
25 Lance LaVine (p. 160)
26 Lance LaVine (p. 160)
27 Lance LaVine (p. 160)
28 Lance LaVine (p. 161)
29 Lance LaVine (p. 162)
30 Lance LaVine (p. 162)
31 Lance LaVine (p. 163)
32 Alberto Moreno Image kindly provided by Casa Barragán and used with the permission of the Barragan Foundation, Switzerland (p. 164)
33 Benjamin Ibarra (p. 165)
34 Benjamin Ibarra (p. 165)
35 Alberto Moreno Image kindly provided by Casa Barragán and used with the permission of the Barragan Foundation, Switzerland (p. 165)
36 Alberto Moreno Image kindly provided by Casa Barragán and used with the permission of the Barragan Foundation, Switzerland (p. 166)
37 Benjamin Ibarra (p. 166)

Chapter 8

Chapter 9

Chapter 10

INDEX

D

Q

R

S

W

Z